## Also by William Poundstone

*Big Secrets* (1983)

*The Recursive Universe* (1984)

*Bigger Secrets* (1986)

*Labyrinths of Reason* (1988)

*The Ultimate* (1990)

*Prisoner's Dilemma* (1992)

*Biggest Secrets* (1993)

*Carl Sagan: A Life in the Cosmos* (1999)

*How Would You Move Mount Fuji?* (2003)

*Fortune's Formula* (2005)

*Gaming the Vote* (2008)

# Priceless

# Priceless

## The Myth of Fair Value (and How to Take Advantage of It)

## William Poundstone

🖋 Hill and Wang

A division of Farrar, Straus and Giroux

New York

Hill and Wang
A division of Farrar, Straus and Giroux
18 West 18th Street, New York 10011

Distributed in Canada by D&M Publishers, Inc.
Printed in the United States of America
First edition, 2010

The perceptual illusion on page 37 is copyright © 1995 by Edward H. Adelson.

Library of Congress Cataloging-in-Publication Data
Poundstone, William.
    Priceless : the myth of fair value (and how to take advantage of it) / William
Poundstone.— 1st ed.
        p.    cm.
    Includes bibliographical references and index.
    ISBN: 978-0-8090-9469-1 (hardcover : alk. paper)
    1. Pricing.    I. Title.

HF5416.5.P66 2009
338.5'2—dc22

                                                                    2009015726

Designed by Jonathan D. Lippincott

www.fsgbooks.com

3    5    7    9    10    8    6    4    2

**To Larry Hussar**

# Contents

## Part I

1 The $2.9 Million Cup of Coffee   3
2 Price Cluelessness   8
3 The Myth of the Boomerang   17

## Part 2

4 Body and Soul   25
5 Black Is White   34
6 Helson's Cigarette   38
7 The Price Scale   42

## Part 3

8 Input to Output   49
9 Lunch with Maurice   56
10 Money Pump   62
11 The Best Odds in Vegas   71
12 Cult of Rationality   77
13 Kahneman and Tversky   81
14 Heuristics and Biases   86
15 The Devil's Greatest Trick   93
16 Prospect Theory   97
17 Rules of Fairness   104
18 Ultimatum Game   109
19 The Vanishing Altruist   116

20  Pittsburgh Is Not a Culture    120
21  Attacking Heuristics    125
22  Deal or No Deal    129
23  Prices on the Planet Algon    134

## Part 4

24  The Free 72-Ounce Steak    143
25  Price Check    149
26  Shilling for Prada    155
27  Menu Psych    159
28  The Price of a Super Bowl Ticket    165
29  Don't Wrap All the Christmas Presents in One Box    169
30  Who's Afraid of the Phone Bill?    172
31  Breakage and Slippage    176
32  Paying for Air    179
33  Cheap and Cheaper    182
34  Mysteries of the 99-Cent Store    184
35  Meaningless Zeros    193
36  Reality Constraint    196
37  Selling Warhol's Beach House    202
38  Groundhog Day    207
39  Anchoring for Dummies    213
40  Attention Deficit    215
41  Drinking and Deal Making    219
42  An Octillion Doesn't Buy What It Used To    223
43  Selling the Money Illusion    230
44  Neutron Jane    234
45  The Beauty Premium    239
46  Search for Suckers    241
47  Pricing Gender    245
48  It's All About Testosterone    248
49  Liquid Trust    252
50  The Million-Dollar Club    255
51  The Mischievous Mr. Market    260
52  For the Love of God    266
53  Antidote for Anchoring    269
54  Buddy System    272

55  The Outrage Theory      276
56  Honesty Box       280
57  Money, Chocolate, Happiness       284


*Notes*      *291*
*Sources*      *311*
*Index*      *325*

# Part One

**"The more you ask for, the more you get"**

# One

# The $2.9 Million Cup of Coffee

In 1994 an Albuquerque jury awarded Stella Liebeck $2.9 million in damages after she spilled a piping-hot cup of McDonald's coffee on herself. This resulted in third-degree burns and precious little sympathy from the American public. Late-night comics and drive-time DJs turned Liebeck into a punch line. Talk radio pundits saw the lawsuit as Exhibit A to What's Wrong with Our Legal System. A *Seinfeld* episode had Kramer suing over spilled coffee, and a website inaugurated the "Stella Awards"—booby prizes for the wackiest perversions of the justice system.

Liebeck's injuries were no joke. Her grandson had driven her to the McDonald's drive-through window. They bought the coffee, then pulled over and stopped the car so that Mrs. Liebeck could add cream and sugar. She steadied the cup between her legs as she pried off the lid. That's when it spilled. Liebeck racked up $11,000 in medical bills for skin grafts on her groin, buttocks, and thighs. The tricky question was, how do you put a price on Liebeck's suffering and McDonald's culpability?

Liebeck initially asked the fast-food chain for $20,000. McDonald's dismissed that figure and countered with a buzz-off offer of $800.

Liebeck's attorney, New Orleans–born S. Reed Morgan, had ridden in this rodeo before. In 1986 he sued McDonald's on behalf of a Houston woman who also had third-degree burns from a coffee spill. In his most mesmerizing Deep South baritone, Morgan advanced the legally ingenious theory that McDonald's coffee was "defective" because it was too hot. McDonald's quality control people said the coffee should be served at 180 to 190 degrees Fahrenheit, and this was shown to be hotter than some other chains' coffee. The Houston case was settled for $27,500.

Morgan monitored subsequent coffee lawsuits closely. He knew that in 1990 a California woman had suffered third-degree burns from McDonald's coffee and settled, with no great fanfare, for $230,000. There was one *big* difference. In the California case, it was a McDonald's employee who had spilled coffee on the woman.

Since Liebeck had spilled the coffee on herself, logic would say that her case was worth a lot less than $230,000. Morgan ignored that precedent and used a controversial psychological technique on the jury. I will describe that in a moment. For the time being, I will represent it with a row of dollar signs:

$      $      $      $      $      $      $      $      $      $      $      $

The technique worked. As if hypnotized, the jury awarded Liebeck just under $2.9 million. That was $160,000 in compensatory damages plus $2.7 million in punitive damages. It took the jury four hours to decide. Reportedly, some jurors wanted to award as much as $9.6 million, and the others had to talk them down.

Judge Robert Scott apparently thought the jury award was as outlandish as almost everyone else in America did. He slashed the punitive damages to $480,000.

Even with the reduced award, an appeal from McDonald's was inevitable. The eighty-one-year-old Liebeck wasn't getting any younger. She soon settled with McDonald's for an undisclosed amount said to be less than $600,000. She must have recognized that she had hit a home run and wasn't likely to repeat it.

Skippy peanut butter recently redesigned its plastic jar. "The jar used to have a smooth bottom," explained Frank Luby, a price consultant with Simon-Kucher & Partners in Cambridge, Massachusetts. "It now has an indentation, which takes a couple of ounces of peanut butter out of the product." The old jar contained 18 ounces; the new one has 16.3. The reason, of course, is so that Skippy can charge the same price.

That dimple at the bottom of the peanut butter jar has much to do with a new theory of pricing, one known in the psychology literature as *coherent arbitrariness*. This says that consumers really don't know what anything should cost. They walk the supermarket aisles in a half-conscious daze, judging prices from cues, helpful and otherwise. Coherent arbitrariness is above all a theory of relativity. Buyers are mainly sensitive to relative differences, not absolute prices. The new Skippy jar essentially amounts to a 10 percent increase in the price of peanut butter. Had they just raised the price 10 percent (to $3.39, say), shoppers would have noticed and some would have switched brands. According to the theory, the same shopper would be perfectly happy to pay $3.39 for Skippy, just as long as she doesn't know there's been an increase.

Luby holds a physics degree from the University of Chicago. In his job as price consultant, he more often thinks like a magician. Like a skillful conjurer, he is asked to manage what buyers notice and remember. Skippy peanut butter's customers often have small children and purchase it so regularly that they remember the last price they paid. For such products, consultants recommend creative ways of "invisibly" shrinking packages. In summer 2008 Kellogg's phased in thinner boxes of Cocoa Krispies, Froot Loops, Corn Pops, Apple Jacks, and Honey Smacks cereals. No one noticed. Shoppers just see the box's width and height on the shelf; by the time they reach for the box, the decision has been made and they're thinking of something else.

Dial and Zest recently changed the sculptural contours of their bars, shaving half an ounce off the weight. The boxes stayed about the same. Quilted Northern made its Ultra Plush toilet paper half an inch narrower. The makers of Puffs tissues shrank the length of their product from 8.6 to 8.4 inches. As the Puffs box remained the same (9.5 inches wide), there is presently over an inch of air hidden inside. You can't see it because the opening is in the middle. In any case, a shopper wouldn't notice the shrinkage unless she archived old Puffs tissues and measured them.

This ruse can go on only so long. Cereal boxes would collapse to cardboard envelopes; jars would become plastic voids. Eventually there arrives a point at which the manufacturer must make a bold move everyone will notice. It introduces a new, economy-size package. In size, shape, or other design features, the new package (and its price) is difficult to compare to the old. The consumer is flummoxed, unable to tell whether the new package is a good deal or not. So she tosses it into the cart. The cycle of shrinking packages repeats, ad infinitum.

If you find this a silly charade, you're not alone. Just about everyone does, *when they think about it*. Many grumble they'd rather pay an inflation-adjusted price for the quantities they've known. Others swear they look at the market's comparison labels, giving price per ounce, and wouldn't be fooled. One of the things that price consultants have learned is that what consumers say and what they do are not the same thing. For the most part, memories of prices are short, and memories of boxes and packages shorter.

It wasn't so long ago that companies priced their products with no strategy beyond the demand curves of Economics 101. In the past generation, firms such as Boston Consulting, Roland Berger, Revionics, and Atenga have prospered by advising businesses on the surprisingly complex psychology of price. No firm has spearheaded the professionalization of pricing more than Simon-Kucher & Partners (SKP). German business professor Hermann Simon and two of his doctoral students founded the firm in Bonn in 1985. SKP is now nearing five hundred employees stationed all over the globe, with U.S. offices in Cambridge, New York, and San Francisco. With sixty Ph.D.s on staff, quite a few in physics, SKP has a reputation as the rocket scientists of pricing. The firm exudes a *Star Trek* cosmopolitanism. Employees from India, Korea, Germany, Switzerland, and Spain mingle in the Cambridge office, and it's the practice to rotate promising consultants among nations. Each year SKP assembles its far-flung employees for a party at a castle on the Rhine.

The influence of SKP on the prices we pay for just about everything is as little recognized as it is staggering. Rules that apply to other types of consultancies don't apply to pricing. An ad agency would not have Coca-Cola *and* Pepsi as clients—but SKP does. In many industries, SKP advises half a dozen of the leading firms. Its current roster of clients includes Procter & Gamble, Nestlé, Microsoft, Intel, Texas Instruments, T-Mobile, Vodaphone, Nokia, Sony Ericsson, Honeywell, Thyssen-Krupp, Warner Music, Bertelsmann, Merck, Bayer, Johnson & Johnson,

UBS, Barclays, HSBC, Goldman Sachs, Dow Jones, Hilton, British Airways, Lufthansa, Emirates Airlines, BMW, Mercedes, Volkswagen, Toyota, General Motors, Volvo, Caterpillar, Adidas, and the Toronto Blue Jays. The same psychological tricks apply whether you're setting a price for text messages or toilet paper or airline tickets. To SKP's consultants, prices are the most pervasive of hidden persuaders.

Though a price is just a number, it can evoke a complex set of emotions—something now visible in brain scans. Depending on the context, the same price may be perceived as a bargain or a rip-off; or it may not matter at all. A few of the tricks are timeless, like shrinking packages and prices ending in the magic number 9. But price consultancy is more than the latest chapter in flat-world hucksterism. It draws on some of the most important and innovative recent work in psychology. In the mundane act of naming a price, we translate the desires of our hearts into the public language of numbers. That turns out to be a surprisingly tricky process.

# Two

# Price Cluelessness

Imagine you are asked to heft a suitcase and guess its weight. How accurate would your guess be? Not very, most would admit. The arm muscles and brain and eye just aren't wired to gauge pounds or kilograms. That's why supermarkets have scales and carnival weight-guessers draw slack-jawed crowds.

Now imagine that the suitcase is lost luggage being auctioned. The lock is picked, and the suitcase is shown to contain some resort clothes, a high-end camera, and other lightly used merchandise. Your task now is to guess the winning bid—the market value of the suitcase and its contents. How accurate do you think this guess would be? Would it be any better than your guess about weight?

Auctions can be unpredictable. Okay, I'll make it easy for you. Pretend you're a bidder in the auction. All you have to do is decide your top bid. You're not guessing what *other* people will do; you're just expressing how much the suitcase is worth to you, in dollars and cents. How exact would that valuation be? It's not the easiest thing to attach a price to something with no clear market value. You may end up wondering whether your top price is any more sharply defined than the other two guesses.

One of the running themes of price psychology is that judgments of monetary value have much in common with sensory judgments like weight—or brightness, loudness, warmth, coldness, or intensity of odors. The study of sensory perceptions is known as *psychophysics*. Back in the 1800s, psychophysicists determined that people are acutely sensitive to differences and not so sensitive to absolute values. Given two identical-looking suitcases, one weighing 32 pounds and one 36 pounds, it's a cinch to tell which is the heavier by lifting. But without a scale, it's hard to be certain whether either suitcase would meet an airline's 44-pound limit.

People display a similar cluelessness about prices. This all-important fact goes largely unrecognized. That's because we live our lives in a media cloud of advertised prices and market values. Because we remember what things are "supposed to" cost, we can adopt the pretense of having an unerring sense of value. Consumers are like a sight-impaired person who can navigate familiar surroundings because he has memorized where the furniture is. This is compensation, not keenness of vision.

Every now and then we get a hint of how myopic the price sense is. Anyone who's held a yard sale knows how difficult it can be to put meaningful prices on household castoffs. "This old Tribe Called Quest CD should be worth twice as much as that Alanis Morissette—I'm sure of that. I'm not so sure whether Tribe should be selling for $10 or 10 cents."

In a 2003 paper, economists Dan Ariely, George Loewenstein, and Drazen Prelec termed this curious mix of conviction and uncertainty coherent arbitrariness. Relative valuations are stable and coherent, while actual dollar amounts can be wildly arbitrary. Yard sales reveal a truth we might not care to admit in a business deal: prices are made-up numbers that don't always carry much conviction.

This book tells the story of a simple finding with far-reaching consequences. The numbers that make our world go around are not so solid, immutable, and logically grounded as they appear. In the new psychology of price, values are slippery and contingent, as fluid as the reflections in a fun-house mirror.

This challenges the credo that "everyone has a price," something ingrained in business sense and common sense alike. Terry Southern's 1959 novel, *The Magic Christian*, riffs on that bit of folk wisdom. Billionaire antihero Guy Grand is a prankster who devotes his life to proving that every man and woman has a price. In a typical caper, Grand buys an office building in Chicago just to tear it down and replace it with a boiling vat of manure, blood, and urine from the stockyards. Simmering in the hellish muck is $1 million in hundred-dollar bills. A sign on the vat announces FREE $ HERE. Grand's doctrine is that there is nothing so degrading that someone won't do it for a sufficiently large pile of cash. *The Magic Christian* permits the reader no scope for feeling superior. We may not all be money-grubbing materialists, but it is difficult for anyone in our society not to believe in the weirdly transcendent power of money.

The "everyone has a price" theory holds that valuations are stable and can be revealed by a little wheeling and dealing. When offered a bargain (Faustian or otherwise), I compare it with an internal price and decide whether to accept it. It is not too much of an exaggeration to say that all of traditional economic theory is founded on this simple Guy Grand premise: everyone's got a price, and those prices determine actions.

There's now overwhelming evidence that this idea is wrong, at least as a model of how real people act. As far back as the late 1960s, psychologists Sarah Lichtenstein and Paul Slovic demonstrated the deep ambiguity of prices. In their experiments, subjects were unable to set prices consistent with what they wanted or the choices they made. Psychologists have been working out the consequences ever since. In the new view, internal prices are "constructed" as needed from hints in the environment. One demonstration of how that works is the "United Nations" experiment of Amos Tversky and Daniel Kahneman.

Tversky and Kahneman are a legendary team of Israeli American psychologists. Kahneman, now in his mid-seventies, is a very active senior scholar at Princeton's Woodrow Wilson School. Tversky, the younger man by three years, died of melanoma in 1996, at the age of fifty-nine. In 2002, Kahneman shared the Nobel Prize in Economic Sciences with American economist Vernon Smith. Tversky was cheated of that honor only by his early death.

Kahneman and Tversky's primary field was a still-young branch of psychology called *behavioral decision theory*. This is the study of how people make decisions. At first encounter, that topic may sound worthy and slightly dull. In fact, it spans the human comedy and tragedy. Life is all about deciding.

The word "behavioral" emphasizes that this is an empirical science, studying how flesh-and-blood people act rather than prescribing how they *ought* to act. Behavioral decision theory is still a small field, much like an extended family. In interviewing some of its most distinguished figures, my talk of "Professor Kahneman" instantly branded me an outsider. To everyone in the field, it's "Danny" and "Amos," and this is no false familiarity. Almost everyone knew them. Seated, with his feet up, in the study of his East Village penthouse, "Danny" was almost apologetic when I mentioned his United Nations experiment, part of the body of work that merited his Nobel Prize.

"At the time," he said, "it was not considered a big sin." The "sin" was using deception in a psychological experiment, something now frowned upon.

He and Tversky used one piece of aparatus, a carnival-style wheel of fortune marked with numbers up to 100. A group of college students watched as the wheel was spun to select a random number. You can play along—imagine that the wheel is spinning right now and the number is . . . 65. Now answer this two-part question:

(a) Is the percentage of African nations in the United Nations higher or lower than 65 [the number that just came up on the wheel]?
(b) What is the percentage of African nations in the United Nations?

Write your answer here (     )—or pause a moment to think of a *specific number*. Got it?

Like many experiments, and some wheels of fortune, this one was rigged. The wheel was designed to produce one of only two numbers, 10 or 65. This rigging was done only to simplify analysis of the results. In any event, Tversky and Kahneman found that the allegedly random number affected the answers to the second question. The effect was *huge*.

When the wheel stopped on 10, the average estimate of the proportion of African nations in the U.N. was 25 percent. But when the wheel-of-fortune number was 65, the average guess was 45 percent. The latter estimate was almost twice the first. The only difference was that the estimators had been exposed to a different "random" number *that they knew to be meaningless.*

Okay, you're saying, people are lousy with geography. The college students didn't know the right answer and had to guess, to pull a number out of the air. You might imagine that someone at a loss for an answer would parrot a number that happened to have been mentioned recently. That wasn't what happened. Respondents weren't simply repeating the actual numbers they'd been cued with (10 or 65). They named their own numbers; but in so doing they were influenced by the magnitude of the number cues.

Tversky and Kahneman used the term "anchoring and adjustment" for this. In their now-classic 1974 *Science* article, "Judgment Under Uncertainty: Heuristics and Biases," they theorized that an initial value (the "anchor") serves as a mental benchmark or starting point for estimating an unknown quantity. Here, the wheel-of-fortune number was the anchor. The first part of the question had the subjects compare the anchor to the quantity to be estimated. Tversky believed that the subjects then mentally adjusted the anchor upward or downward to arrive at their answers to the second part of the question. This adjustment was usually inadequate. The answer ended up being closer to the anchor than it should be. To someone inspecting only the final outcomes, it's as if the anchor exerts a magnetic attraction, pulling estimates closer to itself.

By the way, how did *your* answer compare to the 65-group's average of 45 percent? In case you're wondering, the correct fraction of African U.N. member nations is currently 23 percent.

The initial response to anchoring was denial (and that's not the name of a river flowing through those African nations). "The default reaction to a paper is to ignore it," Kahneman explained. In this case, scholars were convinced the paper had to be wrong. It seemed incredible that a simple parlor trick could have such a large effect on educated people's judgment.

Psychologists have since replicated the anchoring experiment with many variations. You do not need a wheel of fortune, or a random number, to have anchoring. You don't even need a *reasonable* number. Psychologist George Quattrone tried these questions:

- Is the average temperature in San Francisco higher or lower than 558 degrees Fahrenheit? What is the average temperature of San Francisco?
- How many top-ten records did the Beatles release—more than 100,025, or less than 100,025? Now give your estimate of the number of top-ten Beatles records.

These numbers are completely wacko. You'd think they couldn't possibly affect guesses about how warm San Francisco is, or how many top-ten Beatles records there were . . . except that they *did*. People primed with these and other absurdly high anchors gave higher estimates than those who received low anchors.

Now of course no one guessed the temperature of San Francisco was anything close to 500 degrees. Everyone knew it was a two-digit number, somewhere between room temperature and freezing. Anchoring is constrained by whatever people know or believe to be true. A geography wonk who knows the percentage of African U.N. members will give that correct answer and not be swayed by a random number. Anchoring is an artifact of guessing.

A team led by Timothy Wilson of the University of Virginia did an experiment in which they offered a prize—dinner for two at a popular restaurant—for the most accurate estimate of the number of physicians in the local phone book. This was again posed as a two-part question, with high and low anchors for different groups. Wilson and company reasoned that the incentive of an expensive dinner might cause the subjects to *concentrate* on getting the best answer and not to rattle off any silly number that popped into their heads. Instead, they found that the anchoring effect was almost as strong with the incentive as without it.

Wilson's group even tried warning about the perils of anchoring. One set of participants received instructions saying that "a number in people's heads can influence their answers to subsequent questions . . . When you answer the questions on the following pages, *please be careful not to have this contamination effect happen to you*. We would like the most accurate estimates you can come up with."

The warning didn't work. The subjects' estimates were still influenced by meaningless numbers. Most likely, those who got the warning *did* try to correct for anchoring, Wilson's team proposes. But they couldn't do it, any more than someone can obey the instruction *not* to think of an elephant.

"We suggest that because anchoring effects occur unintentionally and unconsciously, it was difficult for people to know the extent to which an anchor value influenced their estimates," Wilson's group wrote. "As a result, they were at the mercy of naïve theories about how susceptible they were to anchoring effects."

For "naïve theories," read: anchoring can't happen to *me*.

It is often necessary to translate personal values into numbers that can be communicated to others. Anchoring appears to be a feature (bug?) of the mental software that lets us do that. Whenever we guesstimate an unknown quantity that cannot be calculated, we are liable to be influenced by other numbers just mentioned or considered. This isn't something we're aware of—it takes experiments with groups to demonstrate it statistically—but it is real nonetheless. Anchoring is part of the process that helps us to make wild guesses and have hunches; to jot offers and counteroffers on cocktail napkins; to rate restaurants and sexual partners on a scale of 1 to 10; and, generally, to function in a number- and money-obsessed society. Anchoring works with all kinds of numbers—including those prefixed with dollar signs.

For a good example of anchoring in action, check out the prices charged for Broadway and Las Vegas show tickets. "Cheap seats don't sell," one candid (and anonymous) Broadway producer told the blog TalkinBroadway in 1999. "You know why they don't sell? Because if you price Orchestra or Mezzanine seats real cheap, people think there is something wrong with them."

Broadway depends on tourists who have a limited time to pick a show and may have only a sketchy notion of what they're buying. Least of all are they in a position to judge how much specific seats are worth. In assessing the value of a seat, there's not much a tourist can do except take a cue from the ticket's price ("you get what you pay for"). A ticket's perceived value is proportional to its price, almost regardless of what that price is. Many believe that the $480 premium orchestra seats for *The Producers* were a factor in that show's long, profitable run. Tourists figured that any show with $480 tickets must be worth seeing—and headed for the TKTS booth.

That's an important point: theatergoers who wouldn't dream of paying $480 for a ticket were still affected by that price. It made whatever
they did pay seem like a deal. (It's the same show, after all.) "Scaling the
house" is the process of assigning prices to theater or concert seats in different parts of the venue. It's a vital part of the business, often making the
difference between a sold-out and half-empty house. The anonymous
producer revealed that

> I now scale all the Orchestra and most of the Mezzanine seats at
> top price. If you do that, you sell them in a heartbeat . . . I can
> scale a house so I got a dozen different prices—from top to real
> cheap—and sell out the top-priced seats and have most of the
> cheaper seats empty. Or, I can scale a house where 70–80% of it is
> top price. You know what, when most of the seats are top price,
> even if I send 40% of the tickets for a performance to the TKTS
> Booth, I still make more money.

For years, the Hollywood Bowl has offered tickets as cheap as one dollar to its summer concerts. The Bowl is run by the County of Los Angeles, and the dollar seats are intended as a public service. The trouble is
that those who've never tried them assume they're awful. The Bowl is a
huge place (17,376 seats), and the one-dollar seats are the farthest from
the stage. But the musical experience is essentially the same (amplified,
and supplemented with the occasional police helicopter). The view of
the sunset and city is better from the dollar seats. Much of the time, the
hundred-dollar seats are packed and unobtainable, while the one-dollar
seats are empty. A lot of music lovers miss out—because the price is
too *low*.

When Amos Tversky received a MacArthur grant in 1984, he joked that
his work had established what was long known to "advertisers and used-
car salesmen." This was not just self-deprecating wit. At the time, those
Machiavellian practitioners were probably more open to what Tversky
was saying than most economists or CEOs were. Marketers had long
been doing experiments in the psychology of prices. In the heyday of
mail order, it was common to print up multiple versions of a catalog or
flyer in order to test the effect of pricing strategies. These findings must

have dispelled any illusions about the fixity of prices. Marketers and salespeople knew too well that what a customer was willing to pay was changeable and that there was money to be made from that fact. Economist Donald Cox has gone so far as to say that much of behavioral economics is "old hat to marketing experts, who have long since booted *homo economicus* out of their focus groups."

Today there is a symbiosis between psychologists studying prices and the marketing and price consultant communities. Many leading theorists, including Tversky, Kahneman, Richard Thaler, and Dan Ariely, have published important work in marketing journals. Price consultant Simon-Kucher & Partners has an academic advisory board with scholars from three continents. Today's marketers talk up anchoring and coherent arbitrariness—and their somewhat unnerving power. "Many people like myself who teach marketing start the course by saying, 'We're not about manipulating consumers, we're about discovering needs and meeting them,'" said Eric Johnson of Columbia University. "And then, if you're in the field awhile, you realize, yes, we can manipulate consumers."

# Three

# The Myth of the Boomerang

Among the first professions to take note of behavioral decision theory was the law. There was some eye-opening research on jury award anchoring published in the years before *Liebeck v. McDonald's*. In a 1989 study, psychologists John Malouff and Nicola Schutte had four groups of mock jurors read a description of an actual personal injury case in which the defendant had been found liable. All groups were told that the defense attorney had suggested a damage award of $50,000. The one variable was the amount that they were told the plantiff's lawyer had requested. A group informed that the plantiff's attorney had asked for $100,000 awarded an average of $90,333. Another group, told that the attorney had demanded $700,000, awarded an average of $421,538.

Had the jurors been able to deduce a "correct" amount, it should have been the same for all the groups. The facts of the case were unchanged. But of course there is no formula for arriving at a legal award. That leaves jurors susceptible to suggestion. When you chart Malouff and Schutte's four data points (they also exposed groups to demands of $300,000 and $500,000), you get a remarkably straight line. Though the jurors always awarded less than the plaintiff's demand, the amounts went up in lockstep with the demand.

In their wildest dreams, few attorneys imagined that jurors were that malleable. This and other studies raised the question: Just how far can you push anchoring in the courtroom? Does a smart attorney ask for a billion gazillion dollars?

The conventional wisdom says no. There is said to be a "boomerang effect." Over-the-top demands backfire by making the plantiff or attorney look greedy. Juries retaliate by awarding less than they would have with a more sensible demand.

Psychologists Gretchen Chapman and Brian Bornstein tested this idea in a 1996 experiment, when *Liebeck v. McDonald's* was much in the news. They presented eighty University of Illinois students with the hypothetical case of a young woman who said she contracted ovarian cancer from birth control pills and was suing her HMO. Four groups each heard a different demand for damages: $100; $20,000; $5 million; and $1 billion. The mock jurors were asked to give compensatory damages only. Anyone who wants to believe in the jury system must find the results astonishing.

| Demand | Award (average) |
|---|---|
| $100 | $990 |
| $20,000 | $36,000 |
| $5 million | $440,000 |
| $1 billion | $490,000 |

The jurors were amazingly persuadable, up through the $5 million demand. The lowball $100 demand got a piddling $990 average award. This was for a cancer said to have the plaintiff "almost constantly in pain . . . Doctors do not expect her to survive beyond a few more months."

Increasing the demand 200-fold, to $20,000, increased the award about 36-fold, to $36,000. Demanding $5 million got another 12-fold increase on top of that.

Chapman and Bornstein's experiment could not rule out a boomerang effect, but it found no evidence for it. Instead, it found diminishing returns. Asking for $1 billion—an utterly insane number—still got more money than asking for $5 million did. It just didn't get much more.

Anecdotal evidence can mislead. Lawyers remember the time they asked for a lot and got less than they hoped. Any attorney crazy enough to ask for $1 billion might be disappointed by a $490,000 award and blame it on a boomerang effect. This experiment showed, however, that the billion-dollar figure fared the best of the four demands tested.

Jurors are instructed to base compensatory awards on pain and suffering. Chapman and Bornstein asked their jurors to rate the plaintiff's suffering on a numerical scale. They found no meaningful correlation between estimates of suffering and the amounts awarded. In other words, the variable that was supposed to matter didn't, and a variable that was supposed to be irrelevant—the plantiff's demand—did.

The psychologists also asked the jurors, "How likely is it that the defendant caused the plaintiff's injury?" The reported likelihood increased modestly with the size of the award. There was thus no evidence that the billion-dollar demand hurt the credibility of the plaintiff's case.

S. Reed Morgan, of the McDonald's coffee lawsuit, has described attorneys such as himself as "entrepreneurs." By seeking liability suit jackpots, professional litigators provide incentives for big companies to worry about the safety of their products. Less sympathetic observers dismiss this as "lottery litigation." Either way, attorneys facing the legal wheel of fortune sometimes refrain from asking jurors for a specific amount. They fear that a reasonable figure might preempt a windfall, and a high-end figure could boomerang. Chapman and Bornstein's experiment suggests otherwise. The title of their paper says it all: "The More You Ask For, the More You Get."

Anchoring research has convinced some that jurors should not directly set damage awards. Daniel Kahneman believes that jurors are trying to express their outrage at the defendant's actions in the incoherent language of dollars. It's as if jurors are from Mars and they don't know what the money is worth on this planet. Essentially, they're rating the defendant's culpability on a scale of 1 to 10. They look to the attorneys for cues on how much that's worth in Earth dollars.

Morgan succeeded in convincing the *Liebeck v. McDonald's* jurors to feel outrage. His case was two-pronged: that McDonald's coffee was hotter than many of its competitors' and that the fast-food chain had been insensitive to the scope of Liebeck's injuries. In the penalty phase of the trial, Morgan asked the jurors to penalize McDonald's in the amount of one or two days of the company's worldwide coffee sales. He wasn't counting on the jury to do the math. Morgan informed them that McDonald's coffee sales came to about $1.35 million a day.

$   $   $   $   $   $   $   $   $   $   $   $

Huh? Well, the accident involved coffee. Morgan didn't say much about why this specific demand was reasonable, maybe because it *wasn't* especially reasonable. The more you think about the request, the less sense it makes. Why one or two days? Why worldwide sales, as opposed to just in the United States, or just in New Mexico, or just the coffee that McDonald's sold to Stella Liebeck on the day in question (49 cents' worth)?

*Thinking about it* was the point. It is believed that an effective anchor must be in short-term memory at the moment a decision is made. On the face of it, that's a serious limitation. Short-term memory, the kind we use to dial unfamiliar phone numbers, lasts only about twenty seconds. This is one reason many were skeptical that anchoring could apply outside the lab. A jury may deliberate for days. Jurors get bored and spend much of the time daydreaming. Who knows how many numbers they're exposed to?

Field studies show that anchoring effects persist over realistic time frames. For an important matter like a jury award, there is not likely to be any single moment of decision. Each juror will consider the matter a number of times in the jury box, separated by intervals of inattention. They will reconsider the decision each time it is challenged by a new argument or confirmed by a new fact. A successful anchor needs to be memorable enough that it is recalled each time the decision is revisited.

Morgan's non sequitur demand was, if nothing else, memorable. A day or two of McDonald's coffee sales has the ring of poetic justice. It framed the deliberations, encouraging the jurors to construct their own two-part question:

(a) Is a day or two of coffee sales fair?
(b) How many days of coffee sales *is* fair?

Jurors are poor at scaling dollar amounts to the size of a crime or problem. In a 1992 survey by W. H. Desvousges and colleagues, people were told that birds were dying because they became mired in uncovered pools of oil at refineries. This (fictitious) problem could be solved by putting nets over the pools. The experiment asked participants to indicate how much they would be willing to pay for nets to save the birds. The researchers tried telling different groups that 2,000 birds were being killed a year—or 20,000 birds, or 200,000 birds. The answers didn't depend on the number of birds! In all cases, the average dollar amount was around $80. Evidently, all that registered was *A lot of birds are being killed. We should do something about it.*

Morgan most definitely wanted the *Liebeck* jurors to scale their award to McDonald's deep pockets. (Not many hot-coffee suits get filed against mom-and-pop diners.) This is another reason "days of coffee sales" was an effective currency. Once the jurors agreed on the right number of days, the scaling up was straightforward.

You may wonder why Morgan asked for "one or two days." Why be indecisive? When people are given three prices (think of those for small, medium, and large coffee), and they have no strong preference, they tend to pick the "middle" price. Morgan could have anticipated he would be competing against a much lower figure from the defense or an unsympathetic juror. By introducing a "middle" option, Morgan gave the undecided an easy out, favorable to his client.

The *Liebeck* jury settled on $2.7 million in punitive damages, exactly two days' worth of coffee sales by Morgan's estimate. It's hard to deny that Morgan's demand was a compelling influence. Going by the research, Morgan's only blunder may have been not asking for one or two *years* of coffee sales.

# Part Two

**"Black is white with a bright ring around it"**

# Four

# Body and Soul

Dr. Eskildsen's new patient was seven months heavy with child and a bit unsteady in her high heels. She had seen the ad in the newspaper offering a free eye exam and figured the price was right. Dr. Eskildsen's office was across from the courthouse in downtown Eugene, Oregon. A businesslike sign announced the OREGON RESEARCH INSTITUTE VISION RESEARCH CENTER. Inside, the lobby was decorated much like any other small town optometrist's office of the 1960s. Nothing was terribly expensive, everything was neat and new looking. There was Philippine mahogany paneling (a veneer) and seafoam-green carpeting. A couple of prints added a splash of color, one of them a travel poster of WONDERFUL COPENHAGEN—perhaps Dr. Eskildsen was Danish? A receptionist greeted the patient and directed her up three steps into the examination room.

Dr. Paul Eskildsen was a serious man of indeterminate age. With the cleft in his chin, he must have looked dashing before his hair receded. He was wearing glasses and gave the impression of being slightly ill—as if this line of work did not agree with him.

"Would you please come over here and toe this mark on the floor?" he asked mildly. "I am going to project some triangles on the wall, and I would like you to estimate the height of them."

The patient complied and soon fell into the tedium of an eye checkup. A few minutes later, Dr. Eskildsen noticed that something had changed in the patient's manner.

"How do you feel?" he inquired.

"Goofy," the patient said. "I was kind of reeling around."

Perhaps it's because you're pregnant, the doctor suggested, without much conviction.

"I never felt this way before," the patient insisted. "It's a feeling of not being able to control my standing." The woman managed a few steps in her heels, bracing herself against the wall. "Are you hypnotizing me? Because that's kind of sneaky."

Dr. Eskildsen spoke not to his patient but to an intercom on the wall: "Okay, Jim, our subject has popped."

Paul Hoffman had been an Air Force navigator in the South Pacific. Home from the war, he earned a Ph.D. in experimental psychology and became an assistant professor at the University of Oregon, where he found he didn't much like teaching. Instead, Hoffman nursed a dream of establishing a think tank to study human decision making. He got his chance in 1960. Using a $60,000 National Science Foundation grant and a mortgage on his home, Hoffman bought a Unitarian church building at Eleventh and Ferry and rechristened it the Oregon Research Institute. Hoffman believed that some research was best done without the red tape of a university. A prime example of that came in 1965.

The designers of a New York office building presented Hoffman with a problem. The tenants on the building's top floors would be paying the highest rents. The architect and engineers were concerned that these top floors would sway in Manhattan's stiff winds. They didn't want their prize tenants to feel vulnerable. To prevent that, they needed to know exactly how much horizontal swaying was noticeable. There did not seem to be any data on that.

As Hoffman recognized, they needed to do an experiment in psychophysics. A "just noticeable difference" is the smallest perceptible amount of a stimulus (in this case, the swaying of a room). There was an extensive psychophysical literature, going back to the nineteenth century, on how to measure just noticeable differences. It would have been easy enough to build some sort of moving cubicle. But Hoffman knew that had he told people the experiment's purpose, they would have been expecting the cubicle to move. That expectation would cause them to detect motion—or *say* they detected it—much sooner. "So I began to think," Hoffman recalled. "How would you invite a person to come down to an office and sit in a room, for some purpose or other, and be able to start that room in motion?"

Hoffman rented a space in a Eugene office building at 800 Pearl Street and constructed a fake optometrist's office. The examining room was on wheels. A soundproofed hydraulic mechanism, originally designed to move logs through a sawmill, caused the room to sway back and forth with increasing speed and displacement. The vibration-free movement could range from an inch to twelve feet. Paul Eskildsen, a psychologist who also happened to be a licensed optometrist, agreed to play that role. During the course of seventy-two bogus eye exams, they slowly cranked up the speed of the room's swaying until the subjects "popped"—that is, said something to indicate they noticed. The data Eskildsen and Hoffman cared about was how much the room had to be swaying for "patients" to notice. Physical descriptions (pregnancy, high heels, etc.) were carefully recorded, as were their words:

*I feel that I'm not stable. I feel like I'm on a boat. Back in Pennsylvania we had to take drunk driving tests by walking on a line . . .*

*It's unpleasant. You probably have me on an X-ray or something. Maybe I'm on Candid Camera . . .*

*I think you're taking away my gravity or something . . .*

Eskildsen was not immune. Every day he got seasick, went home to recuperate, and came back the next morning to get sick again.

The results showed that the threshold for noticeable swaying was about ten times smaller than the building's engineers had been assuming. Though this was not what the clients wanted to hear, they were intrigued by Hoffman's methods. Architect Minoru Yamasaki and engineer Leslie Robertson visited Oregon and insisted on taking a "ride" in the contraption. They were convinced.

A nondisclosure agreement prevented Hoffman from publishing or even talking about his findings. The building developer did not want anything that could be construed as adverse publicity. The Oregon tests did cause the engineers to adopt stiffer exterior columns. The building opened to great fanfare in 1970 as the World Trade Center. Thirty-one years later, two hijacked jetliners crashed into the center's twin towers. Hoffman's recommendations are credited with keeping the towers standing long enough for more than 14,000 people to escape to safety.

Today the Oregon Research Institute (ORI) is revered as a cradle of behavioral decision theory. ORI was the longtime professional home of Sarah Lichtenstein and Paul Slovic, the first to demonstrate clearly just how clueless people are about prices and decisions based on them. For one productive year, ORI was also home to Amos Tversky and Daniel Kahneman, perhaps the most influential psychologists of their age.

Before getting to this illustrious group, it's necessary to say something about their predecessors, and about the peculiar science of psychophysics.

Well into the twentieth century, psychologists had a case of physics envy. There was agonizing over whether psychology was a science at all. In a quest to make their field more quantitative, psychologists collected reams of numbers. What they were going to do with these numbers was not always clear. No one epitomized this epoch better than Stanley Smith Stevens—"S. S. Stevens" in his publications and "Smitty" to just about everyone.

Stevens (1906–1973) grew up among a gaggle of cousins in a polygamous Mormon household in Logan, Utah. Upon coming of age, he was packed off as a missionary to Belgium. There he labored under the handicap of not speaking the languages of the heathens he was attempting to convert. His subsequent academic career took him from the University of Utah to Stanford to Harvard. Stevens's psychology Ph.D. was awarded, per Harvard custom of the time, by the Department of Philosophy.

War made Stevens's reputation. At the behest of the U.S. Air Force, he founded the Psycho-Acoustic Laboratory in 1940. Its location, the basement of Harvard's neogothic Memorial Hall, belied its somewhat incredible mission: to study the effects of extremely loud noises on pilots. Experimental subjects listened to deafening 115-decibel blasts for seven hours a day. Stevens found that the noise did not impair mental performance too much. The main problem was that nobody could hear what anyone else was saying. Stevens's lab took on the task of designing intercoms for noisy cockpits.

Stevens retained a gruff military manner throughout his career. As one colleague recalled,

> I was directed to Dr. Stevens's office and found him in what I came later to recognize as a characteristic posture, legs extended, ankles crossed, feet on corner of desk. As he sat up and turned to greet me I saw a handsome man in his mid-thirties, tall and muscular, round-shouldered with long arms and large hands, a 4-4-4 on the somatotype scales; a long face with a high forehead and excellent features; wavy black hair and a natty moustache; an open, level gaze and an expression that in repose seemed sad, even disapproving, but could break into an irresistibly winning smile . . . In appearance he could have been a matinee idol, but the idea of S. S. Stevens as an actor would strike anyone who knew him as absurd. He could never have spoken lines from another's script. He was his own man, if ever anyone was. I did not actually join the laboratory until eighteen months later; by then I had learned that my first impression was only one side of a very complex personality. Stevens was a primitive—he had in him the force of Nature.

One name "Smitty" Stevens wasn't so keen on being called was "psychologist." He spent his career fretting about the unscientific bunkum, as he saw it, perpetuated under that name. A bone of contention was the popular lectures his Harvard collegues insisted on giving to enraptured undergraduates. Stevens feared that the pop psychology would attract the wrong kind of people to the field—touchy-feely do-gooders. In his ongoing quest to dissociate himself from psychology, Stevens insisted on styling himself a "psychophysicist." By 1962 he managed to persuade Harvard to name him their first (and apparently last) professor of psychophysics.

That term had been popularized in the mid-nineteenth century by German psychologist Gustav Fechner (1801–1887). According to Fechner, "Psychophysics is an exact doctrine of the relation of function or dependence between body and soul." Fechner, unlike Stevens, was a deeply mystical man, bridging German romanticism and German science.

The son of a rural pastor, Fechner penned satires and studied medicine until an allowance from his mother ran out. Forced to get a steady source of income, he became a prolific author, editing *Home Encyclopedia*, a how-to compendium for Biedermeier households. Fechner wrote about a third of the encyclopedia himself, including entries like "Carving Meat and Setting the Table."

He continued his academic studies, now in physics. In 1834 Fechner was appointed professor of physics at the University of Leipzig. "But then I ruined my eyesight by doing experiments in subjective color perception, looking often at the sun through colored glass . . . so that by Christmas 1839 I could no longer use my eyes and had to interrupt my lectures," Fechner wrote in an autobiographical note. "When I finally could no longer bear daylight at all, I gave up my position."

For some time, Fechner believed himself blind, and the citizenry of Leipzig believed him mad. Fortunately, both conditions improved. On October 22, 1850, Fechner woke up with the characteristically mystical insight that sensations could be measured and connected to the physics of the material world. This event is traditionally taken as the starting point for psychophysics. Its anniversary, "Fechner Day," is still celebrated at Harvard and elsewhere.

"People called Fechner a fool and a fanatic," German physicist Ernst Mach confided to the doyen of American psychology, William James. When not experimenting on perception, Fechner attended séances and claimed that plants have souls. Under a pen name he wrote a tome on the popular obsession of the German romantic era (every era, actually) — the *Little Book on Life After Death*.

With psychophysics, Fechner was confronting one of the oldest questions in philosophy: Can subjective experiences be compared or communicated? Colors are often held up as a convenient example: Do people experience colors the same way, or is it just barely possible that one person sees a red STOP sign as red and another experiences the same sign as green? Would there be any way of telling? The person who sees green would still call the sign red because he's been taught to call the color of a STOP sign red.

Taken in a full-bore philosophical spirit, questions like this are unanswerable. This leaves open the question of whether the intensity of sensations can be measured. Nineteenth-century German psychologist Wilhelm Wundt offered a skeptical view:

How much stronger or weaker one sensation is than another, we are never able to say. Whether the sun is a hundred or a thousand times brighter than the moon, a cannon a hundred or a thousand times louder than a pistol, is beyond our power to estimate.

Understand what Wundt was saying. He *wasn't* saying that a physicist couldn't measure the objective intensity of sunlight and moonlight. That was already beginning to happen in Wundt's time. He *wasn't* saying that you couldn't ask people whether the sun looks brighter than the moon and get 100 percent agreement that the sun is way, way brighter.

Wundt was saying (only) that subjective ratios are meaningless. And in this, he was staggeringly wrong. Over the next century, Wundt's contemporaries and successors, who often went by the name "psychophysicists," assembled compelling evidence that people are fairly good at doing just what Wundt thought to be impossible.

A down-to-earth definition of "psychophysics" would say it is the study of the relationship between physical quantities (noise, light, heat, weight) and subjective perceptions of them. Fechner was not the first to explore this, even in Leipzig. As early as 1834, Ernst Weber, a Leipzig physiologist, established what is still one of the field's great overarching results. He blindfolded people and had them judge how heavy various combinations of weights felt. Weber carefully added tiny weights until the subject said his burden felt noticeably heavier (a "just noticeable difference"). He determined that it was the relative (percentage) change in weight that mattered—not the absolute change in grams or pounds. A fly landing on a strongman's barbell does not make it noticeably heavier. The same fly landing on a coin held in a blindfolded person's palm might be noticeable.

Before the age of lightbulbs and loudspeakers, psychophysics was a primitive affair. One early researcher, Julius Merkel, asked people to judge the loudness of noises made by dropping a metal sphere onto a block of ebony. When Merkel wanted to make the noise louder, he had to drop the ball from a greater height. Another pioneer, Belgian physicist Joseph-Antoine Ferdinand Plateau, asked eight artists to paint a gray that was *exactly* halfway between black and white. Just so there was no confusion about what "black" and "white" meant, Plateau supplied swatches. The artists took the samples and went back to their studios to paint their gray. Despite the fact that the lighting must have been different in each of the studios, the resulting grays were virtually identical, Plateau reported. This was taken as proof that perceptions were not so subjective as some proposed. In an experiment oddly like Fechner's ill-fated one, Plateau stared directly at the sun for twenty-five seconds, permanently damaging his eyesight. He died blind in Ghent, steps away from guidebook masterpieces of the van Eycks.

The growth of psychophysics in the twentieth century was largely a matter of better audio-visual equipment. Fitted out with the latest slide projectors, rheostats, and audio oscillators, the field blossomed. Its scope spanned not only the world of the senses but also that of ethical, aesthetic, and economic value judgments. College students were instructed to look at inclined lines, colors, or reproductions of modern paintings; sniff noxious oils or listen to white noise; compare atrocities, salaries, and perfumes. Then the grilling began: *How inclined is that line to the horizontal? Rate the loudness of that tone you just heard on a scale of 1 to 7. Which crime is worse? How intelligent would you say the child in this photograph is?*

S. S. Stevens is renowned for establishing the shape of the curve relating physical intensity to subjective perception. It was long known that this curve is not a straight line. Imagine a completely dark room. Turn on a 60-watt lightbulb. Then turn on a second 60-watt bulb. Does the light look twice as bright? No (says almost everyone). It looks brighter, but not twice as bright. Careful experiments have shown that point sources of light have to be about four times brighter, physically, to look twice as bright, subjectively.

This is characteristic of a *power curve*. Without getting into the math, here's one way of grasping the gist of it: You're decorating your house with Christmas lights and want to outdo your neighbor. Specifically, you want your lights to look *twice* as bright. According to Stevens, it's not good enough to buy twice as many lights. You'll need something like *four* times as many strings of lights in order to *double* the perception of glittery holiday excess.

This rule holds no matter whether your neighbor has a single, environmentally sensitive string, or whether he's one of those obsessives whose houses make the news. Doubling the subjective effect means quadrupling the wattage (and, unfortunately, your December electric bill).

Stevens noted with satisfaction that his power curve rule can be stated in seven words: *Equal stimulus ratios produce equal subjective ratios.* This is often called Stevens's law, or *the* psychophysical law. Within a generation, Stevens and contemporaries established that the power law is a very general one, applying not just to brightness of lights but also to perceptions of warmth, cold, taste, smell, vibration, and electric shock.

The factor connecting the two ratios varies with the type of stimulus. It's not always "four times the stimulus doubles the response." For instance, it takes only about 1.7 times as much sugar, in a watery soft drink, to double the perception of sweetness. The ratio can also depend on how a stimulus is presented. Perceptions of heat follow different power curves depending on whether it's a warm piece of metal touching the arm, the irradiation of a small area of skin, or sauna-like heat enveloping the whole body. But for a given experiment, the curves are remarkably consistent. By 1965, two of Stevens's colleagues could write, "As an experimental fact, the power law is established beyond any reasonable doubt, possibly more firmly established than anything else in psychology."

# Five

# Black Is White

S. S. Stevens tried to explain why the senses obey a power law. He noted that most of the laws of physics (like $E=mc^2$) are power laws. By adapting to the form of physical law, the senses are better able to "tell us how matters stand out there." In his posthumously published text, *Psychophysics*, Stevens wrote,

> For example, is it the differences or the proportions and ratios that need to remain constant in perception? Apparently it is the proportions—the ratios. When we walk toward a house, the relative proportions of the house appear to remain constant: the triangular gable looks triangular from any distance. A photograph portrays the same picture whether we view it under a bright or a dim light: the ratio between the light and shaded parts of the photograph seem approximately the same even though the illumination varies . . . The usefulness of perceptual proportions and relations that remain approximately constant despite wide changes in stimulus levels is immense. Think how life as we know it would be transformed if speech could be understood at only a single level of intensity, or if objects changed their apparent proportions as they receded, or if pictures became unrecognizable when a cloud dimmed the light of the sun.

Put this way, our ratio-based senses are eminently reasonable. There is an Achilles' heel. The price of being so acutely sensitive to ratios and contrasts is a relative insensitivity to the absolute.

Stevens makes this point, too, with characteristic poetry:

The print in this book looks black, but not because there is no light coming from the black area to your eye. Actually the black gives off so much light that, if we could remove all the white paper surrounding the black, the black standing by itself would seem to glow as brightly as a neon sign at night.

The ratio-based nature of perception has many consequences. One of the more trivial ones is that it affects the design of psychophysics experiments. It was discovered that results depend a great deal on the response scale. This is the "answer sheet," a printed form in the old days and a Web page now. There are two popular kinds of response scales: category and magnitude. You're already familiar with both.

*Category scales* are used in consumer surveys and Internet polls. How would you rate your Whirlpool dishwasher? Check one:

- ☐ 1–poor
- ☐ 2–fair
- ☐ 3–good
- ☐ 4–very good
- ☐ 5–excellent

A category scale has a fixed number of possible responses, labeled with words. There is a lowest or worst score and a highest or best score.

A different approach is a *magnitude scale*. In this, you're asked to rate something on an unbounded numerical scale. The lowest rating is zero, and the highest rating is—well, there *isn't* a highest rating. Why should there be? There is no upper limit to physical quantities such as loudness or heaviness, and no obvious limit to subjective perceptions of them.

Sometimes magnitude scales supply a standard of comparison, called a *modulus*. You might be shown a projected disk of light and be told that it's a 100 on a scale of brightness. You would then be asked to estimate the brightness of other disks. One that's half as bright would be a 50, one twice as bright would be a 200, and of course total invisibility would be a zero.

A modulus is supposed to be helpful, like a scale of miles on a map. But Stevens's wife, the former Geraldine Stone, suggested that he try dispensing with the modulus. Stevens found that his subjects gave more self-consistent judgments *without* it. Thereafter his preferred technique was to instruct subjects to give a number, any number, corresponding to *how bright* or *how sweet* or *how unpleasant*.

This sounds like a prescription for chaos. In a way, it was. Different people assigned wildly different numbers to the same thing. This wasn't necessarily a problem. In medieval times, tradesmen's weights and measures varied from town to town. But an ox that weighed twice as much as another ox on one town's scales would weigh twice as much elsewhere, even though the actual number of pounds might be different. In Stevens's experiments, the subjects' absolute judgments were inconsistent, but the ratios were meaningful. It made more sense to let subjects invent their own mental yardstick and scale their answers to that.

Why isn't a modulus helpful? With the modulus, subjects were afraid of making a "mistake." Without it, they went with their first impulse, and this was usually more accurate. "I liked the idea that I could just relax and contemplate the tones," one of Stevens's subjects told him. "When there was a fixed standard I felt more constrained to try to multiply and divide loudnesses, which is hard to do; but with no standard I could just place the tone were it seemed to belong."

In the psychophysics literature, going back to the 1930s, the word "anchor" was sometimes applied to a modulus or to the two endpoints of a category scale. Judgments were said to be "anchored" by these standards of comparison. It appeared, however, that the anchor could distort judgments, like a bubble in a glass window.

Stevens is not remembered as a compelling teacher. He nonetheless had several impressive classroom demonstrations. In one, he showed his students a gray paper disk surrounded by white. In a darkened room, with a spotlight on the gray disk, the gray looked white. Then Stevens illuminated the white around the disk. The "white" central disk turned black— by contrast with the now dazzling white surround.

Similar principles underlie many perceptual illusions. The one on page 37 (by MIT cognitive scientist Edward H. Adelson) is close in spirit to Stevens's demonstration. The gray color of square A is identical to the color of square B. The illusion is so compelling that it makes a great bar bet. To collect, make sure you have some Post-it Notes.

Carefully block off the surrounding checkerboard squares with Post-it Notes, leaving just the squares containing A and B visible. (You'll need about six small notes.) Not until you place the last note does it seem even *conceivable* that the two colors could be the same. Then suddenly, they "snap" to the same medium gray.

It's not hard to understand how the illusion works. The cylinder casts a shadow, darkening "white" square B (which is really gray). In terms of ink dots on paper, B is the same gray value as "black" square A. But the eye and brain have more important things to do than gauging absolute grayscale values. They are trying to make sense of the world, or in this case, a picture. That means attending to contrasts. We see a checkerboard on which all the "white" squares are the same color, and a uniform shadow with blurred edges. The contrast between light and shadow doesn't interfere with the contrast of the checkerboard squares, or vice versa.

One of Stevens's epigrams ran, "Black is white with a bright ring around it." The Orwellian tone of that statement is justified. Stevens knew only too well that you can get people to believe almost anything about their own perceptions with a little sleight of hand. Subjectively, there are no absolutes, only contrasts.

# Six

# Helson's Cigarette

The childhood of Harry Helson (1898–1977) was straight out of Dickens, or Lemony Snicket. He was born to impoverished Ukrainian immigrants who separated when he was four or five. Harry's mother fell on such hard times that she had to pack her son off to live with the father that both despised. Harry hated the new arrangement and ran away from home. He was taken in by a pair of spiritualists.

They were the Dyers of Bangor, Maine, and this was the golden age of séances and bell-ringing spirits. The Dyers opened their home to visiting mediums and lecturers. It is hard to say what young Harry believed or disbelieved about these houseguests, corporeal and otherwise. One friend said that Harry did a few "amateurish experiments" in the occult. Another recalled that "he did have several experiences that he was wholly unable to account for and that, I think, resulted in later years in an openness about all aspects of human experience."

With this grounding in body and spirit, Helson grew up to be a psychophysicist. A manifestation in a darkened room was a turning point in his career. Helson was working under ruby-red light in a photographic darkroom when he noted something odd. The tip of his cigarette glowed green.

The light emitted by the smoldering tobacco would have looked ember-red under ordinary light, of course. This experience helped Helson crystalize an important idea: that of an *adaptation level*. Evidently, Helson's eyes had adapted to the unusual red light of the darkroom. The glowing cigarette was a cooler, yellower red than the red of the safelight.

That made it look green *in comparison*. Helson's eyes and brain were not registering an absolute color (the way a digital camera might), but a difference between the color of the cigarette and the baseline color of the room.

Helson eventually concluded that all the senses adapt to a given level of stimulation and then register changes from that baseline. He demonstrated this in a famous set of experiments with weights. Helson had volunteers lift pairs of small weights, one after the other, and describe how heavy the second weight felt. He found that subjects were biased by the first weight, which served as an anchor, or baseline for comparison. (He was using the word "anchor" in a somewhat different sense from those I've already described.) When the anchor weight was lighter than the second weight, it made the second weight feel heavier. When the anchor was heavier, it made the second weight feel lighter. This relativity of perception could lead to outright contradiction. Helson could arrange things so that a weight that felt heavy after a light anchor could feel light after a heavy one.

Conceptually, this was no big surprise. If you want to look thin, make friends with fat people! We've all noticed contrast effects. Have you ever taken a sip of tea, expecting it to be coffee? For a fleeting moment, the taste is indescribably alien. It doesn't taste like tea, or like coffee. You're tasting the gap between what you expected and what you got.

Almost from the field's inception, psychophysicists cast their nets widely. Gustav Fechner attempted to scientifically gauge aesthetic preferences for two versions of a Hans Holbein Madonna that were baffling connoisseurs of the time. In the 1920s, at the University of Chicago, Louis Leon Thurstone contrived an alarming classroom project. "Instead of asking students to decide which of two weights seemed to be the heavier," he wrote, "it was more interesting to ask, for example, which of two nationalities they would generally prefer to associate with, or which they would prefer to have their sister marry." Elsewhere psychophysicists were putting their measuring rods to everything from the fineness of ivory carvings to the prestige of occupations to the historical importance of Swedish monarchs.

"The fact is that common principles exist in all fields of judgment," confidently asserted American psychophysicist William Hunt. In some of his experiments, Hunt had volunteers rate crimes "for the enormity of the breach of ethics involved." He came up with this puzzler. Part 1: Consider the crime of murdering your own mother, "wilfully and without provocation or justification." Now think of a crime exactly one half as bad. Write it down: _____

Part 2: Once again, think of murdering your mother, "wilfully," etc., etc. . . . Now think of "cheating at solitaire while playing by yourself." Finally, devise a crime that's exactly halfway between those two in seriousness. Write it here: _____

On a scale of evil, cheating at solitaire is about as close to a zero as you can get. You might expect that the answers to Part 1 would have been similar to the answers to Part 2—for much the same reason that Ferdinand Plateau's artists painted the same medium gray. They weren't. In 12 cases out of 14, the Part 1 answer was a more serious crime than the Part 2 answer.

Hunt concluded that the examples supplied in his questions influenced the answers. In Part 1, there was only mother-murder to serve as a frame of reference. This inspired thoughts of other atrocities. In Part 2, there were two examples, one serious and one not. Not many would think of cheating at solitaire as a "crime." The mere fact that the question called it that encouraged subjects to contemplate picayune offenses as crimes. This pulled down the average seriousness of the answers.

Hunt called this effect "anchoring" (using the word in still a different sense). He distinguished two varieties. *Contrast* anchoring occurs when you compare two stimuli. The glare of a streetlight makes the evening star look faint, and woe to the comedian who follows someone 40 percent funnier. *Assimilation* anchoring occurs when you have to invent an answer, given one or more possible responses. This occurs when people name a crime half as bad as another, or when jurors deliberate on a damage award after hearing an attorney's demand. The two types of anchoring have opposite effects. In contrast anchoring, subjective perceptions are displaced *away* from the anchor. In assimilation, responses are drawn *toward* the anchor.

Helson spent a lot of effort trying to understand what qualifies an experience as an anchor, capable of influencing a judgment. His answers were "recency, frequency, intensity, area, duration, and higher-order attributes such as meaningfulness, familiarity and ego-involvement." That isn't such a mouthful as it sounds. Start with *recency*. A 5-ounce weight feels heavy a couple of seconds after you lift a 3-ounce weight. Wait an hour between weights, and the contrast effect vanishes. You forget how heavy the previous weight felt.

Frequency matters too. Lifting a series of 3-ounce weights causes an adaptation to that particular degree of heaviness. Should you then lift a 5-ounce weight, it feels heavy. The effect of the multiple 3-ounce anchors is stronger than the effect of just one anchor.

Helson's most interesting findings were about "higher-order attributes" such as meaningfulness. He pulled a trick on some of his subjects. In the midst of an experiment, he requested that the subject move a tray of weights out of the way. The tray (plus the weights it held) was a "weight" heavier than any of those used in the experiment. But the heavy tray did *not* make the next object lifted seem light in comparison. The subjects were focused on the little metal weights, not the tray, and they tuned it out. This demonstrated that anchoring is not a muscular reaction but a mental one.

# Seven

# The Price Scale

There is a magnitude scale of overwhelming importance in everyone's life. It's called *price*.

Perhaps around 3000 BC, the Mesopotamians realized that the shekel, their unit of weight, could also denote that weight of barley—or the value of whatever might be bartered for that amount of barley. This was the beginning of money and of prices.

To an economist, a "reserve price" is the maximum amount a buyer is willing to pay, or the minimum a seller is willing to accept. Transactions are expected to take place at a price somewhere between these extremes. Economics investigates how market forces affect prices paid.

There is a quite different way of looking at things. Reserve prices can be thought of as a magnitude scale. For a buyer, prices are a numerical measure of desire to possess something. For a seller, prices measure desire to keep what one already has (including such all-important possessions as time, energy, and self-respect).

In the common sense of everyday affairs, prices are one-dimensional, like marks on a ruler. For every commodity, there's a single point on the scale. These points neatly order all the world's stuff by price. The psychological reality of prices is not that simple.

Those in S. S. Stevens's Harvard lab got some free lessons in the psychology of money. "Smitty was a close man with a dollar, and he spent his laboratory budget as if it were his personal checking account," said colleague George Miller. Stevens was notorious for denying raises. When confronted, he had the perfect psychophysical explanation. *You don't want a raise*, Stevens would say. *One day you'll leave Harvard. If you get used to a high salary here, you'll be completely priced out of the market elsewhere.* To Stevens, a good salary was a low salary surrounded by a ring of abject poverty.

Stevens posed this riddle to his classes: "Suppose I were to tell you that I have a special fund for the purpose, and that I am going to give you ten dollars. That would make you happy, would it not? Now think this over carefully: how much would I have to give you to make you twice as happy?"

Philosophers are free to object that a phrase like "twice as happy" is meaningless. But Stevens's students didn't seem to have a problem answering the question in the spirit intended. Their replies would have shocked economists more than philosophers. The average answer was about $40.

Think of it this way. Getting $10 you didn't expect is a nice little surprise. For the next day or two, at odd moments, you'll think about the extra cash in your wallet and feel good. A week from now, the money will be spent and forgotten.

Now: Can you honestly say that getting $20 would be *twice* as good? Everything I just said about $10 applies to $20.

By this line of reasoning, it ought to take more than $20 to make someone twice as happy; and it did. In classrooms, the average answer has ranged from $35 to $50.

Diminishing returns for money was hardly news. No economist would have been surprised in the least had Stevens found that it took $4 million to double the pleasure of getting $1 million. Those are life-changing sums. A million dollars buys much of what money can buy (in Stevens's time, anyway). No one expects one's second million to be as meaningful as the first.

This is known as a *wealth effect*. It can't explain Stevens's little experiment. His subjects were Harvard students, many from wealthy families and most looking forward to a lifetime of financial security. From a lifetime perspective, a few tens of dollars should have been meaningless. The only thing that should have mattered was what the money could buy. Whatever the conversion rate of money to happiness, $20 buys twice as much as $10 does. The "correct" answer should be $20.

Why didn't Stevens's students see things that way? Apparently, they weren't just thinking of what the money could buy. Money itself was a "stimulus" producing a sensation—and it worked much like the other stimuli Stevens studied.

Stevens lived long enough to see a number of careful studies measuring the subjective impact of money. In 1959 the Japanese psychophysicist Tarow Indow showed pictures and descriptions of wristwatches to a group of 127 college students. He had them rate the desirability of each watch, then name a fair price for it in yen. The students believed that in order to get a watch twice as desirable, it was necessary to pay about 8.7 times as much.

To give some contemporary figures, Timex watches hover around $40, you can have your pick of Swatches for around $150, a Cartier Tank watch is $3,000, and a Rolex President costs about $30,000. All are good watches that do what a timepiece is supposed to do. The only difference is status. Wearing a Cartier says you're rich and don't care who knows it. The Rolex says the same thing, only louder. The Rolex presumably has a higher bling rating than the Cartier, but not anywhere near ten times more. As Indow's students appreciated, a massive increase in price buys only an incremental increase in cachet.

There were also studies finding power laws for the social status attached to income and the seriousness of a theft of money. To double your social status, you need to earn about 2.6 times as much, according to one study cited by Stevens. The seriousness of thefts rose the slowest with dollar value. A thief would need to steal 60 times as much to double the seriousness of the crime. At first this may sound odd. But most would agree that stealing *anything* is wrong; the amount stolen is a secondary consideration. Hence, according to the power curve of thievery, stealing $6,000 is only about twice as bad as stealing $100.

Overall this research confirmed Stevens's opinion that perceptions of money were much like those of the senses. Price is a magnitude scale with a meaningful zero (we all know what it means for something to be worthless) and no upper limit. The different characteristic ratios (for gifts, thefts, etc.) are also typical of magnitude scales.

As mad as our culture is about money, we're actually *less* sensitive to it than to a lot of things. There are many sensations that increase faster than the stimulus itself. It takes only 1.6 times the weight to double the perception of heaviness (all weightlifters understand this). Only 1.2 times the electric current doubles the sensation of shock (this is why it's an effective torture). With money, it always takes more than twice the cash to double the thrill. Relatively speaking, there's not much bang for the buck.

In hindsight, this work on the psychophysics of money was original and hugely important. Price is a unique magnitude scale, of course. We care a lot about absolute values—about the actual prices charged for things. However, caring about absolutes does not confer the power to perceive them accurately. When estimating monetary values, people are easily swayed by the legerdemain of anchoring, by illusions trading on contrasts and the power of suggestion. To an extent that few could have anticipated, this work revealed an invisible hand guiding, and misguiding, the world's financial decision making.

Practically no one outside of psychophysics paid the slightest attention to it.

# Part Three

**"Incoherence is more than skin deep"**

# Eight

# Input to Output

Like most of the Jewish mobsters who ran Las Vegas, Benny Goffstein was a family man. When he had a chance to open his own casino, he named it the Four Queens, in honor of his four daughters. Compared to the first casino he'd run, the Riviera, the Four Queens was downtown and downscale, and all the more profitable for it.

One of the Four Queens' investors was utterly unlike the mob types that Goffstein had encountered at the Riviera. He was Charles B. G. Murphy, a Massachusetts aristocrat of somewhat scandalous tastes. Murphy had been a Yale football player, a friend of J. Sterling Rockefeller, an African explorer, a big game hunter, an attorney, and a gambler. He spent his last years in Las Vegas. Murphy came to Goffstein with a problem. He had set up a charitable foundation to avoid paying taxes. The government was pressuring Murphy to disburse some of the foundation money for good works, lest the tax shelter be disallowed. Murphy was determined to fund scientific research on a topic dear to his heart: gambling.

Murphy called around asking for the name of a scientist who was an expert on gambling. He came up with Ward Edwards, a psychologist at the University of Michigan. Edwards had an unusual request. He and a couple of his former students, who worked for an outfit called the Oregon Research Institute, wanted to do some experiments in a Las Vegas casino. They were big on doing experiments on real people in real settings. Would it be possible to use the Four Queens? Murphy, as major backer, had enough of the street in him to make it clear that this was an offer Goffstein could not refuse.

•   •   •

Ward Edwards (1927–2005) spent his career asking difficult questions. Born in Morristown, New Jersey, he was the son of an economist and grew up hearing the table talk of his father's colleagues. This instilled in him a rebellious skepticism toward economics. Ward decided on psychology as a career, studying at Swarthmore and Harvard. It was at Harvard that he read the work of John von Neumann and Oskar Morgenstern, and he wasn't crazy about all he read.

Hungarian-born John von Neumann was one of the great mathematicians of the twentieth century. At the urging of Princeton economist Oskar Morgenstern, von Neumann turned his brilliant mind to the problems of economics. The result was a 1944 book, *Theory of Games and Economic Behavior*. Von Neumann's running metaphor was that economic conflicts were "games," something like poker and equally amenable to mathematical analysis.

The poker chips of economic games are dollars and pounds and yen. Or actually, not quite that. Von Neumann, like economists in general, insisted on playing for a subjective currency called *utility*.

That term dates to the eighteenth century. Swiss mathematician Daniel Bernoulli noted that the value of money is relative. A hundred-dollar birthday check can be undreamed-of riches to a five-year-old child and totally meaningless to a forty-five-year-old billionaire. In predicting what people will do with money, it is necessary to adjust for these differing valuations, just as it is sometimes necessary to adjust dollars for inflation.

You can think of utility as a personal "price tag" that everyone places on things and outcomes. I think this yard sale lamp is worth 50 utility-dollars, you think it's worth zero. The important thing is, people try to amass the most utility, not necessarily the most dollars. Whoever dies with the most utility wins.

Economists took to Bernoulli's idea for two reasons. One, it acknowledged what was always obvious: that psychology (not just simple avarice) determines economic decisions. Two, utility excused economists from paying much attention to psychology. Economists were mainly interested in forging an exact mathematical science. With a few exceptions, they didn't want to bother with measuring the psychological aspects of money. They much preferred to assume it could be done in principle.

Utility is a powerful idea (so goes the prospectus) because its imaginary price tags determine all economic decisions. MIT economist Paul Samuelson developed this notion into his doctrine of "revealed preference." This appealingly sensible thesis says that the only way to learn about utility is to look at the choices people make. Choices reveal all that we can know of utility, and utility in turn determines the prices that consumers are willing to pay.

When someone is given a free choice between A and B, he simply consults his invisible price tags and chooses the one with the higher utility. Decision making is thus reduced to numbers. This assumption leads naturally to most of the standbys of economic theory, from demand curves to the Nash equilibrium.

That brings us back to von Neumann's contribution. Many economic choices are gambles. Given our uncertain world, the difficult and interesting choices are *always* gambles of one kind or another. It is therefore necessary to assign prices to gambles. According to von Neumann, the way to do this is to multiply each possible outcome's subjective price by its probability, and total the results.

Von Neumann and Morgenstern maintained that every rational person uses this kind of mental math (the "expected utility model") to make decisions, from deciding what to order for lunch to what stock to invest in. This premise became the mainspring of their economic theory, a model that economists embraced in the postwar years.

Not all economists applauded the new regime. Herbert Simon was one of the earliest, loudest, most down-to-earth critics of economics' cult of rationality. In a review of von Neumann's book, Simon complained that it is "impossible for the behavior of a single, isolated individual to reach any high degree of rationality." Simon was equally harsh on the tradition that von Neumann was partly upending. "How any grown-up, bright human being can go satisfied with the neoclassical theory is kind of hard to understand," he marveled.

Simon's own career-keynote book, *Administrative Behavior*, was published three years after von Neumann's. It could hardly have presented a more different picture of the "games" people play. Simon analyzed case studies of how corporations and other hierarchies made decisions. His most enduring sound bite is that humans are "boundedly rational." They are too busy, too ill-informed, and occasionally too boneheaded to think things through in the way that von Neumann proposed. Authentic humans don't show the perfect, chessmaster appreciation of consequences that von Neumann's theory demands. Instead, decision makers resort to *heuristics*, or mental shortcuts, to arrive at quick, intuitive choices.

Simon was feinting at the path that psychologists would soon take. He didn't go there himself. For one thing, Simon did not see himself as an experimentalist. Second, he viewed human rationality as being like military intelligence: an oxymoron. Simon held that it was organizations rather than individuals that attained rationality, and thus it was organizations that interested him. These organizations were like anthills, able to muster collective "intelligence" from rather unpromising individual resources.

Ward Edwards was never entirely comfortable fitting into the organizations that so intrigued Simon. Edwards had been fired from his first job, at Johns Hopkins, for lackadaisical teaching. He then found a post with the Air Force in Denver, working for a cryptic bureau called the Intellectual Functions Section. Edwards later claimed that landing the Air Force job was the most fortunate thing that ever happened to him. It exposed him to a constant stream of decision-making problems.

Edwards once visited NORAD, the nuclear defense command center in Colorado Springs. He was curious to see how some of the world's most momentous decisions got made. Edwards was ushered into the command center, dominated by a *Dr. Strangelove* map displaying military information collected from distant early warning radar and ships at sea. In those pre-Google days, the volume of real-time information was mesmerizing. Edwards asked the officer escorting him what was done with all that information. His escort pointed to a red telephone, apparently a direct line to the White House. Edwards asked, "Do you think the ratio of input to output information should be like that?"

Edwards had not gained much academic renown by the time he moved to the University of Michigan's psychology department. "Michigan was a large department, very tolerant and very open," psychologist Barbara Tversky explained. Even in that most liberal context, Edwards stood out. He "was nutty—not really socialized." Two associates recalled that Edwards's "occasional colorful and forthright behavior" perpetually threatened to derail tenure.

With his free-spirited wife, Ruth (a Ph.D. student of B. F. Skinner's), Edwards lived in bohemian splendor. At one point the couple inhabited a dusty building behind a garage, in an industrial part of Ann Arbor; at another, a ruinous farmhouse. The Edwardses raised dachshunds, one named Willy (after psychophysicist Wilhelm Wundt, of course). Dinner parties featured "Ruth's excellent, if often exotic cooking, with the early arrivals required to light dozens of candles placed on every horizontal surface in living and dining rooms."

Edwards is usually credited as the founder of behavioral decision theory. It was certainly he who lent the nascent field a name, in the form of the title of a 1961 paper. But others were exploring decision making, at Michigan and elsewhere.

Many of the early experiments involved gambling. A researcher needs a way of getting subjects' attention in a psychological experiment. A small money prize, that might be won or might not, is an effective motivator. Edwards and Michigan colleague Clyde Coombs did experiments in which volunteers had to choose between gambles or assign prices to them. Sarah Lichtenstein, who took her Ph.D. under Edwards, has the impression that Coombs ("a marvelous person") was not interested in gambling per se. Gambles simply offered a handy way of creating decision problems. Edwards "was actually interested in the economic theories of decision making."

In deciding how much to pay for a car or whom to marry, there are always trade-offs—a process of "comparing incomparables," in Coombs's words. Gambles offer an obvious trade-off between the money to be won and the chance of winning it. So Coombs and Edwards would have volunteers choose between a gamble with a bigger prize and another with a better chance of winning. The psychologists sifted the stated preferences and tried to discern how people decided. A 1960 study by Coombs and D. G. Pruitt found that most of the choices could be explained by simple rules such as "Always choose the bet with the highest payoff for winning."

Welcome to the world of bounded rationality. Anyone who followed this rule was ignoring the odds—betting on the long shots, no matter what. That policy doesn't work well at the racetrack, and it's not much better elsewhere.

Edwards learned poker at the Air Force job and remained an enthusiastic player at Michigan. The game provided some of his experimental supplies. One of Edwards's best-known experiments involved two backpacks filled with equal numbers of poker chips. One of the backpacks contains mostly red chips—say, 70 percent red and 30 percent white. The other is mostly white chips, with the percentages reversed. You don't know which backpack is which. Your task is to decide which is the mostly red backpack. To do that, you draw chips one at a time from one backpack. You must estimate the odds as you go. It's as if you're a bookmaker and have to quote the current point spread. Edwards had students do that as he carefully kept track of the colors of the chips drawn.

Imagine you're drawing from backpack #1. The first chip you draw is red. That bumps up the probability that this backpack is the mostly red one. How much?

The correct answer is simpler than you might think. It's 70 percent exactly. But this wasn't intended as a math puzzle. Most decisions are made by gut, and Edwards wanted to see how accurate these gut instincts were. He found that guesses tended to be less than the correct value. People failed to appreciate that a single red chip could be as informative as it actually is.

This confirmed Edwards's suspicion that people are not especially good at making decisions under uncertainty. But that is exactly what von Neumann and much of the economic profession were taking as a given.

In a 1954 *Psychological Bulletin* article, Edwards sketched the von Neumann–Morgenstern model—few of his psychologist readers would have known much about it—and posed the rhetorical question of whether it had the slightest thing to do with reality. "The method of those theorists who have been concerned with the theory of decision making is essentially an armchair method," Edwards complained. "They make assumptions, and from these assumptions they deduce theorems which can presumably be tested, though it sometimes seems unlikely the testing will ever occur."

High among the untested assumptions was that humans behave like the fiction known as an *economic man* (*Homo economicus*) or *rational actor* or *rational maximizer*. This is a worker/capitalist/consumer/game-player concerned exclusively with personal gain. In Robert Heilbroner's words, economic man was "a pale wraith of a creature who followed his adding machine brain wherever it led him." That adding machine brain enabled economic men to calculate expected utility for decisions big and trivial.

"Von Neumann and Morgenstern defended this model and, thus, made it important," Edwards wrote, "but [by] 1954 it was already clear that it . . . does not fit the facts."

That year of 1954 was not chosen casually. It was the date of Edwards's pivotal *Psychological Bulletin* paper, and it must also allude, in part, to what we now call Allais' paradox. That deserves a chapter of its own.

# Nine

# Lunch with Maurice

In 1952, Leonard "Jimmie" Savage had one of the most excruciating lunches of his life. Savage was a thirty-five-year-old American in Paris attending an academic conference. Seated across the table from him was a man with the expression of a startled terrier. He was Maurice Allais, a forty-one-year-old French economist. Allais had his hair trimmed up the sides of his head, leaving a bushy flat top. Between the trick haircut and the tight smile that might be a frown, Allais' face evoked one of those odd pictures that becomes a different face when turned upside down.

Allais had told Savage he had something to show him. It was a little test he wanted him to take. The important thing is that Savage failed the test.

Savage was a brash statistician, then at the University of Chicago. He had gone into statistics on the advice of John von Neumann himself. Visually, the most remarkable thing about him was his eyeglasses. Their lenses packed enough diopters to reveal the space behind his head. At Chicago, Savage had acquired a second mentor, Milton Friedman — founding father of the Chicago school of economics, future Nobel laureate, and veritable saint to Reagan-era capitalists. Friedman knew quite a bit of statistics for an economist. He and Savage had begun a peripatetic collaboration. Savage was attempting to devise a theory of how people make decisions. The decisions that concerned him tended to be about money. He was interested in how people assign prices to goods and services and how they make choices between them. Savage wanted to show that decisions about money were (or could be) completely logical. Friedman desired just such a theory. It would supply a firm foundation to his utopian economics of the free market.

There was one big problem with that, Allais told Savage: his theory was dead *wrong*.

Proving theories wrong was a hobby with Allais. His parents had owned a cheese shop, and he had worked eighty-hour weeks—while holding down administrative posts with the French bureau of mines—writing the iconoclastic economic works that secured his renown, and ultimately a Nobel Prize. Allais did not limit himself to disproving wrong ideas in economics. He was just then embarking on a grand quest to disprove Einstein's theory of relativity. Allais devised a special pendulum that would one day show Einstein's error, or so he believed. He would spend much of the 1950s attempting to demonstrate that Einstein had cribbed relativity (for what it's worth) from that great Frenchman Henri Poincaré.

Proving that Savage's theory was wrong was much simpler. Like a troll in a fairy tale, Allais posed three riddles.

I will use a streamlined version of the questions Allais published the following year, putting the money amounts in dollars. Though not identical to the riddles Allais posed to Savage, they will give you the flavor of his argument.

Riddle one: Which of the following would you rather have?

(a)  A sure $1 million
   —*or*—
(b)  This gamble: We spin a wheel of fortune with 100 slots. You have an 89 percent chance of winning $1 million, a 10 percent chance of winning $2.5 million, and a 1 percent chance of winning nothing at all.

Allais believed that most people would choose (a), the sure million, over (b), which offers a small chance of ending up with nothing. Apparently, Savage agreed.

Riddle two: This time your choice is

(a)  An 11 percent chance of winning $1 million
   —*or*—
(b)  a 10 percent chance of winning $2.5 million.

Allais thought that most people would choose (b). There isn't much difference in the chances. You might as well go for the higher prize in (b). Again Savage concurred. In so doing, he fell into the Frenchman's trap.

This brings us to Riddle 3. In front of you is a sealed box. Which would you rather have?

(a) An 89 percent chance of winning whatever is in the box, and an 11 percent chance of winning $1 million instead

 —or—

(b) An 89 percent chance of winning what's in the box, a 10 percent chance of winning $2.5 million, and a 1 percent chance of winning nothing at all.

This was a direct thrust at the American's jugular. As Allais knew, one of Savage's axioms of reasonable decision making says (in essence) that when deciding between a burger with diet soda or pizza with diet soda, you can ignore the diet soda because you're getting it in either case. The only thing that matters is whether you like burgers or pizza better. In general, according to Savage, deciders should ignore the common elements of choices and choose based on the differences.

This sounds reasonable to just about everyone. Allais spotted a subtle flaw. By Savage's logic, the choice in Riddle 3 shouldn't depend on what's in the box. Whether you choose (a) or (b), you get the same 89 percent chance at winning the same box.

This doesn't mean that the box's contents are unimportant. The box could contain a billion dollars, or a deadly tarantula, or the phone number of that cool person you met on the subway. But according to Savage, the box shouldn't bear on the choice between (a) and (b). That choice should be based solely on whether it's better to have an 11 percent chance of $1 million or a 10 percent chance of $2.5 million.

In other words, the answer to Riddle 3 should be the same as to Riddle 2. That's not all. Suppose we open the box and discover a million dollars in there. Then the choice in Riddle 3 ends up being identical to that in Riddle 1. In short, the answer to all three riddles should be the same, either (a) or (b) with no flip-flopping. Allais had tricked Savage into betraying his own rule.

A few months later, Allais gave a similar pop quiz to Milton Friedman. Friedman did *not* fall into the trap Savage did and gave consistent answers. I suppose you have to wonder whether Savage clued him in.

•   •   •

In a 1953 *Econometrica* article, published in French, Allais took issue with the axioms of *l'école Américaine* (meaning Detroit-born Jimmie Savage and his Brooklyn-born friend Milton Friedman). The Americans were saying that everyone's got a price (utility) for everything. These subjective prices determine all decisions. Humans are more complex than that, Allais argued. Choices depend on context, and no single number can express how one feels about uncertain outcomes.

This demonstration has since become known as Allais' paradox. Don't worry if you're still unclear on what Allais was driving at and why it's important. Let me give a remix of the paradox, conceived by Richard Zeckhauser of Harvard. You are a contestant on a popular new game show, *Your Money or Your Life*. Like most game shows, it simply recycles an old parlor game. Unfortunately for you, that old parlor game is Russian roulette.

At the beginning of every show, Tiffany, the "Bullet Lady," spins Fortune's Wheel. The wheel is divided into six equal slices. The spin tells Tiffany how many bullets, from one to six, to load into a six-barrel gun and hand to the show's host, Brian. After a brief commercial break, Brian spins the gun's barrel and points it directly at your left temple. Just before he pulls the trigger, he proposes a financial arrangement that you will doubtless find interesting.

*You can buy a bullet.* Should you and Brian agree on a price, he will extract one bullet at random from the gun's barrel and hand it to you in exchange for the money you give him. He will then spin the barrel again, point the gun at your temple again, and pull the trigger.

Here's the odd thing. You'd probably be willing to pay a higher price for a bullet when it's the only one in the barrel. Buy that one bullet, and you're 100 percent certain to survive (versus having a 1 in 6 chance of not making it to the commercial break). You'd pay a lot for that, right?

Just for the sake of comparison, suppose there are four bullets in the barrel. Now how much would you pay to buy one bullet—to have just three bullets rather than four? Somehow this weakens the case for raising every last penny for that bullet. You might even feel you'd be willing to take your chances with the four bullets.

Isn't the human mind a funny thing? A bullet is a bullet, dead is dead. The reduction in probability of your demise is precisely the same in both cases. Why isn't your price the same?

Or imagine there are six bullets in the gun. You're a corpse unless you buy a bullet. This may cause you to flip-flop again and conclude that the bullet is priceless, worth paying everything you've got.

Both this game and Allais' original puzzle reveal a *certainty effect.* There is often a huge subjective difference between an *absolute, 100 percent sure thing* and something that is only 99 percent likely. This difference is expressed in prices as well as choices. Meanwhile, the difference between a 10 and an 11 percent chance is shrugged off.

To a select following of economists, psychologists, and philosophers, the Allais paradox became a sword in the stone. Great minds tested themselves against it, few managing to get much of a grip. In later years, Allais himself thought and wrote extensively about his puzzle. In true economist fashion, he tried to lay out axioms of human decision making and show that they were subtly incompatible, leading to contradiction.

"His paradox was great," one scholar said of Allais. "But if you read his own papers on what he thought the right theory was, they're very hard to understand . . . He's also cantankerous. There were a few conferences of a group called FUR, Foundations of Uncertainty and Risk, and I went to a couple of them. Allais would give this talk, and someone would say, 'Your axioms are wrong, you claim you've proved something that's not proved.' Allais would bluster, and [UC San Diego economist] Mark Machina would literally stand up and try to defend Allais. Then Allais would turn on Machina."

Allais continued his attack in a prickly 1995 paper subtitled "Unceasingly Repeated Errors or Contradictions of Mark Machina." ("As a matter of fact," Allais wrote, "I haven't been able until now to answer Machina's paper. My time has been entirely used up, on one hand by the task of editing the first printed version of my 1943 work, in view of which I have [been] awarded the 1988 Nobel Prize in Economic Science, with a new and long introduction, and on another hand by the task of publishing an important book on Europe . . . The reader will understand that I cannot accept to spend too much of a scarce time to correct Machina's mistakes, *line after line . . .*")

The long-suffering Machina has posted Allais's paper on his website, under the heading "News, Gossip & Games." I'll confine myself to saying a little about why Allais' paradox was so intractable. The stumbling block isn't the certainty effect per se. It's the way that smart people are influenced by mere words, by the way the choices are framed. As Amos Tversky later wrote, "We choose between descriptions of options, rather than between the options themselves." For the most part, economists were not ready to accept that fact of life.

# Ten

# Money Pump

For a psychologist, Ward Edwards could display startling insensitivity to the feelings of others. Sarah Lichtenstein found him exasperating. Fresh out of Swarthmore, she arrived at Ann Arbor for graduate work, with Edwards as her advisor. Edwards proposed that she collaborate on an article with another grad student, Paul Slovic. "When we had written it up and were talking about the order of names to publish it under, Ward very graciously agreed to be the third name," Lichtenstein said. "He suggested—it was stronger than that—that Paul be the first author because he, being a man, would have to earn a living." The article appeared in a 1965 issue of *The American Journal of Psychology*, credited to Paul Slovic, Sarah Lichtenstein, and Ward Edwards. Slovic was three years younger than Lichtenstein.

The patriarchal times dictated Lichtenstein's moves after grad school. "I sort of followed hubby around for several years." Husband Ed was a clinical psychologist who took a job in Los Angeles. When he got an offer from the University of Oregon in 1966, one selling point was that Sarah might be able to land a job at the Oregon Research Institute. "It was a terrific inducement," she explained. ORI "was a marvelous place to work at that time."

Paul Slovic was already there. He had accepted a job after graduation in 1964 and lobbied for ORI to hire Lichtenstein. The two resumed an agreeable collaboration that, among other things, studied how people assign prices to gambles.

For example: A wager offers a 1 in 8 chance of winning $77. How much would you be willing to pay for the privilege of playing this bet?

The obvious approach is to compute how much you can expect to win, on the average, each time you play. This comes to ⅛ times $77, or $9.63. Of course, the numbers here make it hard to do the math in your head. The psychologists were interested in intuitive judgments, and they observed that the prices subjects assigned to simple bets were usually too high. People apparently paid more attention to the prize amount than to the chance of winning it.

This could explain why lotteries are so popular. A lottery offers, let's say, a one-in-a-zillion chance of winning $58 million. Players are essentially buying the right to fantasize about the jackpot. The "one in a zillion" is in the fine print, literally *and* in the minds of players. When lottery boards want to drum up business, they raise the jackpots, not the chances of winning.

A similar phenomenon pertains to losing bets. How much would you pay to get out of a situation in which you have a 1 in 12 chance of losing $63? People were typically willing to pay *more* than the average loss. The dollar amount of the penalty loomed more important than the probability in their decision making.

This suggests an explanation for why people buy insurance. They are willing to pay "too much" for coverage because they worry more about the dollar value of catastrophes than the remoteness of the odds.

Lichtenstein and Slovic asked some of their subjects to rate the "attractiveness" of bets on a scale of 1 to 5. They found that the ratings correlated most strongly with the probability of winning. People liked bets that were easy to win.

Okay, fine. But the *prices* assigned to bets correlated with the amount to win. It was as if people had two ways of valuing bets, and they were subtly in conflict.

"I remember we were in Paul's office, I can't tell you what year it was," Lichtenstein said. "We were getting an idea of what subjects were paying attention to. I don't recall who said it first, or whether we said it at the same time. But it struck us that we could design bets that would encourage subjects to do one thing under one response mode and another under another response mode. When we saw it and said it aloud, we were sure it was going to work—and it did."

Their brainstorm was that prices might not reflect what people want.

They could invent a pair of bets—call them A and B—such that most people would say they preferred A, but, when asked to assign prices to them, they would give a higher value to B.

The strangeness of this might be easier to appreciate if you pretend that A and B are fancy gift boxes wrapped in paper and bows. I don't know for sure what's in either box. I have had a chance to shake them and form some opinion about what's inside. Okay, I've decided that I'm willing to pay $40 for Box A and $70 for Box B. I've also decided that I'd rather have Box A.

This is crazy! My prices don't jibe with my desires or actions. Lichtenstein and Slovic found something crazier yet. For certain types of gambles, *most* people have valuations just like this.

They called this a "preference reversal," and here's an example. In the figure below, the two circles represent dartboards. Pick one; then a "dealer" is going to toss a dart at the center of your chosen target, so that the dart is equally likely to land anywhere within the circle. That determines how much (if anything) you win. Which target would you rather use?

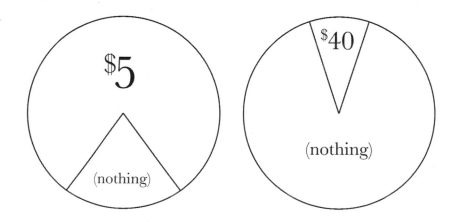

The target on the left offers an 80 percent chance of winning $5 (otherwise nothing). The one on the right has a 10 percent chance of winning $40, and otherwise nothing.

The expected value happens to be the same for both bets ($4), so that provides no grounds for choosing. Yet a majority prefer the target on the left. Lichtenstein and Slovic termed gambles like the one on the left *P* (for *probability*) bets. A P bet offers a high chance of winning. The bet on the right is a $ (*money*) bet offering a bigger prize and a lesser chance of winning it. When asked to choose, most people prefer P bets to $ bets.

There is nothing peculiar about that. Choosing the P bet increases the odds of walking away a winner. What *is* odd is that the same subjects regularly assign higher prices to $ bets, like the one on the right above. The prices contradict the preferences.

In the actual experiments, a dozen distinct bets were used. They were somewhat more complicated than the examples above, in that the player stood a chance of losing money as well as winning it. (This is more like familiar sports or casino bets: you have to put up some money to play and risk losing it.) The experimental subjects were first shown bets two at a time and asked to choose which they preferred. Then they were shown the same set of bets one at a time and asked to price them. In this part, they were told that they "owned" the bet in question and could sell it back to the house for sure cash. What was the minimum price they would accept?

Out of 173 subjects, 127 *always* chose the P bet, yet *always* assigned a higher price to the $ bet. Almost everyone reversed preferences at least some of the time. They weren't necessarily aware of what they were doing. It would have been hard to remember all one's responses and enforce a consistency. The volunteers went with their instincts, and those instincts showed a striking pattern.

"These reversals clearly constitute inconsistent behavior and violate every existing theory of decision making," the psychologists wrote in a 1971 issue of *The Journal of Experimental Psychology*. This time the byline read "Sarah Lichtenstein and Paul Slovic."

The experiment revealed that most people do not assign prices consistent with their choices. The psychologists' careful methodology underscored this startling finding. In one set of trials, Lichtenstein and Slovic went all out to make sure their subjects were answering after due reflection. This group of participants played their bets with a roulette wheel and won real money, though not much of it. (Psychologists often have to resort to penny-pinching in experiments. The subjects played for "points" convertible into dollars, and the maximum winning was $8.) Players were shown each pair of bets three times and reminded of previous choices. They were allowed to change their minds. Only the third choice was binding. With all these safeguards in place, the players *still* assigned higher prices to bets they rejected.

In another set of trials, the instructions for pricing bets were changed. Subjects were asked to pretend that they wanted to *buy* each bet and to state the maximum price they would be willing to pay for it. Logically, there shouldn't be a difference in buying and selling prices for a simple money bet. The bet is worth whatever it's worth. But Lichtenstein and Slovic found that people buying bets were less likely to assign high prices to the $ bets. The number of preference reversals greatly diminished.

This was an early description of what's now known as the *endowment effect* (a name coined by the University of Chicago economist Richard Thaler in 1980). In the absence of market values, selling prices are typically twice as much as buying prices (above and beyond any strategic exaggeration for the sake of bargaining). Lichtenstein and Slovic thus tried three ways of assessing value and found them all potentially contradictory.

In the years since 1971, psychologists and economists alike have tried to explain preference reversal—or explain it away. It was apparent to all that the subjects were using mental shortcuts. Whether pricing gambles or choosing between them, they simplified things.

Here is one of the choices Lichtenstein and Slovic tested:

[P bet]:  A 10 in 12 chance of winning $9, otherwise you lose $3
      —*or*—
[$ bet]:  A 3 in 12 chance of winning $91, otherwise you lose $21.

By design, it is hard to look at this and intuit which bet is "better." How do you choose, then? One subject in an early experiment explained: "If the odds were . . . heavier in favor of winning . . . I would pay about ¾ of the amount I would expect to win. If the reverse were true, I would ask the experimenter to pay me about . . . ½ of the amount I could lose."

Any bookmaker would shudder at this. This subject was ignoring much of the information he'd been given. We *all* do that. In splitting a restaurant bill or guessing how much time to buy on a parking meter, everyone rounds mathematical corners. We do it because there's not much money at stake, and our time and effort may be worth more than the rounding error.

Another factor might be the limits of memory. Short-term memory—roughly, the set of recalled concepts residing in your consciousness *right now*—is said to be limited to around seven elements. Though you may have a great long-term memory for figures, and have gigabytes of financial models on your laptop, these exist only for reference. At the decisive moment (assuming there *is* a "decisive moment") you can access only about seven numbers or concepts.

The choices in the preference reversal experiments must have brushed against this limit. Participants were given six explicit numbers (a probability of winning, a win amount, and a loss amount, for each of two bets). A conscientious subject might try to calculate additional numbers, like the probabilities of losing or the expectation for each bet. Only so many of these numbers will "fit" in consciousness at once. Thinking about the calculated numbers means forgetting, at least temporarily, some of the original numbers. In Lichtenstein and Slovic's words, "The strain of amalgamating different types of information into an overall decision may often force an individual to resort to judgmental strategies that do an injustice to his underlying system of values."

This isn't true of just some exotic bets cooked up in a psychology lab. Most big price decisions present us with too much information. When setting a price for a used car, a house, or a corporate acquisition, we sift dozens, if not hundreds or thousands, of relevant numbers. Data must be reduced like a fine sauce, to the few most telling numbers and reasons. Doing that means making intuitive judgments about what information may be safely ignored. Anyone who's ever sat in on a meeting where colleagues justify a new vendor, ad campaign, or vice president hears boiled-down half-truths and heuristics. "I went with the Korean offer because it's basically a sure thing" . . . "I always offer 75 percent of what I expect to pay—sometimes it works" . . . "This way, we're guaranteed to make our money back and have a shot at a lot more." We oversimplify because, simply, there's no other way of getting by in the world.

•   •   •

After the experiment, Lichtenstein debriefed the preference reversal subjects. In each case, she tried to convince them that they had been
"wrong" in order to see whether they would stand their ground or recant.
ORI made audio recordings of these conversations. In them, Lichtenstein's tart delivery is as perfect as an Elaine May routine. I will give a
few excerpts from a 1968 debriefing (and encourage you to listen to the
full audio on the Web):

SARAH LICHTENSTEIN: I see. Well, how about the bid for Bet A? Do you
    have any further feelings about it now that you know you are choos-
    ing one but bidding more for the other one?
SUBJECT (male college student): It's kind of strange, but no, I don't have
    any feelings at all whatsoever really about it. It's just one of those
    things. It shows my reasoning process isn't so good, but, other than
    that, I . . . no qualms.
LICHTENSTEIN: No qualms. Okay. Some people would say that that pat-
    tern of responses is not a reasonable pattern.
SUBJECT: Yeah, I could see that.
LICHTENSTEIN: Well, supposing I asked you to make it reasonable.
    Would you say, well, it's reasonable now, or would you change some-
    thing?
SUBJECT: Actually, it is reasonable.
LICHTENSTEIN: Can I persuade you that that is an irrational pattern?
SUBJECT: No, I don't think you probably could . . .

You may be wondering whether we should cut those poor preference-
reversal subjects a little slack. ("A foolish consistency is the hobgoblin of
little minds," Ralph Waldo Emerson wrote, endearing him to the inconsistent ever since.) There are a few things to be said for the quaint virtue
of self-consistency, though. Inconsistency in *prices* is different from inconsistency in music tastes. Behind every corner stands a sharp character ready to profit from prices gone askew. That practically everyone's
normal, thoughtful pattern of price setting presents an ongoing arbitrage
opportunity was a shock. Consider an amusing confidence game called
the money pump:

LICHTENSTEIN: Well, now let me suggest what has been called a money-pump game and try this out on you and see how you like it.

SUBJECT (same as above): Okay.

LICHTENSTEIN: If you think Bet A is worth 550 points, you ought to be willing to give me 550 points if I give you the bet. Does that sound reasonable?

SUBJECT: If I were to give you . . . yeah, that would be reasonable.

LICHTENSTEIN: So first you have Bet A.

SUBJECT: Okay.

LICHTENSTEIN: And I have Bet B, and I also have your 550 points. That was reasonable, wasn't it?

SUBJECT: Yeah.

LICHTENSTEIN: That I should take your 550 points?

[Both say "Okay."]

LICHTENSTEIN: So, you have Bet A and I say, "Oh, you'd rather have Bet B, wouldn't you?"

SUBJECT: Yeah, it's a sure thing.

LICHTENSTEIN: Okay, so I'll trade Bet B. Now . . .

SUBJECT: I'm losing money.

LICHTENSTEIN: I'll buy Bet B from you. I'll be generous; I'll pay you more than 400 points. I'll pay you 401 points. Are you willing to sell me Bet B for 401 points?

SUBJECT: Well, certainly.

LICHTENSTEIN: Certainly. Okay, so you give me Bet B.

SUBJECT: Uh-huh.

LICHTENSTEIN: I give you 401 points, and you'll notice that I kept your 550 and . . .

SUBJECT: That's right.

LICHTENSTEIN: I gave you 401 . . . I'm now ahead 149 points.

SUBJECT: That's good reasoning on my part. [laughs] How many times are we going to go through this?

LICHTENSTEIN: Well, . . .

SUBJECT: Okay, I see your point you're making.

LICHTENSTEIN: You see, you see the point, I can go through it indefinitely if I simply stick to the pattern of responses you have told me. Now that you see that in that money-pump sense that pattern of responses just doesn't . . .

SUBJECT: Doesn't fit.

LICHTENSTEIN: Doesn't fit.

SUBJECT: It ain't so good.

LICHTENSTEIN: . . . Do you still feel that you would not want to change any of your three responses here?

SUBJECT: I'd have to think a lot more time on it.

The money-pump game can indeed be repeated ad infinitum. Lichtenstein and the "mark" keep swapping A and B, and with every cycle, Lichtenstein picks up 149 points. Talk about taking candy from a baby! There's one difference between this "con" and the ones pulled on street corners: here there's no deception. Each step of the way, the victim understands what's going on and makes a choice grounded in his so-called values.

Lichtenstein's inquisition failed to budge this subject. At one point, he toyed with recanting "just to make myself look rational," but he couldn't bring himself to do it. To be "rational" would be to deny what he felt inside. Like a perverse Galileo, he knew his valuations still moved.

# Eleven

# The Best Odds in Vegas

"Roulette Bet May Decide Man's Fate," ran a curious headline in the March 2, 1969, *Las Vegas Review-Journal*. A photo showed the avuncular Ward Edwards playing a game "designed by scientists to probe what makes man tick."

> A 25-cent bet on a Las Vegas roulette table could be a factor in the greatest decision ever to confront mankind.
>
> That would be the unimaginably catastrophic decision to plunge the world into nuclear war. Some place, at some time, as long as a human being is able to poise his finger over a nuclear button, that is a possibility.

The journalist doubtless got that cold-war spin from Edwards, a RAND Corporation consultant and advisor to governmental agencies. Edwards talked up the Las Vegas game as "one of the few decision-making experiments ever conducted." Never was it mentioned in the article that this particular game was devised not by Edwards but by two of his former students.

Sarah Lichtenstein had heard that Edwards had an "angel." This was the attorney and casino backer Charles B. G. Murphy. Over a period of years, Murphy's Wood Kalb Foundation disbursed several hundred thousand dollars—a fortune at the time—to Edwards. Edwards in turn used it to finance his own research and that of colleagues, much of it done at the Four Queens with the permission of Benny Goffstein and his successor, Thomas Callahan. The idea was to present decision experiments as casino games. Players would bet money out of their own pockets, and they'd be playing for keeps.

Lichtenstein thought the preference reversal experiment "would be perfect for Vegas." One criticism of the original study was that the subjects might not have been motivated to make sound decisions. College kids doing repetitive experiments for little or no cash get bored. After a while, they may not even try. Outside the lab, people are motivated to devote more time and attention to a decision when the stakes are high. A Las Vegas trial would be an acid test of whether preference reversal was for real.

The main hitch turned out to be the Nevada Gaming Commission. Any gambling "experiment" conducted in a casino had to be approved. Edwards was called in to meet Wayne Pearson, the commission's head. Lady Luck was smiling on him: Pearson turned out to be a psychologist, with a Ph.D. from Cornell, who had read Edwards's work. He quickly green-lighted the project.


For ten weeks in 1969, the Four Queens offered the best odds in Vegas — a fair game with no house advantage. "Stakes and Odds," as the experiment was called, occupied a balcony space within earshot of a lounge band and the clatter of a casino restaurant. It used a standard roulette wheel, chips, and layout. Pit boss John Ponticello played the role of croupier. Hulking behind him was a PDP-7 minicomputer the size of several tall bookcases. The monitor, looking like an Ed Wood prop, was hexagonal with a circular screen. Any profits were promised to go to a home for unwed mothers.

Lichtenstein and Slovic spent only a few days in Las Vegas. Lichtenstein played the game herself to check up on the dealer. Unlike roulette, Stakes and Odds was strictly solitaire. Because the game was completely unfamiliar and required choosing among and pricing 40 bets, Ponticello had to warn each player that a complete game would take anywhere from one to four hours. For scientific validity, they needed players to go through the whole game. Those who didn't want to make that time commitment were discouraged from playing.

At the outset, each player was asked to buy 250 chips. He or she got to name the value of the chips, anywhere from 5 cents to $5 each. There weren't any high rollers; nobody chose a higher denomination than 25 cents. In the first stage of the game, the player chose between pairs of bets presented on the computer's monitor, indicating a choice by hitting a set of push-buttons set into the roulette table. The customer then played the chosen bet on the roulette layout. The win probabilities were all divisible by 12, to fit a 36-number roulette layout. Ponticello spun the wheel, tossed the little ball, and called the number. (Any zeros that came up didn't count. Ponticello ignored them and spun again.) Winnings were paid, losses taken.

In the second stage of the game, players named prices for bets. These prices could be positive or negative, as half the bets were in the house's favor, the other half in the player's favor. (The game as a whole had no net advantage for the house.) It can be tricky to get a gambler to name an honest price. We are all so used to bargaining that we instinctively shade asking prices up and offering prices down, figuring we can always come down or up later. This is potentially a serious problem in this kind of experiment. Lichenstein and Slovic needed their off-the-street subjects to name a candid price X, such that they'd be happy to sell the bet for X or anything more, but would truly prefer not to sell for anything less than X.

To ensure candor, they used the Becker-DeGroot-Marschak system, which is a good deal simpler than its name. This is the protocol they used in some of the lab experiments as well. A seller (of a bet, or of anything) is asked to state an honest minimum price. The dealer then spins a roulette wheel to generate a random "bid." Should the bid be higher than the stated reserve price, the sale goes through at the randomly selected bid price. (The seller is happy because she gets more than her minimum.) If the bid is lower than the seller's price, there's no sale. (The seller is happy because she wouldn't want to sell for less than her honest minimum.) The best strategy here is to name your honest price.

By Las Vegas standards, Stakes and Odds was a flop. According to Slovic, casino patrons like simple, repetitive bets like slot machines. This game was *hard*. Ponticello kept wanting to "improve" the game, over the psychologists' dogged insistence that he stick to the rules. The game did succeed at drawing the curious. Ponticello noticed that it attracted a diverse crowd: an Air Force pilot, a mathematician, a TV director, college students, a sheep rancher, a computer programmer, a bus line ticket agent, a real estate broker, and seven fellow Las Vegas dealers.

They managed to get 86 games started. Because some players quit out of boredom or befuddlement, 53 games were completed. That was more than enough.

"The results of this experiment," Lichtenstein and Slovic reported, "were strikingly similar to the findings of previous experiments based on college students gambling with hypothetical stakes or small amounts of money." The downtown Las Vegas crowd preferred the P bets when choosing, yet priced the $ bets higher. This time, it was the players' own money on the line. The highest winning for the complete game was $83.50, and the greatest loss was $82.75. (These figures are around $500 in today's dollars.) Though the game was fair, the average player lost money to the house. That was the money pump in action.

"There is a natural concern that the results of any experiment may not be replicated outside the confines of the laboratory," the psychologists wrote. What they learned from Las Vegas was expressed in a masterpiece of understatement: "the widespread belief that decision makers can behave optimally when it is worthwhile for them to do so gains no support from this study."

From today's perspective, Lichtenstein and Slovic started a revolution. The preference reversal experiment can with some justice be compared to the Michelson-Morley experiment in physics. That experiment refuted the absolute velocities of nineteenth-century physics, laying the groundwork for Einstein's relativity. It is tempting to draw a parallel between the physicists' "ether" and economists' utility. Both were invisible, impalpable, tasteless somethings that "existed" because everyone assumed they *had* to exist. By showing that there are no invisible valuations dictating all economic decisions, Lichtenstein and Slovic heralded the relativity of prices—a keystone of what would be called behavioral economics.

Lichtenstein and Slovic proposed a simple explanation for preference reversals: anchoring. When asked to price bets, players direct their attention to the prize amounts. The most likely or biggest prize amount becomes a starting point or anchor. The players knew they had to adjust from the anchor to take into account the probabilities and any other prizes or penalties. This adjustment required tough mental math. Everyone cut corners and guesstimated, with the result that the adjustment was usually inadequate. The final answer was too close to the anchor. It was an acorn that didn't fall far enough from the oak.

Asking people to *choose* between bets activated a different thought process. Dollar amounts are less relevant, since many gambles are long shots. Obviously, everyone likes winning. There's a strong tendency to pick the bet most likely to provide that happy outcome. Here, too, players tried to make allowances for dollar amounts and other complicating details. Once again, the adjustments tended to be inadequate.

Amos Tversky and Paul Slovic later generalized this idea into a "compatibility principle." This rule says that decision makers give the most attention to information that is most compatible with the required answer. Whenever you have to name a price, you will focus on prices or other dollar amounts in the problem. In deciding how much to offer for a used car, Kelley Blue Book value and prices on Craigslist command attention. Everything else that ought to matter (condition, repair history, color, options, whether you *want* the options) gets short shrift. The latter factors are not so easily mapped onto the dollar scale.

Lichtenstein and Slovic used shifting attention to engineer an "impossibility." The players were convinced their choices and prices had been reasonable throughout, and that they had not been tricked into saying anything they didn't mean. Yet their values were suddenly revealed to be topsy-turvy. The final twist was the money pump—presto, change-o, your money disappears.

However marvelous the illusions of a conjurer, we know that the woman is not cut in two; the jet plane does not vanish. When perceptions contradict the laws of physics, physics is right and perceptions are wrong. The audience goes home convinced that things are the same as they've always been, that the good solid core of reality has not been breached.

No such reassurances are possible with the preference reversal experiment. Nobody is more of an expert than I am on what I want and how much I'm willing to pay for it. In such matters, honest convictions are the only underlying reality there can be. The "illusion" of preference reversal is genuine.

•   •   •

Magic is only one of many metaphors that have been used in coming to terms with Lichtenstein and Slovic's finding. Another popular trope says that valuations are constructed and not revealed—like architecture, not archaeology. To name a price is to *build* a valuation (rather than to excavate deep into the psyche and uncover one).

A 1990 paper by Amos Tversky and Richard Thaler took its imagery from America's great wellspring of metaphors, baseball. It involves the old joke about the three umpires:

> "I call them as I see them," said the first. "I call them as they are," said the second. The third disagreed. "They ain't nothing till I call them." Analogously, we can describe three different views about the nature of values. First, values exist—like body temperature— and people perceive and report them as best they can, possibly with bias (I call them as I see them). Second, people know their values and preferences directly—as they know the multiplication table (I call them as they are). Third, values or preferences are commonly constructed in the process of elicitation (they ain't nothing till I call them). The research reviewed in this article is most compatible with the third view of preference as a constructive, context-dependent process.

What *did* gain support was the relativity of prices. What people want, and how much they're willing to pay, depends on the granular details of how you phrase the question. "It would be an overstatement to say of preferences, as Gertrude Stein said of Oakland, that 'there is no there there,'" wrote legal scholar Cass Sunstein in this connection. "But frequently what is there is far less fixed, and far more malleable, than conventional theory predicts."

Values may not be Oakland, but they are something like the elephant in the parable of the blind men. A man who feels the trunk reports that an elephant is like a snake; a man who feels the side says an elephant is like a wall; one who feels a leg compares the elephant to a pillar. "Each of the blind men was partly right," says a character in an old Walt Kelly *Pogo* cartoon. "Yeah," his friend adds, "but they were all mostly wrong."

# Twelve

# Cult of Rationality

The Las Vegas experiment threw down the gauntlet. By using real people and real money, Lichtenstein and Slovic had invaded economists' turf. Their experiment was a challenge to Paul Samuelson's doctrine of revealed preference, a bulwark of modern economics. In some situations at least, revealed preferences weren't so revealing at all. Choices failed to predict the prices people would pay. As Lichtenstein put it: "If you can't talk about a preference, what the hell can you talk about?"

There was a knee-jerk, visceral rejection of preference reversal. "The first time I talked about it to a group of economists, I was astounded," Lichtenstein recalled. "They were picking at it in trivial ways . . . asking these nit-picking little questions . . . It wasn't until the economists jumped all over us—and the economists were jumping all over Amos and Danny—that I began taking seriously the incredible hostility."

The vehemence of that reaction, and those to follow, may puzzle anyone who was not a part of it. It is worth saying a little about economists' long, complex love-hate relationship with psychology.

Economists live in the same world as everyone else. They have friends who buy overpriced time-shares and brothers-in-law who just don't *think*. Adam Smith devoted many words to human foibles and their inevitable influence on markets. Psychology was in the lexicon of economics until the Second World War. Then things started to change.

Under the influence of people like Samuelson and Milton Friedman, the field became progressively more mathematical. Much as dogs grow to resemble their owners, the new economics took on the features of the people now building it. Economists embodied a math-smart, self-controlled stereotype and built theories describing people exactly like themselves.

Colin Camerer, a behavioral decision theorist at Caltech, encountered the rationalist mind-set at its holy of holies, the University of Chicago, in the 1970s. "I was very young, I was seventeen, and here were these brilliant people preaching this crazy gospel," he said. "To me it was just kind of ludicrous. I think there was a misplaced, almost religious fanaticism saying that if there is a principle of rationality, you have to obey it. If you don't obey it, it's because you didn't realize you were disobeying it. But when it's pointed out, you'll quickly correct yourself."

Part of the Chicago doctrine was that Savage-Friedman-type rationality was a prerequisite for survival in the cold, hard business world. Those failing to toe the Chicago line "would get taken advantage of in the markets. They wouldn't go on to govern companies and be successful leaders," Camerer said. "These rationality principles were like commandments. You're either good or evil—and evil people get punished."

It was nonetheless an open secret that economic theories did not predict human behavior especially well. There was more than one way of waving that aside. Economic models typically assume two things: that people are perfectly reasonable, and also that they are perfectly well informed. Some economists adopted the position that the inhabitants of their models were ignorant, not stupid. Much of the 1970s was spent working out the ramifications of this hopeful (?) prospect.

There was also Milton Friedman's pet idea that quirks of individual psychology might not matter so much to the economic big picture. Markets, by embodying a wisdom of crowds, could be more rational (read: more like the economic models) than the individuals composing them. By the 1970s, few economists were in a mood to believe otherwise.

It fell to two Caltech economists to defend the honor of their profession. They were David M. Grether and Charles R. Plott, and their goal was simple: "to discredit the psychologists' work as applied to economics."

In a 1979 article, Grether and Plott described with alarm the decade-old preference reversal experiments. "Taken at face value," they wrote, "the inconsistency . . . suggests that no optimization principles of any sort lie behind even the simplest of human choices."

"We knew Charlie Plott," Sarah Lichtenstein said. "He called several times" during the course of his mission to demolish her and Slovic's work and was "jocular" about it. "Plott is pretty good at spotting an interesting phenomenon," Colin Camerer explained. "I think he knew that if they could replicate all this stuff, that would be interesting because it's so startling. And if they destroyed it, that would be great too because economists could say 'silly psychologists don't know how to do this.' It was perfectly hedged."

The Caltech team began by making a laundry list of everything they could think of that might account for the Lichtenstein-Slovic results. Their list came to thirteen explanations. Item No. 13 is an interesting social document. It reads, "The Experimenters Were Psychologists." "In a very real sense," Grether and Plott warned sternly, "using psychologists as experimenters can be a problem" because "psychologists have a reputation for deceiving subjects."

As Camerer had it, the paper is "written as if 'this can't possibly be true, these guys are crummy experimenters.'" The economists were concerned about "Unsophisticated Subjects" (psychology undergraduates fell into that category), "Confusion and Misunderstanding," "Strategic Responses," "Misspecified Incentives," including the use of imaginary rather than real money, and a number of subtle procedural points. Of course, they conceded that the "game" had already been played for real money in Las Vegas.

Grether and Plott replicated the preference reversal experiments using economics and political science students only (informing them that this was an *economics* experiment) and paid up to $40 for the richest $ bet. Their results were essentially identical to Lichtenstein and Slovic's. Caltech economics students flip-flopped just like Oregon psychology students and downtown Las Vegas gamblers.

"Needless to say, the results we obtained were not those expected when we initiated this study," Grether and Plott wrote. "We remain as perplexed as the reader who has just been introduced to the problem . . . Our design controlled for all the economic-theoretic explanations of this phenomenon that we could find. The preference reversal phenomenon . . . remains."

They ruled out twelve of their thirteen possible explanations, leaving only Lichtenstein and Slovic's own hypothesis, the "anchoring and adjustment mechanism." As Grether and Plott explained it—making a heroic effort to reconcile preference reversal with the economic zeit-geist—"it is as though people have 'true preferences' but what they *report* as a preference is dependent on the terms in which the reporting takes place. Certain words or contexts naturally induce some dimensions as anchors whereas others induce other dimensions."

Even with the "as though" qualification, these were radical words for economists in 1979. Appearing in one of the top economic journals (*The American Economic Review*), Grether and Plott's replication was an "amplifier." It not only alerted the economic profession to the findings but also convinced them that the results were solid, real, and profoundly incompatible with what they believed.

Slovic remembers receiving a few admiring letters from economists. They said his work had been an inspiration, and that the writer was doing research along much the same lines. Slovic's initial pleasure was dashed when he looked at the enclosed reprints. They were crankish lunacy. Among economists, only the freaks and weirdos could "appreciate" his work.

# Thirteen

# Kahneman and Tversky

During the 1956 Sinai war, Amos Tversky was a platoon commander in an Israeli paratroop regiment. Chief of Staff Moshe Dayan came to observe Tversky's platoon in exercises one day. A soldier was assigned to blow up some barbed wire. The man set the explosive, lit the fuse, and then froze in a panic attack. Tversky was just yards away. He ran up to the stricken soldier, ignoring the shouted orders of his commanding officer, and pulled the man to safety. When the explosive detonated, the panicked soldier was unharmed. Tversky caught some shrapnel that he kept for the rest of his life.

This story became emblematic. Tversky, who spent most of his career as a psychologist studying how people make decisions, impressed those around him as the one sane, humane person in the midst of chaos. "Amos was something special, really something special," recalled Sarah Lichtenstein. "You were happy being in his presence," said mathematician Persi Diaconis, who knew him at Stanford. "There was a light shining out of him."

Amos Tversky (1937–1996) was born in the biblical city of Haifa, then part of British Palestine. His mother, Genia, a social worker, would later serve fifteen years in the Knesset. His father, Yosef, was a physician turned veterinarian. "The story is that he got tired of people's complaints," Tversky's wife, Barbara, said. "Cows don't complain."

Israeli high school students were required to choose between the humanities and the sciences. Amos "surprised everyone by taking the humanities option, for he had such aptitude for math and science," Barbara said. "The math he knew was all self-taught." Self-education was a lifelong project. "He didn't like to learn anything the schoolbook way. He took tennis lessons but he didn't like the way they were taught, so he invented his own way of learning tennis."

Tversky began his academic career at Hebrew University, an institution with the éclat of having Einstein and Freud on its first board of governors. He studied both philosophy and psychology. "Growing up in a country that's fighting for survival, you're perhaps more likely to think simultaneously about applied and theoretical problems," Tversky once explained. He became one of the first Hebrew University students to get a psychology degree after an Arab ambush had killed virtually the entire psychology department in 1948.

After earning his B.A. in 1961, Tversky went on to doctoral work at the University of Michigan. There he met a stimulating group including Ward Edwards, Clyde Coombs, Sarah Lichtenstein, Paul Slovic, and—most significant—Barbara Gans, who became his wife. Initially Tversky struck the Americans as quiet. He had grown up speaking Hebrew, and English was the language of the enemy—the British occupation. Tversky's verbal skills were formidable, however. He wrote Hebrew poetry ("a little mechanical, but perfectly structured," said Barbara) and was a friend of the Israeli poet Dahlia Ravikovich. At Michigan, Tversky honed his English to the point where he was able to coauthor a mathematical psychology textbook with his doctoral advisor, Coombs, and Robyn Dawes. When the manuscript was sent to press, Edwards warned the editor that one of the authors was not a native speaker of English. "Amos's writing was perfect," Barbara said. "The problems were with Coombs, an American."

With greater confidence in the language, Tversky blossomed into an extrovert, a man with a mission. "I remember walking home with him once in graduate school," Barbara said. "He was working on his dissertation, and he anticipated his whole research program in judgment—and he was a twenty-seven-year-old grad student. I was mesmerized at this young man who really had a vision for a life's work that would make a difference."

After taking his Ph.D. in 1965, Amos and New York–born Barbara moved to Israel. He spent a dozen years teaching psychology at Hebrew

University. There, in 1968, colleague Daniel Kahneman asked him to give a talk for a graduate seminar. This turned out to be a "life-changing event," in Kahneman's words.

Kahneman's parents were Lithuanian Jews who had moved to Paris in the 1920s. His father headed research at a chemical company. His mother was visiting family in the Palestinian city of Tel Aviv when she gave birth to Daniel in 1934.

Kahneman's early years were spent in Paris, a city changed irrevocably by the Nazi occupation in 1940. In his Nobel autobiography, Kahneman wrote,

I will never know if my vocation as a psychologist was a result of my early exposure to interesting gossip, or whether my interest in gossip was an indication of a budding vocation. Like many other Jews, I suppose, I grew up in a world that consisted exclusively of people and words, and most of the words were about people. Nature barely existed, and I never learned to identify flowers or to appreciate animals. But the people my mother liked to talk about with her friends and with my father were fascinating in their complexity. Some people were better than others, but the best were far from perfect and no one was simply bad. Most of her stories were touched by irony, and they all had two sides or more.

In one experience I remember vividly, there was a rich range of shades. It must have been late 1941 or early 1942. Jews were required to wear the Star of David and to obey a 6 p.m. curfew. I had gone to play with a Christian friend and had stayed too late. I turned my brown sweater inside out to walk the few blocks home. As I was walking down an empty street, I saw a German soldier approaching. He was wearing the black uniform that I had been told to fear more than others—the one worn by specially recruited SS soldiers. As I came closer to him, trying to walk fast, I noticed that he was looking at me intently. Then he beckoned me over, picked me up, and hugged me. I was terrified that he would notice the star inside my sweater. He was speaking to me with great emotion, in German. When he put me down, he opened his wallet, showed me a picture of a boy, and gave me some money. I went home more certain than ever that my mother was right: people were endlessly complicated and interesting.

The Kahneman family spent the war years trying to stay a step ahead of the Nazis. The first sweep of Jews sent Kahneman's father to Drancy, a way station to the extermination camps. He was quickly released owing to the pull of the director of his chemical firm—who, it turned out, had been a major financial backer of the French anti-Semitic movement. The family decamped to the Riviera, then to central France, where Daniel's father died of improperly treated diabetes six weeks before D-Day.

Kahneman's mother moved the family to Palestine to be close to her relatives. Daniel studied psychology and mathematics at Hebrew University, then was drafted into the Israeli army in 1954. Among his duties was administering a battery of psychological tests inherited from the British Army. In one test, eight soldiers, stripped of all rank insignia, collaborated on moving a telephone pole over a wall or similar obstacle. The rules said the telephone pole must not touch the wall or the ground; if it did, the soldiers had to start over.

The test was intended to distinguish the true leaders from the followers. Kahneman found himself more interested in what the test said about the psychologists. A monthly "statistics day" brought the staff together to compare their evaluations with the grades from officer training school. "The story was always the same," Kahneman remembered. "Our ability to predict performance at the school was negligible."

In 1958 Kahneman and his new wife, Irah Kahn, moved to Berkeley for grad school. His eclectic curriculum included studies on subliminal perception, personality testing, and Wittgenstein. One of his teachers was Tom Cornsweet, whose name is now attached to a famous perceptual illusion (opposite page).

Everyone thinks the left half is darker. Wrong! Try placing a finger over the boundary between "dark" and "light" regions. You'll see that nearly the whole rectangle is the same shade of gray. The boundary region only has been shaded slightly darker on the left, lighter on the right, to create a contrast.

The Cornsweet illusion is an open-ended metaphor. People are the same all over; boundaries of various kinds make us think we're different from "them." On a more mundane level, it demonstrates the leitmotif of psychophysics. Contrasts matter, and absolute values don't. It is perhaps not too much of an exaggeration to say that some of Kahneman's most

celebrated papers applied this general principle to price setting and other types of decision making.

The "most significant intellectual experience" of Kahneman's grad school years came on a road trip his first summer in America. Kahneman drove to the Austen Riggs Clinic in Stockbridge, Massachusetts, a psychoanalytically oriented asylum for the wealthy. The staff included such famous analysts as Erik Erikson. Each Friday, the doctors met for a group interview of a patient, followed by a freewheeling discussion of the case. Kahneman was permitted to sit in on some of these conferences. The one that lingered in memory was typical except for the fact that the patient didn't show up. He had committed suicide the night before.

"It was a remarkably honest and open discussion," Kahneman mordantly observed, "marked by the contradiction between the powerful retrospective sense of the inevitability of the event and the obvious fact that the event had not been foreseen."

# Fourteen

# Heuristics and Biases

Tversky and Kahneman found they shared a skepticism about the wisdom of experts in psychology or anything else. Tversky mentioned Ward Edwards's experiment with poker chips. The subjects had failed to appreciate how informative a single poker chip could be. Kahneman countered that the opposite bias was more common. His army psychologists believed that a single data point—performance on the telephone pole test—could predict a future military career, when such things are really not very predictable at all.

Jovial back-and-forth led to the pair's writing a six-page semi-humorous article for the *Psychological Bulletin*, "Belief in the Law of Small Numbers." The title is a play on the "law of large numbers" of probability theory. This says that flipping a fair coin a large number of times will give you a percentage of heads close to 50. That is all you can ask of a fair coin. You can't predict the outcome of a small number of tosses. However, Tversky and Kahneman noted, people want to believe just that. They suppose that flipping a coin ten times will yield five heads and five tails, or something close to it. In reality, lopsided outcomes (like eight heads and two tails) are more common than people believe. Tversky and Kahneman surveyed some mathematical psychologists at a meeting and found that even the experts were subject to this error. The article's most memorable line displays a playful wit rarely encountered in scientific papers: "People's intuitions about random sampling appear to satisfy the law of small numbers, which asserts that the law of large numbers applies to small numbers as well."

This modest paper, published in 1971, inaugurated a decade of intensive collaboration so productive that friends called the pair "the dynamic duo." Since it was impossible to determine who had contributed more to a given paper, they flipped a coin to determine whose name came first in a publication's byline.

"There was a lot of irony in our whole research program," Kahneman told me. "It was not an attack on humanity, it was an amused and ironic look at ourselves." Tversky had a funny line, or a funny story, for every situation. "In his presence, I became funny as well, and the result was that we could spend hours of solid work in continuous mirth."

Amos "was the opposite of Danny" in Barbara Tversky's analysis. "He was a perfectionist in everything, including the words. Amos always wanted to get it right, to do it over and over until it was right. Danny was always moving on to the next idea; he always had a wealth of new ideas." Amos "couldn't write a paper without having a title, and the title had to be just the right title." He rectified any remaining deficiencies in his English by grilling Barbara for just the right word. " 'Is it this or this? This or this?' he'd ask. 'It's your language!' " Barbara protested. "You're looking for words that don't exist!"

Kahneman and Tversky spent the 1971–72 academic year at the Oregon Research Institute. Paul Hoffman was an adept fund-raiser, and ORI then had "a pile of money," as Kahneman remembered. "We had no schedule, no classes." He rated the year at ORI "by far the most productive of my life."

He and Tversky quickly settled in the routine that would define their collaboration. As Kahneman was a morning person and Tversky a night owl, they dovetailed their schedules by meeting for lunch and an afternoon of work. For the most part, "work" meant talking.

"They were so *verbal*," said Sarah Lichtenstein. "I remember once, with Amos and Danny and Paul, I put my hand up to speak. There were just the four of us—I couldn't get a word in." The group at Oregon tossed around ideas such as anchoring, preference reversals, and intuitive conceptions of probability. These discussions grew into Tversky and Kahneman's now-famous article "Judgment Under Uncertainty: Heuristics and Biases."

It was a long time in gestation. After the year in Oregon, both Kahneman and Tversky returned to Israel and spent much of the next year hammering out every precious word. They were simultaneously doing research. The paper is essentially a review article citing recent results by the two authors and others. Published in *Science,* "Judgment Under Uncertainty" immediately reached an audience outside the field of psychology. In so doing, it ignited a firestorm of controversy that has only now started to cool.

A "heuristic" is a rule of thumb, something like "No matter how much you're offered, you can probably get 10 percent more." The paper discusses three more fundamental examples, named *representativeness, availability,* and *anchoring and adjustment.* Anchoring has the most to do with prices. Let me briefly explain the other two.

The best-known example of the representativeness heuristic is "Linda the Feminist Bank Teller" (who makes her first appearance in a later paper, from 1983).

> Linda is 31 years old, outspoken, and very bright. She majored in philosophy. As a student, she was deeply concerned with issues of discrimination and social justice, and also participated in anti-nuclear demonstrations.

In a study at the University of British Columbia, 142 undergraduates who read this capsule description were asked which of the following was more likely to be true:

> Linda is a bank teller.
> Linda is a bank teller and is active in the feminist movement.

Eight-five percent rated the second statement more likely than the first.

That's *ridiculous.* The only way Linda can be a bank teller *and* a feminist is if she's also a bank teller. At the risk of beating a dead horse, I'll draw you a diagram (opposite).

Apparently, in judging how likely it is that Linda is a bank teller, people look at how well the information we have about Linda fits our preconceived notion of bank tellers. The question was written so that Linda fits the stereotype of a feminist and doesn't fit the stereotype of a bank

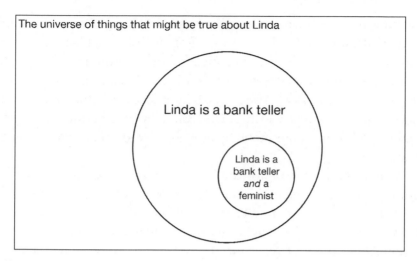

The universe of things that might be true about Linda

Linda is a bank teller

Linda is a bank teller *and* a feminist

teller. Hunches about Linda defied logic. Those hunches were amazingly tenacious, though.

Tversky and Kahneman resorted to "a series of increasingly desperate manipulations" intended to get their subjects to obey simple logic. They tried giving volunteers the Linda problem, followed by two arguments about what the answer *should* be. The subjects didn't have to commit to an answer, just to say which argument they believed was more convincing.

> Argument 1. Linda is more likely to be a bank teller than she is to be a feminist bank teller, because every feminist bank teller is a bank teller, but some women bank tellers are not feminists, and Linda could be one of them.

> Argument 2. Linda is more likely to be a feminist bank teller than she is likely to be a bank teller, because she resembles an active feminist more than she resembles a bank teller.

Even in this case, 65 percent favored the second argument. After the survey, when the matter was explained at length, many subjects remained unconvinced, uncertain, or unrepentant. Said one in defense of his answer, "I thought you only asked for my opinion."

· · ·

Which is more common, words that begin with *r* (like "road") or words with *r* as the third letter (like "car")? Most say that words beginning with *r* are more common. It's easy to rattle off words beginning with *r*; harder and slower to free-associate words with *r* in third place. This is an example of the availability heuristic, and here it leads us astray. Words with *r* in third place happen to be more common. But because words beginning with *r* are more mentally available, we overrate how common they are.

A familiar example of availability is the way we all assume that the tastes, politics, education level, and TV viewing habits of our social set are widely shared. We marvel when such-and-such show is a hit or so-and-so gets elected. "Nobody would vote for that jerk!" Well, they *did*.

Another example: Every year, thousands of kids aspire to become a pro athlete, despite long odds and near-certain disappointment. Why? It's easy to list names of athletes who beat the odds and became rich and famous. Now try to name some guys who went out for the NBA or NFL and never made it. Can you name any? Hmm, maybe the odds aren't so bad after all . . .


Anchoring and adjustment had already been proposed as a cause of preference reversal. In Lichtenstein and Slovic's experiment, the anchors—prize amounts—were at least relevant to the value of the gambles. Tversky and Kahneman supected that anchoring would work even with anchors that were known to be irrelevant. To test this hypothesis, they devised the United Nations experiment. The wheel of fortune was stagecraft, a way of emphasizing that the anchor numbers were completely random and meaningless. The anchors worked nonetheless. Of all of psychology's challenges to rationality, anchoring is "the easiest to demonstrate," wrote Fritz Strack and Thomas Mussweiler, but "the hardest to explain."

The United Nations experiment has become the classic demonstration of anchoring. Yet the 1974 *Science* paper is the only article to report it, and it gives scant data. Tversky and Kahneman published other, more detailed papers on representativeness and availability—but not on anchoring. "Amos and I didn't quite agree on the interpretation of anchoring," Kahneman explained. "The question was whether it's adjustment or (in modern terms) it's priming. Amos liked the idea of actual adjustment."

Tversky's idea was this. When asked to guess the percentage of African U.N. members, people start at an anchor value (the number that came up on the wheel of fortune) and adjust it downward or upward. They would continue adjusting until they reach the outskirts of a broad, fuzzy zone of plausible values. Then they'd stop. The stopping value will be on the anchor's side of the plausible zone. The greater the uncertainty, the broader the zone and the greater the anchoring effect.

It's as if I asked you to go get me a hamburger. You would probably stop at the first hamburger place you saw and bring me one of their hamburgers. You wouldn't search the whole city for the *best* hamburger.

By Tversky's theory, people adjusting from an anchor stop too soon. Instead of racking their brains for the "best" answer, they settle for the first plausible answer they come to. With a high anchor, that answer will be too high, and with a low anchor, it will be too low.

Originally, Tversky instructed the participants to start at the wheel of fortune number and mentally adjust it upward or downward. This instruction embodied what Tversky thought was actually happening. It's now clear that this instruction is unnecessary. The important thing is that there be some kind of mental comparison between the anchor and the quantity to be estimated. This happened naturally in the preference reversal experiments. When the anchor is blatantly uninformative—a random number or an obviously wrong one—a comparison can be prompted by asking a preliminary question of the form "Is the percentage of African U.N. members more or less than 65?"

Tversky's adjustment theory can't readily account for the anchoring seen with plausible values. Was the year of Einstein's first visit to America earlier or later than 1939? German students who heard this question gave a later estimate of the year than those asked whether Einstein's first visit was before or after 1905. Both dates are reasonably believable (the real date was 1921). It should not be necessary to adjust a figure that is already plausible.

Many other explanations for anchoring have been proposed. It has been argued that anchoring is logical, that subjects clutching at straws reasonably take a "conversational hint" from the experimenter. The experimenter would not be asking whether Einstein visited America before or after 1939 unless that was a reasonable answer. Therefore, you can't look too stupid by naming a year close to 1939.

Kahneman had a distinct theory. "I didn't know about priming," he said, explaining that "the term didn't exist. But I was pushing an idea that was very close to priming, that it's a suggestibility thing."

# Fifteen

# The Devil's Greatest Trick

"Priming" is a fairly new term for phenomena that have long been part of the world's store of knowledge, not necessarily of the scientific kind. Have you ever bought a car and suddenly noticed that "everyone" on the freeway, practically, is driving that model? Have you ever learned a new word (or heard of an obscure sea mammal or an ethnic dance) and then encountered it several times in the space of a few days? You come across it in the news, you overhear it mentioned on the bus and on public radio, and the old issue of *National Geographic* you're thumbing through falls open to an article on it . . .

This is priming (fortified with a few low-grade coincidences). When you skim the newspaper, half-listen to TV, or drive on the freeway, you ignore most of what's going on around you. Only a few things command attention. Paradoxically, it is unconscious processes that choose which stimuli to pass on to full consciousness. Prior exposure to something (priming) lowers the threshold of attention, so that that something is more likely to be noticed. The upshot is that you have probably encountered your "new" word or car many times before. It's just that now you're noticing.

Priming affects not only what you notice but what you do. In this case, priming can be identified with the power of suggestion. A yawn becomes contagious in a boring meeting, a cough in a concert hall. Visit Scotland, or Alabama, and you start talking that way.

"When it comes to our behavior from moment to moment, the big question is, 'What to do next?' " said the Yale psychologist John Bargh, author of a number of papers on priming. That question is unlikely to have a clear-cut, logical answer. Instead, says Bargh, "we're finding that we have these unconscious behavioral guidance systems that are continually furnishing suggestions through the day about what to do next, and the brain is considering and often acting on those, all before conscious awareness."

In the current understanding of priming, words and other stimuli activate relevant mental processes. Once "switched on," this cognitive machinery remains accessible for a while, influencing subsequent thoughts and actions. When priming affects the estimation of number values, psychologists call it anchoring.

"Anchoring effects are (mostly) caused by the fact that when I ask you if the tallest redwood is more than 800 feet tall, I have primed you to think of very tall trees," explained Kahneman. "The sample of trees you recover from memory is biased upward." You think of redwoods and giant sequoias and eucalyptus, and everything you ever read or half-remember seeing on the Discovery Channel about extremely tall trees. You think of things that are 800 feet tall, and reasons why a tree might or might not be that tall. All these trains of thought remain active and help to legitimize high estimates for the height of the tallest redwood. Meanwhile, other ideas must compete with the anchor for attention. The final answer is to some extent a weighted compromise between the values considered—reflecting any biases in the set of considered values. Even if you conclude (correctly) that no tree on this planet is anywhere near 800 feet tall, you cannot completely ignore what you've just been thinking. "What I tell you three times is true," said the Bellman in Lewis Carroll's "The Hunting of the Snark." Thinking is believing—to a degree, anyway.

Some decisions are the result of logical deliberation. These decisions come with an inner dialogue you "hear"—a dialogue that is often voiced aloud to spouses, accountants, agents, and corporate boards. The conscious mind flatters itself that *all* decisions are like that. Other decisions are completely unconscious, though, like whether to cough. Most important decisions fall somewhere in between these two extremes.

Despite their numerical nature, price decisions usually have a strong intuitive component. A price is not an answer to a math problem; it's an expression of desire or a guess about what other human beings will do (accept your offer or turn it down). You name a price that "feels" about right. As the rest of this book will show, price numbers are influenced by factors the conscious mind would reject as irrelevant, irrational, or politically incorrect.


In the film *The Usual Suspects*, Kevin Spacey plays a con man who fabricates a confession to a crime. His deception is exposed when his police interrogator swivels in his chair to gaze at the bulletin board behind his back. He realizes that every name or detail in Spacey's story has been lifted from one or another of the posted memos. The detective is so shocked that he drops his coffee mug. Picking up the shards, he notices that the cup's manufacturer, Kobayashi Porcelain, is identical with the name of an attorney Spacey has just mentioned.

The ability to confabulate—to tell stories smoothing over the rough edges of experience—is part of being human. The mind generates an ongoing fiction in which it knows more and acts more logically and nobly than it does in reality. We *believe* this fiction. Anchoring is one small part of it. We feign accuracy in mapping our feelings onto numbers or dollars. In truth, we are always grabbing handy numbers in the environment and transforming them into guesstimates and prices.

This somewhat unsettling idea raises an extreme possibility that University of Virginia psychologist Timothy Wilson called the *basic anchoring effect*. "There are many, many arbitrary numbers in our minds throughout a given day, such as the temperature that was just announced on the radio, the numbers on a computer keyboard that we just pressed, the numbers on the dial of the clock we just consulted, or the page numbers of a book or questionaire we read," Wilson and colleagues wrote in a 1996 paper. "It seems unlikely that numbers considered as briefly as these would be used to make an unrelated judgment."

Wilson and company tried to find out how subtle a "background" anchor could be. In one experiment, volunteers were given questionaires with adhesive notes attached. Written on each sticker was a four-digit "ID number" between 1928 and 1935. One group of participants was required simply to copy this number onto the questionnaire. They were then asked to estimate the number of physicians in the local phone book. The average estimate was 221 doctors.

The important thing here is that the ID code was just a number that happened to be there, not a meaningful part of the problem. Other groups were given slightly different instructions that caused them to pay a little more attention to the ID number. Some were told to note whether the ID number was written in red or blue ink (on the pretext that this would determine which page of the questionnaire to fill out). For these people the average answer was 343 doctors. A split second's extra attention to the number had raised the estimate 55 percent. (All the ID numbers were big. As anchors they would have pulled the estimates up.)

Another group was asked to note whether the ID number was in the range of 1920 through 1940 (as they all were). Unlike the question about ink color, this forced participants to consider the number as a number. This group put the number of doctors in the phone book at 527.

One group was asked a two-part question. They first had to guess whether the number of physicians in the phone book was greater or less than their ID number, and then give their estimate of the number of physicians. This group's average was 755.

The anchoring effect was by far the strongest when people had to make an explicit comparison between their anchor and their estimate. Still, the anchor numbers "leaked through" and affected answers even when they were fairly peripheral.

The researchers later asked some participants whether they thought their judgments might have been influenced by the ID number on the adhesive sticker. The answer, overwhelmingly, was no. As Kevin Spacey says in *The Usual Suspects* (quoting Baudelaire): "The greatest trick the devil ever pulled was convincing man he didn't exist."

# Sixteen

# Prospect Theory

For part of the 1970s, Barbara Tversky's husband drove her and the kids up the wall. "I would go batty because he'd be asking questions all the time. 'Yeah, we had that question yesterday,' " she'd protest. " 'No, no, it's different,' " Amos would insist.

Maurice Allais was to blame—his paradox, anyway. Early in his collaboration with Tversky, Kahneman decided that Allais' paradox was the foremost unsolved problem in the psychology of decision making. The great prize would be to give a proper accounting of it. In an attempt to do that, he and Tversky began devising "interesting choices." When a choice seemed interesting enough, the families became guinea pigs. One example:

> Would you rather have $3,000 (a sure thing) *or* an 80 percent chance of winning $4,000 (and a 20 percent chance of ending up empty-handed)?

Just about everyone preferred the $3,000 sure thing to the gamble. That's not surprising. Tversky had a clever idea about how to make things more interesting. "Reflect" a question by putting a negative sign in front of each dollar amount. To make it realistic, imagine you're being sued for $4,000. Would you rather settle for $3,000 right now (a sure loss, −$3,000) or go to trial, knowing there's an 80 percent chance you'll lose and owe the full amount (−$4,000), and a 20 percent chance you'll win and owe nothing at all? (Ignore legal fees.)

Were attitudes toward risk consistent, the answer to this second question seemingly ought to be the same as to the first. But that's not the way most people think. A majority rejects the sure loss and prefers to take its chances with the trial. The train of thought is, "I don't want to lose thousands of dollars, and the gamble is my only shot at avoiding it. The difference between a $3,000 loss and a $4,000 loss isn't all that great."

By posing many other questions of this kind, Kahneman and Tversky were able to probe attitudes toward gains, losses, and risk from all directions. They stopped annoying family members and started doing careful surveys of student volunteers. This led to their 1979 article, "Prospect Theory: An Analysis of Decision Under Risk." The newly coined title was intentional, Kahneman said. "We reasoned that if the theory ever became well known, having a distinctive label would be an advantage."

Prospect theory is founded on several simple, powerful ideas. One is the relativistic nature of money (or gains and losses generally). Kahneman and Tversky invoked the parallel to psychophysics:

> Our perceptual apparatus is attuned to the evaluation of changes rather than to the evaluation of absolute magnitudes . . . an object at a given temperature may be experienced as hot or cold to the touch depending on the temperature to which one had adapted.

Likewise, people get used to a certain level of wealth or income and react mainly to changes. For instance: You expect your rich aunt to give you a $1,000 check for a wedding present because that's what she's given all your siblings. Instead she gives you a lousy $25 gift card! You are apt to feel you've "lost" $975 rather than gained $25.

In Kahneman and Tversky's terminology, the anticipated $1,000 is a *reference point*. This is much like the "adaptation level" of psychophysics. The reference point determines whether something is entered as a gain or a loss on the mental ledger. That can make a huge difference in behavior.

A second key idea of prospect theory is *loss aversion*. Losing money (anything of value) hurts more than gaining that same thing delights. You can demonstrate loss aversion by offering a bet on a coin toss. Tails you lose $100, and heads you win X. How big does X have to be for you to take the bet?

Surveys show that few want to accept a "fair" bet with X = $100. Few accept X = $110, which offers a nice expected profit. (Those who do accept at this price tend to be gamblers, arbitrageurs, or economists.) The average person requires roughly a $200 prize to balance the prospect of an equally probable $100 loss.

Neither gains nor losses are additive. The pleasure of a $20 windfall is less than twice that of getting $10. This was the moral of S. S. Stevens's little riddle, where it took about $40 to feel "twice as good" as $10. Economists always knew that *large* gains and losses aren't additive, but prospect theory extends this rule to amounts that may be completely trivial. People act as if "wealth effects" apply to small change.

One pop metaphor expresses some of the ideas behind prospect theory: "Money is a drug." The addict, of crack or of cash, adapts to a certain level of the abused substance. Thereafter he must score more than that baseline to achieve a new high. When the addict fails to achieve the baseline, he experiences a painful withdrawal. The withdrawal is more painful than the high is pleasurable.

Kahneman observed that loss aversion "extends to the domain of moral intuitions, in which imposing losses and failing to share gains are evaluated quite differently." There's a law against being a thief, not against being a tightwad. And while avarice makes the list of seven deadly sins, and charity the top three Christian virtues, the Ten Commandments forbid only stealing or coveting someone else's wife and property. Charity is just a suggestion.

A third important idea of prospect theory is the *certainty effect*. Kahneman and Tversky's surveys confirmed Allais' thesis, that there is a subjective chasm between the certain and the merely very probable (between 100 percent and 99 percent probability, say). This finding too can be reflected: there is also a big psychological difference between the very unlikely and the guaranteed-not-going-to-happen (between 1 percent and 0 percent probability).

Between gains and losses on the one hand and likely and unlikely events on the other, there are four domains of behavior. This can be

|  | Likely events | Unlikely events |
|---|---|---|
| Gains | **Risk-averse behavior**<br><br>("A bird in the hand"— investing in bonds rather than stocks; accepting an okay offer rather than holding out for a better one) | **Risk-seeking behavior**<br><br>("No guts, no glory"— buying lottery tickets; trying to make the big leagues) |
| Losses | **Risk-seeking behavior**<br><br>("Go for broke"— playing double-or-nothing to make up for gambling losses; con games where victim has too much invested to quit) | **Risk-averse behavior**<br><br>("Better safe than sorry"— buying insurance; wearing seat belts; not eating sushi because of parasite risk) |

summarized in a simple four-cell diagram (see above). The fourfold pattern of prospect theory explains not only Allais' paradox but also such mysteries as why compulsive gamblers buy insurance.

Take Allais' first riddle. You can have (a) a sure $1 million *or* (b) a tempting gamble that carries a 1 percent risk of coming away empty-handed. No matter what you do, you are almost certain to end up with a million dollars or more. In other words, you are in the happy position of choosing from among likely gains. That puts you in the upper left cell above.

That cell is marked "risk-averse behavior." You are likely to feel that a million dollars is within your reach—all you have to do is choose option (a). You'd be *sick* if you gambled on (b) and lost. This makes the risk of (b) unacceptable.

Allais' second riddle presents a choice of an 11 percent chance of $1 million or a 10 percent chance of $2.5 million. These are still gains; the all-important difference is that winning is now unlikely. You'd be telling yourself, *Don't get too excited—you're probably not going to win*. This changes the psychology, triggering risk seeking, as shown in the upper right cell. You are willing to gamble on the higher prize, and the 1 percent difference in probability doesn't seem so important.

Flipping the gains to losses flips the types of behavior. When losses are likely, reckless gambles become acceptable (lower left cell). At the end of the day, racetrack bettors are willing to "throw good money after bad" in the hope they can recoup their losses. When losses are unlikely (lower right), people are willing to insure themselves against them.

Financial advisors tell clients to consider their "risk tolerance" in making money decisions. The trouble is, these four domains of behavior coexist in all of us. A person who is risk-averse in one situation will turn reckless in another. All it takes is a changed reference point.

Investors regard bonds as "safe" and stocks as a gamble offering a higher average return. Since both investments promise gains, many investors are risk-averse (upper right cell) and load their portfolios with bonds. There are other ways of looking at it. When you factor in inflation and taxes, bonds may have zero or negative real return. "Put your money in bonds, and you're sure to lose purchasing power!" This is a highly effective argument—for anyone trying to sell someone stocks.

When real estate bubbles collapse, sellers remember what their home would have fetched at the top of the market. This becomes the reference point, and selling at the current market price becomes a "loss" (lower left cell). Rather than accept a reasonable current-market offer, they say no and gamble on getting a better offer—someday. It can take years for sellers to readjust their reference points to the new realities. During that time, few transactions take place.

Kahneman has said he believes the concept of loss aversion to be his and Tversky's greatest single contribution to the theory of decisions. The basic idea has certainly been around for a while. In his *Philosophical Enquiry into the Origin of Our Ideas on the Sublime and Beautiful* (1757), Edmund Burke wrote, "I am satisfied the ideas of pain are much more powerful than those which enter on the part of pleasure." What Kahneman and Tversky offered was a degree of rigor and scope never attempted before. "The major points of prospect theory aren't hard to state in words," Harvard's Max Bazerman said. "The math was added for acceptance, and that was important." Tversky, the self-taught mathematician, gave prospect theory the full mathematical treatment needed for economists to take it seriously.

They published their theory in *Econometrica*, possibly the toughest of all economic journals. Economists had long shed demonstrations of human unreasonableness as ducks do water. These dismissals were often reduced to one word: "psychology." The implication was that psychology was not a very serious or important topic. "Prospect Theory" did a great deal to change that mind-set. By one account, it had become, by 1998, the most cited article ever to appear in *Econometrica*.

In 2009 German billionaire Adolf Merckle committed suicide by jumping in front of a train. He was distressed over financial reverses. His net worth was still apparently in the billions.

Traditional economic theory deals in absolute states of wealth. A billion dollars is a billion dollars, and you should be happy with it. The human reality is that a billionaire who's lost half his fortune can feel destitute, and a $5,000 lottery winner can feel on top of the world. It's all about contrasts.

The unanswered question is why losses sting more than gains feel good. Why is the deck stacked against us? In the years since Kahneman and Tversky's paper, evolutionary explanations have become popular. "Humans did not evolve to be happy, but to survive and reproduce," Colin Camerer, George Loewenstein, and Drazen Prelec wrote. Picture a starving animal in the dead of winter. To forage for food is risky; it exposes the animal to predators. To play it safe by staying in the den is to slowly starve to death. It makes sense for the animal to gamble on finding food. In the summer, the same animal has plenty of food, and its strategy should change. It should *not* bet its life on finding berries it doesn't need.

Replace "food" with "money" or any other gain, and you have prospect theory. We act as if losing $500 at poker is a life-or-death issue. Camerer suggests that loss aversion is a form of unreasoning fear, like that an acrophobic experiences looking out the window of a penthouse.

"Many of the losses people fear most are not life-threatening, but there is no telling that to an emotional system overadapted to conveying fear signals," Camerer wrote. "Thinking of loss-aversion as fear also implies the possibility that inducing emotions can push around buying and selling prices."

# Seventeen

# Rules of Fairness

Kahneman and Tversky spent the 1977–78 academic year at Stanford, polishing their prospect theory paper. This time was a watershed in their lives and careers. In short order, both decided to accept permanent appointments in North America—Tversky at Stanford and Kahneman (along with his new wife, psychologist Anne Treisman) at the University of British Columbia.

In 1982, Tversky and Kahneman traveled to Rochester for a meeting of the Cognitive Science Society. They had a beer with a psychologist named Eric Wanner, vice president of the Alfred P. Sloan Foundation. Wanner told them of his interest in bringing together economists and psychologists to encourage them to learn from each other's fields. He wanted advice on how to do that. Kahneman and Tversky's answer was that there was no way to "spend a lot of money honestly" on that goal. Wanner couldn't force people to be interested in another field if they weren't. They did believe that there were a few economists willing to learn psychology, and they mentioned Richard Thaler.

Shortly thereafter, Wanner was appointed president of the Russell Sage Foundation. The long-dead Russell Sage, a Wall Street speculator and notorious miser, left a tax-free $100 million fortune to his second wife, Margaret Olivia Sage, in 1906. The following year, Margaret established the Russell Sage Foundation, devoted to "the improvement of social and living conditions in the United States"—a subject in which the late Mr. Sage had shown no particular interest. Sage's foundation, still handsomely endowed, has been a principal financial backer of behavioral research in economics. One of the first Sage grants under

Wanner's tenure allowed Thaler to spend the 1984–85 academic year working with Kahneman at the University of British Columbia. As Kahneman put it, "That was the year that behavioral economics began."

Thaler, then a Cornell associate professor, was just shy of forty, personable and witty. He joined Kahneman and another economist collaborator, Jack Knetsch of nearby Simon Fraser University. There was then a Canadian public works project that paid unemployed university graduates to conduct nationwide telephone surveys on public issues. "They were short of questions," Kahneman said, "and Jack and I had been feeding them questions every day. It was like a dream come true—every day we had an opportunity to get a national sample."

The group became interested in *fairness*. Listen in to any real estate negotiation, union contract talk, focus group, or executive compensation meeting. Sooner or later, the speakers will say the magic word—"I only want what's *fair*." A visitor from another planet might conclude that fairness is the secret ingredient of prices and wages. Yet most 1980s economists wouldn't have known what to do with a fuzzy concept like fairness. So Kahneman, Knetsch, and Thaler set out to discover the "rules of fairness."

They devised little scenarios and passed them on to the survey takers. Their telephone subjects were simply asked to judge how fair a hypothetical action was.

A hardware store has been selling snow shovels for $15. The morning after a large snowstorm, the store raises the price to $20.

Eighty-two percent judged this unfair. "Supply and demand" was no excuse for raising prices.

Thaler, who had a young daughter, came up with a question about Cabbage Patch dolls. (Kahneman had never heard of them. They were grotesque dolls that became so popular they caused shortages and even riots during the 1983 Christmas shopping season.)

A store has been sold out of the popular Cabbage Patch dolls for a month. A week before Christmas a single doll is discovered in a storeroom. The managers know that many customers would like to buy the doll. They announce over the store's public address system that the doll will be sold by auction to the customer who offers to pay the most.

Seventy-four percent of the public found this unfair.

Another question had a football team selling limited seats for a big game. The team has three options: auction the tickets; have a lottery in which randomly chosen fans get to buy the tickets; or have a line, with tickets sold on a first-come, first-served basis. The subjects overwhelmingly rated the line fairest. The auction was overwhelmingly judged the *least* fair.

> A severe shortage of Red Delicious apples has developed in a community and none of the grocery stores or produce markets have any of this type of apple on their shelves. Other varieties of apples are plentiful in all of the stores. One grocer receives a single shipment of Red Delicious apples at the regular wholesale cost and raises the retail price of these Red Delicious apples by 25% over the regular price.

This question throws the oddness of the price-gouging taboo into stark relief. A 25 percent increase is less than ordinary seasonal swings in produce prices. The scenario makes it clear that children aren't starving for lack of Red Delicious apples. They can eat a Granny Smith. Yet raising the price of Red Delicious was rated unfair by 63 percent of the public.

"We had a very good time making up those questions," Kahneman said. "In fact they're pretty funny." The group also found that the survey answers became reasonably predictable. "You ask a few of these questions, and you get a sense."

The public was realistic enough to appreciate that prices sometimes *have* to go up. It was okay for stores to pass on their own increased costs. It was okay for a company that's losing money to cut wages. But it *wasn't* okay to take advantage of market forces (say, to raise prices on existing stock during a shortage). The cardinal rule of fairness appeared to be *Don't increase your profit at my expense.*

This reflects the thesis that losses hurt more than gains feel good — and perhaps a melancholy picture of the world in which everyone's out to squeeze a few extra dollars out of everyone else. Yet the framing of "gains" and "losses" was easily manipulated by words in the working vocabulary of any real estate agent or con artist. One survey question began:

> A company is making a small profit. It is located in a community experiencing a recession with substantial unemployment but no inflation. There are many workers anxious to work at the company. The company decides to decrease wages and salaries 7% this year.

Sixty-two percent judged the wage cut unfair.

In an another version of the question, the community was said to have "substantial unemployment and inflation of 12% . . . The company decided to increase salaries only 5% this year." Now 78 percent said this was acceptable. But of course the workers' lot is almost identical in both versions. Getting a 5 percent "raise" when prices rise 12 percent translates into nearly a 7 percent cut in buying power.

One conclusion is that inflation is the Scroogish employer's best friend. A similar principle applies to bonuses. It was judged okay for a troubled company to skip an annual 10 percent bonus it had been in the habit of paying, but *not* to cut wages 10 percent for a year. (Wall Street employers, at the mercy of a volatile market, have long made use of this.)

Kahneman, Knetsch, and Thaler wrote,

> Conventional economic analyses assume as a matter of course that excess demand for a good creates an opportunity for suppliers to raise prices, and that such increases will indeed occur. The profit-seeking adjustments that clear the market are in this view as natural as water seeking its level — and as ethically neutral. The lay public does not share this indifference . . . The gap between the behavior that people consider fair and the behavior that they expect in the marketplace tends to be rather small.

The shock was in how self-serving the folk rules of fairness are. Philosophers of left and right have always felt the need to be logically consistent. The public had no such inhibition. Overwhelming majorities rejected the laissez-faire capitalist view of property and free enterprise, and equally rejected any consistent notion of workers' rights and the common good. The public displayed Ayn Rand selfishness to such a degree that it judged free markets unfair—for free markets are as likely to work against one's selfish interests as for them.

# Eighteen

# Ultimatum Game

Imagine a postapocalyptic future in which nothing survives of American culture except some Farrelly brothers movies. That is virtually what happened with the earliest Roman literature: all is lost, save for the appealingly lowbrow farces of Plautus (c. 254–184 BC). Thanks to this accident of survival, one of the West's earliest descriptions of bargaining is a comical one. It occurs in the pivotal scene of Plautus's play *The Rope*. A slave named Gripus dreams of buying his freedom with a trunk of gold he found in the sea. Gripus crosses paths with the conniving Trachalio, who recognizes the gold as the property of a notorious pimp and senses a blackmail opportunity.

TRACHALIO: Right, then; listen. I saw a robber robbing—I knew the man he robbed from—I went up to the robber—I offered him a bargain— "I know the man you robbed from," I said—"you give me 50-50—I'll say no more about it." He wouldn't listen to me. Well, I ask you, wasn't half a fair share?

GRIPUS: You should have asked more than half. If he won't give it you, I'd say you ought to tell the owner.

TRACHALIO: Thanks, I will. Now see here: this is where you come in.

GRIPUS: What do you mean?

TRACHALIO: You've got a trunk there. I know who it belongs to. I've known him a long time.

In modern terms, this is an "ultimatum game." One person (Gripus) has some loot, and another (Trachalio) has the power to make the loot disappear. Does that entitle the latter to a share? It assuredly does in Plautus's tale. Unless he gets half the gold, Trachalio threatens, he will tell the rightful owner. Then neither slave will get anything. Gripus snaps, "The only share you're going to get is a share of trouble, I can promise you that." He vows he would sooner get nothing than give anything to Trachalio.

As a metaphor for the absurdity of the human condition, Plautus found all he needed in two actors and a series of ridiculous ultimatums. Gripus's trunk is said to be snared in the fishing net in which he caught it, attached to a rope (hence the play's title). The play's viewers must have witnessed the slaves' comic war of words devolve into a literal tug-of-war. The message is timeless: "bargaining" is a polite word for extortion, and logic has little to do with the outcome.

Kahneman, Knetsch, and Thaler presented their fairness research at a University of Chicago conference. Their talk was published (in a 1986 issue of the *Journal of Business*), and that article included the diabolical little experiment now known as the *ultimatum game.*

You are given $10 to split with a stranger, and you get to propose how the money is divided—for example, "$6 for me and $4 for the other guy." The twist is that the other person gets to decide whether to accept your split or reject it. Provided he accepts, the money is split exactly as you specified. Should he reject the split, neither of you gets a penny. As the game's name indicates, this is a take-it-or-leave-it deal with no counteroffers.

You are under no obligation to be "fair." You can demand as much of the $10 as you think you can get away with. Naturally, you want to stop short of the point where your partner will be so upset with his "unfair" allotment as to veto the deal.

You might want to decide how you would play the game before you read further. First, pretend you're the person splitting the money (the "proposer" or "allocator"). How much of the $10 prize would you offer to a complete stranger? (You will never learn this person's identity, nor will s/he learn yours.) Write down the figure.

*I offer $_____ out of $10*

Next, you're the other person, the "responder." Since you're playing alone here, it is necessary to decide how you would respond to every possible offer you might receive. These offers could range from nothing at all to the full $10. For simplicity, proposers are often restricted to whole dollar amounts. Circle your minimum acceptable offer (indicating you would accept the circled offer, and any offer bigger than that, but no smaller offer).

*I will accept*
$0   $1   $2   $3   $4   $5   $6   $7   $8   $9   $10

To a rational maximizer, the ultimatum game should be a no-brainer. The responder should never turn down "free money." He should accept a pittance rather than veto. In turn, a reasonable proposer should anticipate that and offer a token amount, in blissful confidence of its being accepted.

That didn't happen. When Richard Thaler tried this game on students at Cornell, he found that a "fair" fifty-fifty split was by far the most common proposer offer. He also found that responders were willing to reject stingy offers. The average responder would accept $3 but reject $2.

It's not hard to understand what was going on. The proposers had enough social intelligence to know they had to give the responders enough to keep them satisfied. One thought that must have occurred to all is that a fifty-fifty split is "fair." That makes a case for offering an even split, as a plurality of Cornell students did.

The thing is, neither life nor the ultimatum game is necessarily fair. The two participants have different choices and different powers. Unless the responder is *so* upset that he is willing to cut his own throat, the proposer has power and incentive to shave a little off the even split. Why not offer $4, or $3 . . . , uh, or even $1?

You can see where this is going. For any responder, there's a point where he gets so angry that he vetoes. A greedy-though-prudent proposer would want to approach that point as closely as possible without exceeding it. Where is that point, exactly? That is one question that the ultimatum game asks.

It's easy to recognize echoes of the ultimatum game in your own life. Every day people use pushiness, entitlement, and chutzpah to get their way in the world. Those making unreasonable demands succeed because everyone else sighs and puts up with them—*up to a point*. The ultimatum game explores the not unreasonable anxiety that fair dealing will get us only so far in the world. To do that, it creates an ambiguous ethical space. The proposer did not do anything to deserve the $10. The responder did not do anything entitling him or her to a share. By stripping away all the customary social, legal, financial, and ethical entitlements, the game lays bare the issue of inequality, something that all societies struggle with.

In a way, the ultimatum game is the monetary version of S. S. Stevens's classroom demonstration that black is white. The value of money depends on context and contrast. How would you feel about getting $100 for doing nothing? You'd feel pretty good. How would you feel if that $100 was your share of a $1,000 windfall—and your "partner" had unilaterally decided to keep $900 for himself? That *wouldn't* feel so good. The $100 is insultingly small next to the $900, even though it would be a nice piece of change in another context. The contrast creates emotions, and emotions influence actions. There are those who seize advantages because they think they can get away with it, and others who find their only bargaining chip to be a self-destructive veto. In a real sense, we *all* play the ultimatum game.

"We were very pleased with the ultimatum game," Kahneman said. "We thought it was a very good idea—we didn't realize how good it was. Then, just as the piece was written, Dick Thaler was doing a routine research of the literature just before publishing, and he says, 'Sorry, guys . . . we've been scooped.' "

The same game had already been published in 1982 by a German game theorist, Werner Güth, and two colleagues. Güth, then at the University of Cologne, well understood that game theory is no predictor of human behavior. As a child he had been taught game theory's method of sharing a treat: "divide and choose." One child cuts the cake into two slices, and the other gets first pick. "My brother and I always relied on divide and choose to limit the amount of fighting," Güth told me. "However, we weren't too successful."

Starting in the mid-1970s, Güth became interested in ultimatum bargaining—the kind in which one party makes an offer, take it or leave it. Güth returned from a 1977 academic conference with 1,000 deutsche marks in his bag, a grant for running economic experiments. He and colleagues Rolf Schmittberger and Bernd Schwarze did the first ultimatum game experiments during the 1977–78 academic year.

Güth said it was never his intention to demonstrate that humans don't behave as economists assumed. "That would have been overkilling an already dead man." He was interested in devising "the easiest nontrivial ultimatum bargaining games with only two players" and seeing how real people would play them.

He came up with two games, calling one the "complicated game" and the other the "easy game." In the former, a player had to split some black and white chips into two piles, then the other player got to pick one pile for himself. The complication was that all the chips were worth 2 marks each to the first player, but the white chips had only half this value for the other. University of Cologne students were not especially good at finding the optimal split.

So Güth tried the "easy game," now known as the ultimatum game. In the first experiment, forty-two graduate economics students were paired off. One person in each pair split a variable cash prize that ranged from 4 to 10 marks. The offer was conveyed to the partner, who was limited to a simple *ja* or *nein*. The most common offer, made by seven of the twenty-one proposers, was a fifty-fifty split. According to Güth, one of the more common reactions to this research among economists was a simple question: "Are those students in Cologne stupid?"

Kahneman remembered "being quite crestfallen" when he learned of the Güth paper. "I would have been even more depressed if I had known how important the ultimatum game would eventually become." He, Knetsch, and Thaler didn't revise their paper, aside from mentioning Güth and adding him to the references. Fortunately, they had taken a different approach from the German group and had new things to offer.

Güth did not ask his responders to state a minimum acceptable amount. Because most proposer offers were close-to-even splits, the German group did not get many chances to observe how responders reacted to grossly unfair allocations. Kahneman, Knetsch, and Thaler were more interested in the responder. "All our questions on fairness had to do with, 'Do you think the behavior of that guy, the powerful guy, is fair?' " Kahneman explained. "As a psychologist, I like the idea of people wanting to be fair. But Dick was enough of an economist to take the responder as the key."

They therefore grilled the responders on what offers they would accept. This involved a series of yes-or-no questions. ("If the other player offers you $0.50, will you accept the offer or reject it?") This approach is known as the strategic method of playing the ultimatum game, now widely used. In effect, it reveals the responder's reserve price.

The results were similar to Güth's, half a world away. An even split was the most popular offer, and the average amount offered was about $4.50. Responders were willing to reject offers less than about $2.30.

The vetoing responder is the game's starkest challenge to economic theory. "It's the resentment, the willingness to punish at cost, that is the whole thing," Kahneman explained. The player who vetoes is rejecting logic no less than "free money" and making an economic decision on the basis of emotion. And it wasn't just an occasional subject who acted contrary to the theory; practically everyone did.

"The thing that's truly bewildering," said Kahneman, is that "the theory can stand for hundreds of years, unchallenged, until someone says, 'look at the emperor, no clothes.' The counterexample was trivial."

"Is the Ultimatum Game the Ultimate Experiment?" asked the title of a 2007 paper by Yoram Halevy and Michael Peters. They were referring only half-facetiously to the academic industry the game has become. The ultimatum game is claimed to be one of the most frequently performed of all human experiments today. Psychology and economics grad students are often assigned it as a training exercise in recruiting subjects, getting consent forms signed, and doing chi-square tests. Yet the main reason for its enduring popularity is the belief that the game tells us much about the psychology of prices and bargaining.

What does the game mean, and why should we care? As Güth now sees it, the game has two messages: that "money alone does not rule the world" and that "simple games can be very complex." Kahneman views the game as a milestone in establishing the importance of psychology in even simple economic decisions. "Something special had to happen for economists to pay attention," he explained. "The ultimatum game had that feature."

One reason economists paid attention is the evident parallels to price setting. The $10 can represent the potential profit ("surplus") on a sale. The person splitting the money is a "seller," and the responder is a potential "buyer." The seller may choose to keep all the profit for himself (set a high price) . . . or surrender all the profit to the seller ("sell at cost") . . . or share the profit with the buyer. The buyer decides whether to accept the price or reject it as too high.

The game can also be seen as a bare-bones model of negotiation. Lemuel Boulware, General Electric's labor negotiator in the 1950s, was notorious for putting a wage package on the table and refusing to budge. *It was not GE policy to negotiate.* Boulware's offers were chosen after much research. They were apparently intended to be the minimum offer that the union leaders would accept, albeit through gritted teeth. Boulware (and the many labor negotiators who attempted to emulate him) was acting like a strategic proposer in the ultimatum game.

The more usual back-and-forth kind of bargaining can be thought of as a sequence of ultimatum games. Offers on real estate are structured as ultimatums: This offer must be accepted by 6:00 p.m. Tuesday, or it's null and void. Unless you accept the latest offer, you run the risk that the other side will walk away.

Bargaining is often a polite, socially sanctioned ritual. I lower my offer and you raise yours in stairstep increments. We meet somewhere in the middle. Sometimes fake "ultimatums" are part of that ritual. "That's my final offer, take it or leave it. I'm leaving . . . I'm actually walking out the door . . ." Each side may know the other isn't serious.

The crux of negotiation is how to deal with tough bargainers making lopsided demands. The ultimatum game presents, in concentrated form, the truly *difficult* part of negotiation. Where one or more hard-line bargainers are involved, there must come a moment of truth in which feints, bluffs, and built-in bargaining room are cast aside, leaving only an ultimatum. What do you do then—allow yourself to be exploited, or walk away, leaving money on the table?

## Nineteen

# The Vanishing Altruist

New York governor Nelson Rockefeller had the perfect Fifth Avenue penthouse with a panoramic view of Central Park. He also had a problem. There were plans to put up a skyscraper public housing project on the West Side. It would have been a big middle finger blocking Rockefeller's sunset view. The sponsor of the housing project bill was Meade Esposito, last of the cigar-chomping Democratic party bosses. Rockefeller invited Esposito to his penthouse to discuss the matter as gentlemen. "If you stop construction of that skyscraper," Rockefeller announced, "I'll give you that Picasso."

He pointed to one of the modernist works on the wall. Esposito agreed to do what he could. The skyscraper was never built, and Rockefeller made good on his promise. Esposito got a Picasso, and Rockefeller got a story to tell for the rest of his life. For years afterward, Rockefeller lovingly recounted every detail of the bribery, capping it with the punchline: "It was only a print!"

Negotiation isn't a pretty picture. Much of the time, the skillful negotiator is the one who best misrepresents value. It is not "fairness" so much as the appearance of fairness that drives the psychology of prices. (In the name of journalistic fairness, I must add that Rockefeller was not the lone scoundrel. Esposito may not have known art, but he knew the art of the deal. In 1987 he was convicted of influence peddling, resulting in a $500,000 fine and a two-year suspended sentence.)

Some of the early commentaries on the ultimatum game experiments mentioned *altruism*. Proposers don't stiff the responders. They typically offer a little more than they have to, to get the statistically average responder to okay the deal (through gritted teeth). The game therefore demonstrates an innate and noble generosity.

You still come across this interpretation in some feature stories. Sad to say, this happy notion has mostly been torn to tatters by later research. Bargainers are indeed less concerned with fairness than with what other people will think.

Kahneman, Knetsch, and Thaler took on the altruism question in their first article on the game. They devised what is now called the dictator game. Psychology students at Cornell were given $20 to split with an unknown stranger. The money was divided as the proposer—uh, "dictator"—decreed. That was it; the other player had no say.

In this first experiment, the dictators were allowed only two options. They could be greedy and keep $18 for themselves ($2 for the partner), or be fair and split the money evenly. Seventy-six percent of the subjects opted for the even split.

Kahneman's group described this result with the noncommittal "resistance to unfairness." Dictators avoided being unfair. Altruism could be one explanation for that, though not the only one.

The researchers further explored that resistance in another game, "altruistic punishment." After a round of the dictator game, new subjects were presented with this choice:

(a) They could share $12 evenly with one of the players in the previous dictator game experiment. The player they were sharing with had been a "greedy" dictator (taking $18 for himself, leaving $2 for the other person).

(b) They could share $10 evenly with a different player in the dictator game. This player had been "fair" (chosen the even split).

The majority chose (b). They were willing to penalize themselves a dollar in order to "punish" someone who had done nothing to them personally—but was known to be an "unfair" player.

So far, this sounds encouraging. Dictators were mostly fair, and those who weren't got their comeuppance. The original dictator game at Cornell was limited, though. It allowed only two options, a fair split and an *extremely* greedy one (keeping 90 percent of the prize). Not many were comfortable being *that* piggish. Since then, other researchers have done experiments where dictators are allowed a full range of splits. These experiments generally report that dictators are much less generous. When they are free to make any split, they offer around 30 percent on average to the powerless partner. About one in five dictators gives nothing.

Elizabeth Hoffman and colleagues at the University of Arizona performed the definitive dictator game experiment. Hoffman suspected that dictators were being generous only because someone was watching. The experimenter is often the subject's teacher, someone who would be grading him for months to come. Is it worth a few dollars to have the professor know you're a greedy bastard?

Hoffman's group therefore took pains to ensure that no one would know how any specific participant had acted. Each dictator was handed a plain white envelope and directed to the back of the room. There he opened the envelope inside a cardboard box to shield it from prying eyes.

Most of the envelopes contained ten one-dollar bills and ten blank slips of paper cut to dollar-bill size. The dictator was to take as many of the ten bills as he wanted for himself, leaving the rest inside the envelope for his partner. He was then to remove enough blank slips so that the envelope would contain exactly ten pieces of paper (blanks plus bills). This done, he handed the envelope to a "monitor" (who was not the experimenter, and who could not infer anything from the weight or feel of the envelope). The monitor took the envelope into another room to give to the partner.

The scheme's pièce de résistance was that everyone was informed that a few of the original envelopes contained no bills, just twenty slips of paper. An unlucky dictator who got such an envelope would have to remove ten slips and leave the other ten slips for the partner. The upshot is that even a partner who received nothing could not conclude that he or she had been intentionally stiffed.

Under these conditions, about 60 percent of dictators took *all ten bills* for themselves, leaving only blank slips of paper in the envelopes.

There is no point in being shocked. (No IRS examiner would be.) Concepts like "greedy" and "generous" always depend on a frame of reference. *Right this instant*, you have the opportunity to share the money in your wallet with a fine charity such as Doctors Without Borders. I'll give you their address: PO Box 5030, Hagerstown, MD 21741-5030, www.doctorswithoutborders.org/donate. You really should donate . . . but no one will be the wiser if you keep practically all of the money for yourself. No one will know if you skip it and don't send anything at all.

The pessimistic interpretation of Hoffman's experiment is that it shows how hypocritical people are. When no one was watching, *but only then*, subjects were nearly as selfish as the economists postulated. Colin Camerer and Richard Thaler proposed an alternative interpretation: The outcomes of ultimatum and dictator games have less to do with altruism than with manners. Social norms of fair play are not easily cast off. Even "hypocrisy" is not always a bad thing. Sometimes, just by pretending to be a better person than you are, you end up being that better person, for all intents and purposes.

# Twenty

# Pittsburgh Is Not a Culture

The ultimatum game has become an ur-experiment, the scientific equivalent of a catchy riff that lends itself to endless sampling and remixing. It has been played with members of the globe's diverse cultures; with children, the autistic, the high-IQ, and men having exceptionally high levels of testosterone; with players who have been given a hormone that increases trust in strangers; even with chimpanzees splitting a prize of ten raisins. The game's continuing fascination rests on how behavior changes, or doesn't change, with context. Like a well-oiled weathervane, the experiment's archetypic economic choice is sensitive to subtle pressures that affect us all the time yet usually go unnoticed.

Many simple variables dramatically affect behavior. Elizabeth Hoffman's group at the University of Arizona did a set of trials in which players had to earn the right to be the proposer by winning a trivia quiz. This made proposers *less* generous. They apparently felt they had merited their position of privilege and had a right to the perks. The responders agreed, it seems. They were willing to accept less from someone who had won the proposer role fair and square. Most proposers offered $3 or $4, and these offers were never rejected.

Hoffman's team also tried presenting the game as a retail transaction. The proposer was called a "seller," the responder a "buyer" who had to decide whether to buy at the seller's price or pass. Both parties received a table telling how they would profit from any possible price. The payoffs were identical with the standard ultimatum game.

This shouldn't make any difference (for a rational actor), but it did. Sellers were greedier, usually allotting $3 or $4 to the buyer. Yet the latter usually bought. Apparently, participants felt that sellers had a right to set a price. A high price was judged less worthy of punishment than an unequal split in the standard presentation.

One of the most interesting findings of Hoffman's experiments was that proposers and responders were mostly in sync. When presented with a newly minted variation of the game, proposers instantly sensed how much more or less they should offer, and responders adjusted their expectations too. This happened without communication.

"My Israeli game theory professor was proud to note that Israel is one of the few places where low offers were given and accepted" in the ultimatum game, economist Presh Talwalkar wryly noted. For what it's worth, the "Israeli myth" owes to a 1991 study comparing behavior in Pittsburgh, Ljubljana, Jerusalem, and Tokyo. The most common proposer offer was 40 percent among Israelis, versus 50 percent for Americans. That's not much of a difference, really (as we will see). But it led to a mystique of Israelis as the chosen rational people—or else it played into the old Shylockian stereotypes. One of the four-city study's coauthors, Hebrew University's Shmuel Zamir, recalls a young Israeli coming up to him, "visibly upset." He complained, "I did not earn any money because all the other players are *stupid*! How can you reject a positive amount of money and prefer to get zero? They just did not understand the game! You should have stopped the experiment and explained it to them."

When Colin Camerer described this "crosscultural" study to UCLA anthropologist Robert Boyd, Boyd objected that it was no such thing. "Pittsburgh is not a culture," he said, "it's a place on a map."

To an anthropologist, all four cities were part of the same homogenized global culture. The story got more interesting when one of Boyd's grad students, Joe Heinrich, performed ultimatum game experiments with the Machiguenga people of eastern Peru. "He came back and said, can you come and look at my data?" recalled Camerer. "So I went over to UCLA, and Joe said, 'I think I made a mistake because they made a lot of low offers, and they were all accepted. Except for one, and that was even suspicious because I had a Spanish-speaking assistant with me who spoke the local dialect, and that guy kind of bullied him into it: "I don't think you should take that." So I think they *all* were accepted.' "

The Machiguenga are among the most asocial peoples on earth.

They don't cooperate on building schools or irrigation systems as neighboring peoples do. They rarely interact with those outside their clan. The Machiguenga don't even use proper names for outsiders (much as Westerners don't use proper names for sparrows). "They'd say 'the guy in the red shirt' or 'the real tall guy,'" explained Camerer. "It's like the opposite of *Cheers*: nobody knows your name."

Heinrich's discovery was deeply ironic. Finally, in the Peruvian outback, he had discovered people who behaved the way traditional economists postulated. They were people with no economy to speak of.

"We both expected the Machiguenga to do the same as everybody else," Boyd said. "It was so surprisingly different that I didn't know what to expect anymore." The finding precipitated an ambitious effort to compare ultimatum game play among the globe's cultures, a sort of human genome project of bargaining behavior. The MacArthur Foundation kicked in money, followed by the National Science Foundation.

One hypothesis was that ultimatum game behavior was a function of the importance of markets within a culture. "That's actually a tricky thing to measure," admitted Camerer. At one meeting, Oxford's Abigail Barr suggested that the anthropologists line themselves up against a wall according to how market-oriented the cultures they studied were. The most market-oriented were to be at one end, and the least market-oriented at the other. The anthropologists were to have discussions with their neighbors, comparing their field cultures, and to swap order as necessary. "We called this the Barr scale," Camerer said. "Absent a better scale, it was pretty good."

They found that the kind of behavior seen with European or North American college students appears to exist wherever there is a market economy. It does not require industrialization. The Orma people of Kenya live by trading cattle. A study put their average offer at 44 percent, in line with Western cultures. Whatever the differences between African cattle traders and American day traders, both cultures put a premium on members who make the best deals. That means naming prices fair enough to be accepted, and knowing a rip-off when you see it.

Where game behavior is much different, it is in relatively isolated, small-scale cultures. There can be great differences in game play between nearby cultures (that are likely to be close genetically). This supports the idea that the ultimatum game is a cultural X-ray (in Camerer's words), a way of understanding how societies deal with economic in-equality.

Many nonmarket cultures are founded on elaborate codes of social cooperation. The Lamalera whalers of Indonesia and the Aché hunter-gatherers of eastern Paraguay are societies in which the most esteemed members contribute to a hunt and share the meat generously. When these people play the ultimatum game, they are "hyperfair." Proposers offer *more* than 50 percent of the prize to responders.

The Au and Gnau of Papua New Guinea are hyperfair, and respon-ders typically *reject* offers of more than 50 percent. In Au and Gnau cul-ture, gifts and favors come with strings attached. They create an obligation to reciprocate, and most people would prefer not to have that burden. "Offering too much money, rather than being extremely gener-ous, is actually being kind of mean," Camerer explained. "Adam Smith had this famous quote, 'It is not from the benevolence of the butcher, the brewer, or the baker, that we expect our dinner, but from their regard to their own interest.' That invites the interpretation that markets flourish when people are just looking out for themselves. The message of this study was, cultures where people trade a lot seem to have this norm of fair sharing. In cultures where they don't trade a lot, the norm is, just keep whatever you've got and I don't expect you to give me anything, so I'm going to settle for a pittance."

The closest species to *Homo sapiens* is not the mythic *Homo econom-icus* but the authentic *Pan troglodytes*, the chimpanzee. A 2007 study by Keith Jensen, Josep Call, and Michael Tomasello, all of the Max Planck Institute for Evolutionary Anthropology, Leipzig, found that chimps were more selfish ("rational") than humans.

In their ingenious experiment, two chimps in adjacent cages faced a cabinet containing two sliding drawers. Each drawer had two trays of raisins, one tray for each chimp. The proposer chimp had to pick a drawer and tug on a rope to slide it within reach of the responder. Then the responder had to grab a projecting rod and pull the drawer's trays within reach of the cage. This allowed each chimp to eat the raisins in its respective tray.

In a typical setup, one drawer contained a fair split of five raisins in both trays. The other drawer had a greedy split, eight raisins in the pro-poser's tray and two in the responder's. Seventy-five percent of the time, the proposer chimps picked the greedy split. Ninety-five percent of their slighted partners let them get away with it. They accepted the two raisins rather than punishing. "It thus would seem," Jensen's group concluded, "that . . . one of humans' closest living relatives behaves according to traditional economic models of self-interest, unlike humans, and that this species does not share the human sensitivity to fairness."

# Twenty-one

# Attacking Heuristics

The brightest minds of economics had labored for a century on a powerful mathematical theory based on marvelously simple premises: that choices reveal authentic preferences and that reserve prices are real. There was no easy way to retrofit economic theory to fluid prices and constructed preferences. "I don't know how much [Amos] anticipated the effect on economics," Barbara Tversky said. "He must have anticipated some of it because he read Savage." She added, "Economists, some of our closest friends, still don't get it at all."

It was not just economists who were uneasy with the new psychology. At a Jerusalem dinner party in the early 1970s, Kahneman was asked what he was working on. He started to explain the heuristics and biases research when a visiting American philosopher turned away. "I am not really interested in the psychology of stupidity," he said.

That reaction was prophetic. Heuristics and biases rubbed some people the wrong way. To catalog the limitations of human rationality was perceived in some quarters as nihilistic, threatening, and/or postmodern. The "irony" of Kahneman and Tversky's research program, not to mention its abiding scientific curiosity, got overlooked.

"Human incompetence is presented as a fact, like gravity," complained University of Iowa psychologist Lola Lopes. She blamed Kahneman and Tversky for letting their "evident exasperation with their subjects' answers" color the wording of their 1974 *Science* article. As journalists discovered Tversky and Kahneman's work, their inevitable simplifications only irked the critics more. Lopes quoted a *Newsweek* piece offering the breezy factoid that most people are "woefully muddled information processors who often stumble along ill-chosen shortcuts to reach bad conclusions."

A key document of the critique was Oxford philosopher L. Jonathan Cohen's article, "Can Human Irrationality Be Experimentally Demonstrated?" Cohen's thinkpiece, along with twenty-nine responses by noted philosophers, psychologists, and mathematicians, filled a rollicking 1981 issue of *The Behavioral and Brain Sciences*. Cohen advanced an argument that only a philosopher's mother could love: Humans are the only possible standard of rationality; ergo, nothing humans do, including their performance in behavioral experiments, can prove humans to *not* be rational.

Other critics, among them Harvard cognitive scientist Steve Pinker, wondered how evolution would permit such things. We can't be all *that* stupid, or we'd be dead already. Gerd Gigerenzer of the Max Planck Institute for Human Development in Berlin—best known to Americans from Malcolm Gladwell's book *Blink*—felt heuristics to be parlor tricks, contingent on trivial details of the experiment and basically not all that important. For Gigerenzer, the story getting lost in the heuristics hoopla was how accurate hunches are. In making this case, he took a tendentious spin on what Kahneman and Tversky were saying. (One person close to both told me succinctly: "Gigerenzer was lying.")

Most would agree that evolution is not a Santa Claus that gives us everything we might wish for. It is more a loving parent that gives us what's realistic. As early as 1954, Ward Edwards remarked that it might be "costly" to have self-consistent preferences. The design of the human mind entails complex trade-offs. Survival often requires us to make quick decisions without complete knowledge of the problem. The mind is presumably optimized for mostly accurate hunches and an improvisitory approach that constructs desires and beliefs on the fly. This can lead to inconsistent prices and choices—if you look hard enough for them.

Do these inconsistencies matter, then? Perhaps they didn't much in the world of our distant ancestors. But things have changed in the past few millennia (a blink of the eye in evolutionary terms). Inventions like writing, numbers, law, and money have introduced new types of challenges. Today's conflicts are resolved by committing to a number—a price, a wage, a boundary, a no-fly zone—that casts a shadow far into the future. In these situations, we can have cause to regret the arbitrary in our choosing and pricing. As Tversky and Kahneman wrote, "Incoherence is more than skin deep."

Ward Edwards lived long enough to see his reputation eclipsed by those of his former students. He too became an acerbic critic of Tversky and Kahneman's work. "Why are experts interesting only if they are not too expert?" Edwards asked in a 1975 article. He answered his own question: "I believe the answer is that psychologists want to believe in the severity of human intellectual limitations."

Edwards was married to the understandable position that a heuristic was a "lapse in judgment" to be "cured," in Colin Camerer's analysis. Edwards could never understand why heuristics had suddenly become the focus of attention. To him, the younger generation was obsessing over the flaws in the marble and ignoring the statue.

In defense of his position, Edwards remarked that people could not drive cars unless they could judge uncertainties accurately, that heuristics "may explain how to get to a mental hospital, but not how to get to the moon." (Years later, Kahneman would recall that unkind crack in his Nobel Prize autobiography.) "We frequently hear about human memory limitations," wrote Edwards, "suggesting that we can remember somewhere between seven and twelve things at a time. But I know someone who can quote from memory all of Shakespeare. When we see comparable feats on the stage, we are so little surprised that we do not even comment on them, preferring to discusses shades of interpretation of character. We frequently hear of human irrationality; it would be difficult to imagine that men so limited could produce a single issue of a newspaper, much less of *Scientific American*."

I asked Kahneman why Edwards had never embraced the heuristics research. He quickly corrected the question: "Not only did he not embrace it, he was *annoyed*. He was quite upset with us." Kahneman then gave this explanation: "In the first place, what we did was very much in his face . . . So that's one thing. The other is—and I have a lot of sympathy because it's one of those things that happen in science regularly—when something half-new comes on the scene, there is a big asymmetry.

People who are bringing in the new stuff think they're doing something very different, but the people who were there before say this is just a minor variation on a theme." Edwards "didn't see the point of the fuss being made."

In Kahneman's modest account, "Everything we wrote was *obvious*. In some sense, nothing surprised Ward. Nothing of what we were saying surprised him."

# Twenty-two

# Deal or No Deal

Amos Tversky told almost no one of the metastatic melanoma that was killing him. Deathly ill, he went into the office and worked up to three weeks before his death, on June 2, 1996. In the years since, behavioral decision theory has gained much ground with mainstream economists and even businesspeople. For the most part, the hair-splitting objections of Cohen and Gigerenzer and company have receded to near invisibility. Of late, a more pressing concern has been cheap prizes.

In the United States the ultimatum game is usually played with the sum of $10, an amount that won't buy a movie ticket in Manhattan. Yet the psychologists and behavioral economists conducting such studies do so in the belief that their results have something to say about the wide world outside the lab. The ultimatum game responder (and implicitly all of us) is supposed to care a lot about how his share compares to the proposer's and to be relatively insensitive to absolute dollar amounts.

Imagine a $10 million game, then. The proposer keeps $9 million for himself, leaving you a measly million. Do you pass up the million in order to teach him a $9 million lesson he'll never forget?

Presumably not. Given that, proposers might demand a larger percentage . . . There has been a lot of speculation about how different a million-dollar ultimatum game would be. Some economists have argued that their kind of rationality kicks in after a certain number of zeros in the prize amount.

Elizabeth Hoffman, Kevin McCabe, and Vernon Smith got sick of hearing this talk. Their economist critics weren't even necessarily thinking of million-dollar prizes. Some were saying a $100 game would be different. Sure, people reject a dollar or two, but nobody in their right mind would turn down $10 or $20.

Hoffman and colleagues scraped together the money to run some $100 ultimatum games. That meant raising about $5,000 to run the game enough times to have statistical significance. In these experiments, done at the University of Arizona, there was no significant difference in behavior between the $100 games and the standard $10 games.

There was this note of drama. One proposer (illegally) scribbled a note to the responder on his offer form: "Don't be a maryter [*sic*]; it is still the easiest $35 you've ever made."

This proposer was offering a "cheap" $30 out of $100, and everyone got $5 just for showing up. The responder rejected the $30, adding the note: "*Greed* is driving this country to hell. Become a part of it and pay."

In 2002, Dutch TV debuted a game show called *Miljoenenjacht* (*Chasing Millions*). It became a hit and led to local versions in more than sixty nations, from Mauritius to Argentina to the United States—where it's called *Deal or No Deal*. The show poses dilemmas much like those studied by decision theorists, except that the sums of money are large and real. A 2008 article by Thierry Post, Martijn van den Assem, Guido Baltussen, and Richard Thaler notes that *Deal or No Deal* "almost appears to be designed to be an economics experiment rather than a TV show."

Aside from the leggy models, there's *no* TV show, just an economics experiment. In the U.S. version the game involves twenty-six female models, each carrying a briefcase that contains an unknown cash amount ranging from 1 cent to $1 million. The contestant begins by picking one of the twenty-six briefcases. He "owns" whatever is in the chosen briefcase. Rather than revealing the prize immediately, host Howie Mandel plays an extended cat-and-mouse game. He begins by revealing the prizes in a random group of briefcases that the contestant *didn't* pick. By process of elimination, this provides indirect information about what might be in the chosen briefcase. All the prize amounts are posted on a scoreboard visible to contestants and the audience, and amounts are eliminated from the board as they are revealed.

A "banker" then offers the contestant a deal. Communicating by telephone from a darkened office overlooking the stage, the banker offers to buy the contestant's briefcase for a stated price. The player must therefore choose between the banker's price and a gamble (keeping the briefcase and continuing with the game, with all its possible outcomes). The first banker offer is always small. If the contestant rejects it, more briefcases are opened, and the contestant comes to have a better picture of what is or isn't in his briefcase. The banker makes further offers. Should the contestant keep rejecting offers, it ultimately comes down to a situation in which just two briefcases remain unopened. The banker names his final price. If the contestant refuses it, his briefcase is opened, and he gets whatever amount is inside.

Before any briefcases have been opened, the average of the twenty-six prizes in the standard American show is $131,477.54. That average changes as briefcases are opened. For instance, learning that an unchosen briefcase contains $1 million is bad news for the contestant, and it accordingly downsizes his prospects.

The only part of the show that isn't completely transparent is how the banker computes his offers. In the early rounds, the offers are such a small fraction of the expectation that you'd be crazy to accept them. The offers grow more generous, relative to expectation, throughout the course of a game. The last offer is nearly the full expectation (in the U.S. game) or modestly more (in some other nations).

Thierry Post and colleagues got videotapes of several years' worth of the Dutch, German, and U.S. *Deal or No Deal* games. They painstakingly analyzed every choice made by some 151 contestants in three countries. Consider Frank, a particularly luckless contestant on the Dutch show. Without batting an eye, Frank rejected banker offers as large as 75,000 euros, a comfortable year's income. Frank ended up with 10 euros, enough for a good stiff drink.

Just before Frank opened his briefcase, there were two prizes in play, 10 and 10,000 euros. The banker offered 6,000 euros—more than the expected value of Frank's briefcase, and a sweeter deal than is offered on the American show. Anybody's mother, accountant, or fee-only financial advisor would have told Frank to take the deal. He wouldn't take it; he was too intent on getting the 10,000 euros.

This behavior is hard to explain with any theory that assumes that choices depend on final wealth levels and nothing more. Anyone who watches the whole episode will understand where poor Frank was coming from. He was reacting to all the bum luck that had befallen him prior to this final choice. Like every other contestant, Frank started out with high hopes and a high reference point. The top prize in the Dutch show is 5 million euros, far richer than the U.S. version. Frank saw his millionaire dreams dashed as the three biggest prizes were taken out of play in the first two rounds. Thereafter he felt like a loser. He did not see the banker's offers as found money but as losses (relative to the fortunes he could have won). This made him willing to take risks.

The 1979 prospect theory article discusses dilemmas not unlike like Frank's. Kahneman and Tversky report on this choice. In addition to whatever else you own, you have been given 1,000 Israeli pounds. You are now asked to choose between a 50 percent chance of an additional 1,000 pounds or what I'll call a "banker offer" of 500. Eighty-four percent of Kahneman and Tversky's subjects said "deal." They preferred the sure thing to the gamble.

Then they rephrased the question and presented it to a different group. You've been given 2,000 Israeli pounds and must choose between a 50 percent chance of a 1,000 *loss* or a "banker offer" that in this case is also a loss, of 500. Here 69 percent said no deal. They'd rather gamble than accept a sure loss.

The two versions of the problem are equivalent, going by what you walk away with. The second version just gives you an extra 1,000 up front and subtracts from that to arrive at the same two net outcomes of the first version. The wording of the second question encourages you to adopt the initial 2,000 pounds as a reference point. By framing the options as losses, it encourages risk taking.

Frank's string of bad luck had the same effect. The banker's final price registered as a loss—even though, under happier circumstances, Frank would have seen it as a windfall. This made him willing to play double or nothing.

Post's team compared the performance of the expected utility model to prospect theory in predicting *Deal or No Deal* contestants' decisions. They found that expected utility was correct 76 percent of the time, versus 85 percent for prospect theory. When serious money was at stake, prospect theory beat utility theory for predicting behavior.

*Deal or No Deal* choices must be made on the spur of the moment. Post and colleagues conjecture, however, that the decisions made on the show may be about as carefully considered as those made in choosing mortgages or retirement portfolios. Like someone making a big financial move, *Deal or No Deal* contestants solicit advice from in-studio family and friends. Most contestants are undoubtedly fans of the show and probably plan their strategy long before their appearance. (A lot of people think mortgages and investments are *boring* and try not to think about them any more than they have to. Decisions are put off and put off, then finally made on the spur of the moment.)

The researchers also conducted two home versions of *Deal or No Deal* at Erasmus University, Rotterdam. They replicated the show "as closely as possible in a classroom" with a host (a popular lecturer) and a live audience, the better to "create the type of distress that contestants must experience in the TV studio." They followed the script of televised games as closely as possible, using the same bank offers and random choices of which briefcases to open. This allowed comparison of the students' behavior to the TV contestants'. The one difference was the size of the prizes. In one version, the prizes were 1/10,000 of those on the Dutch TV show, and in the other they were 1/1,000. The latter meant the top prize was 5,000 euros, and the average amount won was about 400 euros. That put this among the richest of all behavioral economics experiments.

If money is a magnitude scale, you'd expect the behavior to be about the same—and it was. The students in the cheaper experimental game played about the same as in the game where the stakes were ten times higher. Both groups' behavior was similar to TV contestants playing for a thousand or ten thousand times more. Whether a banker's price was judged "fair" was strongly influenced by a contestant's history. Subjects who had been disappointed were, like Frank, less likely to accept a good price. Kahneman and Tversky could have been talking about *Deal or No Deal* when they wrote that "a person who has not made peace with his losses is likely to accept gambles that would be unacceptable to him otherwise."

## Twenty-three

# Prices on the Planet Algon

A Monty Python sketch concerns a mission to the planet Algon. Fifth world in the system of Aldebaran, Algon is suspiciously like 1972 Britain—except for its truly *astronomical* prices. As John Cleese has it,

> Here an ordinary cup of drinking chocolate costs four million pounds, an immersion heater for the hot-water tank costs over six billion pounds, and a pair of split-crotch panties would be almost unobtainable . . . A new element for an electric kettle like this would cost as much as the entire gross national product of the United States of America from 1770 to the year 2000, and even then they wouldn't be able to afford the small fixing ring which attaches it to the kettle.

Later in the bit, Michael Palin breaks in with the announcement that attachments for rotary mowers are "relatively inexpensive!—still in the region of nine to ten million pounds, but it does seem to indicate that Algon might be a very good planet for those with larger gardens."

You might wonder how different Algon is from Earth, really. We are born onto the third world of Sol having no idea what things should cost. Perhaps we never learn. All we can do is take cues from the people around us. We act as if they're sane and their prices make sense.

A Descartes of prices might deduce that the only thing we can truly know is relative values. In some deep sense, I can't ever know whether 10 million pounds is a good price for a rotary mower attachment, but I can know it's cheaper than other prices. In a few short years, this daft view of prices, in which relative values matter and absolutes are almost meaningless, has become widely accepted due to some remarkable experiments. They show, you might say, that we all live on planet Algon.

Dan Ariely is another brilliant Israeli American who has thought deeply about the psychology of pricing. He traces some of his research to his first experience in a pricey chocolate store. Before him was an array of incredibly beautiful truffles with equally incredible prices. "I was thinking about what I wanted," he said, "and I realized two things. One was that I quickly adapted to the level of prices. I didn't think about how much chocolate costs in the supermarket." The other thing was that "I was very susceptible—willing to take whatever suggested price the store was going to tell me was the right price to think about."

Now a professor of behavioral economics at Duke University, Ariely is responsible for some of the most compelling demonstrations of how fluid prices are. One such experiment, done in collaboration with George Loewenstein and Drazen Prelec, was a silent auction of fancy chocolates, bottles of wine, and computer gear. The bidders, MBA candidates at MIT's Sloan School, were asked to write down the last two digits of their social security numbers. Then each bidder had to indicate whether he would pay more or less than that two-digit number, in dollars, for each item being auctioned. Finally, bidders wrote how much they were willing to pay for it (an honest reserve price). Winning bidders paid money out of their own pockets and got to keep any items they won.

One of the items auctioned was a bottle of 1998 Côtes du Rhône. My social security number ends in 23, so the first question I would have had to answer is "Would you pay more or less than $23 for this bottle of wine?" The second question is "How much would you be willing to pay?"

As expected, the results showed impressive anchoring. Bidders with "low" social security numbers (defined as those ending in the digits 00 through 19) were willing to pay an average of $8.64 for the bottle of Côtes du Rhône. Those with "high" numbers (ending 80 through 99) were willing to pay an average of $27.91. It wasn't just the wine mystique. There were similar differences in bids for the chocolates, a cordless keyboard and trackball, and a design book—all because of the social security numbers. For the most part, the students who happened to have higher-ending social security numbers walked away with the merchandise. The lower-number people missed out. I will leave it to you to decide who were the real winners—and who were the suckers.


Ariely was serving in the Israeli military when a magnesium flare, used to illuminate battlefields at night, exploded near him. He received third-degree burns over 70 percent of his body. For the next three years, Ariely was a veritable "English patient," covered in bandages and largely immobile. His treatment required regular replacement of the bandages. There was no way of making this anything but torture. Ariely's nurses were compassionate souls with experience in this unpleasant task. They believed in ripping the bandages off quickly. It produced a burst of agony, fading to mere pain. Ariely had a lot of time to ponder the psychophysics of pain. He concluded it was better to pull gradually, for the pain to be less intense yet of longer duration. One can become adapted to slow, steady pain. There was no way to become adapted to the nurses' high-contrast technique. He had little luck in convincing his nurses of this. They had a different perspective. It hurt them, too, to see their patients suffer, and they preferred that this distasteful part of their work be accomplished quickly.

Once he was able to leave the hospital, Ariely studied psychology at Tel Aviv University. (He met Amos Tversky, who gave a lecture there.) Ariely acquired a grounding in psychophysics, reading the work of S. S. Stevens and others. He did experiments on pain, sometimes with himself as a subject, using heat, cold water, pressure, and loud noises. As his interests turned to economic decisions, it was natural to see money as a stimulus, and price as a magnitude scale.

Ariely pioneered a widely influential thesis: that remembered prices obscure how inexact the human price sense is. Were a shopper required to guess the price of an elliptical trainer, he would try to remember what he'd paid for exercise equipment in the past, or what he'd seen elliptical trainers advertised for. He'd make adjustments for quality and features and come up with a figure that might not be too far off. Yet in some sense, he'd be like Oscar Wilde's definition of cynic, knowing the price of everything and the value of nothing.

The MIT auction was designed to strip away some of the effects of memorized prices. They chose items that MIT students were unlikely to have purchased and items known to have a large range of prices. (Wine and fancy chocolates are popular gifts in part because it's hard for the recipient to guess how much the giver paid.) The question was not *Do you remember the price?* but *How much is this worth to you?*

The auction's results looked much like those of S. S. Stevens's experiments with magnitude scales. There was consensus on ratios, though little on absolute values.

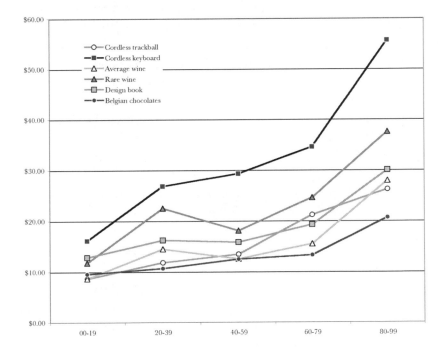

The chart above shows the average bids, broken down into five ranges of social security number endings. Each line indicates the bids for a different item. For the purposes of this experiment, social security numbers can be considered random. You'd normally expect that five random groups would have the same average valuations. Instead, all the lines trend upward. The people with the low social security numbers (left) bid much less than the ones with the high numbers (right). This indicates anchoring.

Within any social security number range, the relative valuations of different items were approximately the same as in every other group. All groups concurred that the keyboard was the most valuable item, and the chocolates were at or near the bottom. The rare wine was consistently valued higher than the average wine, and by approximately the same ratio (1.5 times more) in all groups.

Ariely, Loewenstein, and Prelec theorized that their subjects were retroactively imposing self-consistency. They wrote,

> Suppose that a subject with a social security number ending with 25 has an a priori WTP [willing to pay] range of $5 to $30 for wine described as "average," and $10 to $50 for the "rare" wine. Both wines, therefore, might or might not be purchased for the $25 price. Suppose that the subject indicates, for whatever reason, that she would be willing to purchase the average bottle for $25. If we were to ask her a moment later whether she would be willing to purchase the "rare" bottle for $25, the answer would obviously be "yes" because from her perspective this particular "choice problem" has been solved and its solution is known: if an average wine is worth $25, then a rare wine must be worth more than $25! Moreover, when the subject is subsequently asked to provide WTP prices for the wines, then that problem, too, is now substantially constrained: the prices will have to be ordered so that both prices are above $25 and the rare wine is valued more.

Ariely's group published these results in a 2003 paper in *The Quarterly Journal of Economics,* " 'Coherent Arbitrariness': Stable Demand Curves Without Stable Preferences." The same paper includes yet more impressive proof of the memory theory.

"We wanted something where people don't have a strong reference price," Ariely explained. They needed a brand-new product to price, and the product was pain. One hundred thirty-two MIT students listened to an annoyingly loud high-pitched tone (a 3,000-Hz triangular wave similar to that used for emergency warnings) through headphones. On-screen instructions read,

> In a few moments we are going to play you a new unpleasant tone over your headset. We are interested in how annoying you find it

to be. Immediately after you hear the tone, we are going to ask you whether you would be willing to repeat the same experience in exchange for a payment of 10 cents [50 cents for another group].

Participants were asked to name their prices for listening to 10 seconds, 30 seconds, and 60 seconds of the annoying sound. As expected, those who received the low anchor (10 cents) quoted consistently lower prices than those who got the high value (50 cents). Everyone's prices were scaled appropriately to the length of exposure. Furthermore, repeated trials with the same subjects did not erase the effect of the initial anchor. Most stuck with their original pricing, unaware that it was prompted by a meaningless anchor.

Some volunteers were asked to name their price for the sound and also to rank it on a list of minor annoyances. The peeves included "discovering you purchased a spoiled carton of milk," "forgetting to return a video and having to pay a fine," "having your ice cream fall on the floor," and seven other items. Overall, the annoying sound came in #2 on the list, behind "missing your bus by a few seconds." The telling thing is this. The 10- and 50-cent price anchors had no effect on the *ranking* of the annoying noise. Everyone approximately agreed on how bad the noise was, relative to life's other little annoyances.

Another group of volunteers consented to put a finger in a vise. The experimenter tightened the vise until the subject said he was beginning to experience pain (the "pain threshold"). Then the vise was tightened a millimeter more. The subject was instructed to remember that level of pain. Their fingers released from the vise, the volunteers were then asked which torture they would prefer: 30 more seconds in the vise, or 30 more seconds of the annoying sound.

Most opted for the sound. Again, the anchoring had no statistical effect on whether people preferred the sound or the vise. The anchors affected only the prices.

Economists had long articulated an ideal of decisiveness and self-consistency in financial matters. Apparently, this was not just an abstraction for Ph.D.s; it is a widely shared ideal that average folks try to live up to. We all pretend to have the self-consistent reserve prices of theory and common sense. But the unspoken truth is, all we know are relative valuations. We are ratio wise and price foolish.

# Part Four

**"Pricing is a dangerous lever"**

**Twenty-four**

# The Free 72-Ounce Steak

One of America's longest-running Guy Grand pranks takes place every day just off I-40 in Amarillo. A giant steer statue is blazoned with a sign advertising a FREE 72 OZ STEAK. It's the signature dish of the Big Texan Steak Ranch, and it comes with salad, shrimp cocktail, baked potato, roll, butter, and a very big catch. The catch is that the customer has to consume everything within one hour. Otherwise, the price is $72.

In our litigious age, a deal like that merits some fine print. Customers must pay the $72 up front, to be refunded if and when they clean their plate. Rule #5: "You don't have to eat the fat, but we will judge this." No third party is allowed to touch the food (lest they palm a baked potato?). Diners must sign a waiver accepting responsibility for any and all health risks. Those ordering the 72-ouncer are the Big Texan's de facto floor-show: they have to sit on a special platform, in view of all, and aren't allowed to leave the table during the meal. And just in case you're wondering, anyone who vomits is disqualified even if they want to continue. A bucket is supplied.

Whatever the 72-ounce steak does to the Big Texan's ambience, it has earned the restaurant more publicity than it knows what to do with. It's become a perennial favorite of TV food and travel shows. A *Simpsons* episode had Homer tackling a 256-ounce "free" steak.

Since 1960 (when the price was $9.95), about 60,000 trenchermen have taken the challenge. The restaurant reports that 8,500 have managed to eat everything, an overall success rate of about 14 percent. Not many women try, but about 50 percent have succeeded. Those who order the 72-ounce steak probably feel it's a good deal no matter what. It's a dollar per ounce of beef, and unlike all-you-can-eat promotions, the customers are allowed to take home leftovers.

It's a can't-lose proposition—uh, until you realize you just paid $72 for dinner in Amarillo.

The "free" 72-ounce steak stands at the nexus of vernacular and professional pricing. Big Texan owner Bob Lee came up with the gimmick on his own in 1960, long before the age of menu consultants. His promotion anticipates several principles now espoused by academics and marketing professionals alike. Most important, the 72-ounce steak is an anchor. You can't come anywhere near the Big Texan without being exposed repeatedly to the *idea* of eating a 72-ounce steak. Though the vast majority of Big Texan customers will never order it, the exposure subtly raises diners' estimates of how much they can eat and what they're willing to pay. One of Daniel Kahneman's anchoring experiments is worth mentioning in this connection. He and Karen Jacowitz tried asking:

(a)  Does the average American eat more or less than 50 pounds of meat a year?
(b)  How much meat does the average American eat in a year?

The median answer was 100 pounds of meat. They asked another group whether the average American ate more or less than *1,000* pounds of meat a year. For this group, the median estimate was 500 pounds.

The Big Texan promotion is also a simple example of *nonlinear pricing*. "Nonlinear" means that the price (or price per ounce) is not a straight line—it varies with the amount consumed. The 72-ounce steak costs $72 until you finish everything, and then the price plummets to zero.

This type of pricing casts a hypnotic spell. It is one of the most common tricks of price consultants, used for everything from cell phone bills to airfares. A hungry customer at Big Texan does not know whether he's going to be paying $72 or nothing. That uncertainty renders the $72 a bit less real. There is an alternate way of judging the deal: by price per

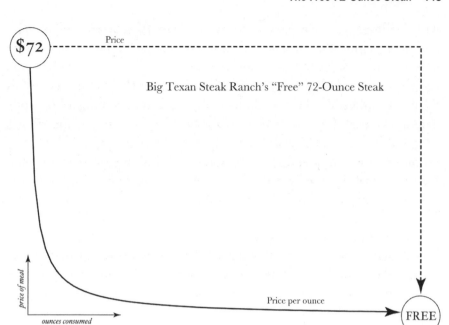

ounce. A chart of the price per ounce is a curve slanting steeply down-ward, then slowly approaching $1, and finally dropping to zero. A diner who ordered the 72-ounce steak, ate a 1-ounce mouthful, and put down the fork would be paying the outrageous price of $72 an ounce. But someone who ate a couple of pounds of meat would be paying $2.25 an ounce, and someone who ate nearly the whole thing would be paying just over $1 an ounce. That's pretty reasonable. The customer is so con-cerned with getting a "deal" that he pays a price he wouldn't otherwise stomach.

Hermann Simon is a man who can get upset about being offered a 35 percent discount on a Nikon camera (as he was recently). He was hap-pily buying the camera when the salesperson insisted on knocking 35 percent off the price. This went against Simon's core business philoso-phy, which one of his papers puts in plain language: "willingness to pay must be exploited to the full."

The imperative tone of such pronouncements, coupled with Simon's teutonic diction, can be startling at first encounter. Simon's fascination with "willingness to pay" is infectious, however. As much as any individual, he is behind the professionalization of pricing in the past couple of decades. In the early 1980s Simon was a University of Bielefeld business professor, occasionally consulting with corporations and often seeing his advice go unheeded. The psychology of price was becoming a hot topic. There was a confluence of reasons for that. For one thing, the ripples from Kahneman and Tversky's work spread ever outward, sparking interest among marketers and retailers. Consider this survey question, published by Tversky and Kahneman in 1981 (itself loosely inspired by a puzzle that Jimmie Savage wrote about in 1954):

> Imagine that you are about to purchase a jacket for $125 and a calculator for $15. The calculator salesman informs you that the calculator you wish to buy is on sale for $10 at the other branch of the store, located 20 minutes' drive away. Would you make the trip to the other store?

Most respondents said they would. Another randomly selected group heard a different version of the question in which the jacket was only $15 and the calculator $125. The calculator was on sale for $120 at the other store. Was *that* worth the trip? Most said no.

Retailers spend their lives trying to understand what makes Joe and Jane Consumer willing to pay a higher price *here* than a lower price *there*. This was a provocative result (assuming that the survey applied to real consumers), and it was completely outside the understanding of standard economics. In both versions of the question, the buyer is planning to spend $140 total and the drive saves exactly $5. "Why are we more willing to drive across town to save money on a small purchase than a large one?" Richard Thaler asked. "Clearly there is some psychophysics at work here. Five dollars seems like a significant saving on a $15 purchase, but not so on a $125 purchase."

The past decades have seen mounting optimism among psychologists and behavioral economists about the practical relevance of their work. Thaler envisions a benign future in which "choice engineers" use the science to help people make decisions better reflecting their inner values— to the extent that inner values exist in the brave new world of constructed prices and preferences. Sendhil Mullainathan, a former student of Thaler's, talks of using decision theory to help nations break out of the cycle of third-world poverty. "What we're saying is that there is a technology emerging from behavioral economics," Kahneman said. "It's not only an abstract thing. You can do things with it. We are just at the beginning."

The same decades have seen a parallel, less idealistic conception of what to do with the science: make money off it. Some of the academics, among them Thaler and Tversky, started connecting the dots for businesspeople in articles published mostly in marketing journals. There was a new scientific curiosity about venerable marketing tricks—prices ending in 9, rebates, discounts, outright gimmicks like "free" steak meals— and whether, or how, they worked. The Professional Pricing Society, founded in 1984, began bringing together Fortune 1000 businesspeople to share ideas.

Simon, though steeped in the work of the behavioralists, was skeptical about its application to the business world. A scientific result is valued for its simplicity and abstraction. The prospect theory paper is one example. The *Scientific American* crowd loves it because it's a simple idea that explains *everything*. That in itself does not help businesses. Companies are more interested in specific solutions to their narrow, complicated (and sometimes *uninteresting*) problems.

A key development was technological. On June 26, 1974, a pack of Wrigley's Juicy Fruit gum was scanned at Marsh's Supermarket in Troy, Ohio. It was the first consumer product to be scanned at checkout, the culmination of an effort by IBM to design a scannable product code. Over the next years, scanners became common on both sides of the Atlantic. They produced a mountain of information. Everyone figured the data ought to be useful, but no one quite knew what to make of them.

One of Simon's doctoral students, Eckhard Kucher, did his dissertation on scanner data. Kucher and Simon realized that the data offered a way to bridge price psychology and practical reality. They let analysts run decision "experiments" retroactively, looking at how consumers reacted (or didn't react) to a price increase, sale, or rebate. The data capture any and all behavioral effects, as well as the traditional economic ones, and the results are specific to the business and its customers. Kucher proposed starting a consultancy offering businesses advice on how to fine-tune pricing. Simon was already thinking along those lines and quickly agreed. Their partnership went into business in early 1985.

A company may not be able to do much about its costs, Simon and Kucher argued, but it usually has freedom to set prices. The partners found that few businesspeople have any clear idea of what their customers are willing to pay, or how prices affect profits. This is one of the things that scanner data can help uncover.

Since the 1980s, the price consultant industry has burgeoned. Software is an important part of the toolkit. A supermarket or department store or online retailer has so many prices that only software can manage them all. Pricing software is in its fourth generation, according to Todd P. Michaud, CEO of Revionics. A client business inputs its scanner data and gets out profit-optimized prices (for each UPC code), illustrated with neat graphs showing why the price should be higher or lower. "Indeed, retail pricing software is now capable of teaching itself," Michaud bragged.

It's not just software, of course. Prices have become more creative than ever. Simon sees his consultants as architects of "price structures." These are billing plans (think of your cell phone plan) that, one way or another, elaborate on the Big Texan gimmick of nonlinear pricing. The customer is encouraged to pay more than he intended in a paradoxical quest to get a low price. The psychology of decision making has much to say about why this works—and almost nothing to tell anyone who frets about its ethical ramifications. Many will feel that the customer has been duped into buying more meat, or minutes, than he truly wanted. The new psychology counters that "what the customer wants" is not nearly so clear-cut. It is constructed on the spot, influenced by details the conscious mind may believe to be immaterial. The price consultant's job, needless to say, is to devise situations favorable to the client.

One SKP maxim runs, "Pricing is a dangerous lever." A small change in prices can make a huge difference in profitability, for good or bad. Simon estimates that optimizing a company's prices typically increases profit margins by about 2 percentage points, say from 5 percent to 7 percent. Michaud claims a similar 1 to 4 percent as a representative range. Because profit margins are small to begin with, adding a percent or two can boost profits immensely. Very few interventions can have such an effect on the bottom line. For hundreds of corporations, this sales pitch has been well-nigh irresistible.

# Twenty-five

# Price Check

You'll find one of the most Machiavellian applications of coherent arbitrariness at any checkout stand. It's the supermarket "loyalty card." Customers who use loyalty cards are a self-selected group of cheapskates. They identify themselves as such every time they fumble to swipe a card because they can't bear the thought of missing a 50-cent discount on Brawny towels. These are the customers who just might drive across town to save $5.

Loyalty card data tell the market what brands and items their cost-sensitive customers buy most regularly. According to Jim Hertel of Willard Bishop, a supermarket consulting firm, chains generally set aside their five hundred or so most frequently purchased items for special treatment. Markets know that customers will notice price increases on Coca-Cola or beef or Maxwell House coffee. As much as possible, they try to raise prices where it's least likely to be noticed. Hardly anyone gets upset when they raise the price for chervil—or other infrequently purchased items like gourmet pasta sauce, pomegranates, goat cheese, or fresh-squeezed orange juice. "There's an opportunity to make some margin back on those items," Hertel explained. That's because customers can't remember what they paid last time and don't otherwise have a precise notion of what these items should cost.

Supermarket consultants leave few stones unturned in determining what boosts consumers' willingness to pay. One of the more intriguing of recent findings is that shoppers open their wallets wider when moving through a store in a counterclockwise direction. On average, these shoppers spend $2 more a trip than clockwise shoppers.

This was determined in studies of shopping cart movements. Herb Sorensen of Sorensen Associates has fitted carts with RFID tags emitting a radio ping every five seconds. This PathTracker technology allows sensors to triangulate each cart's location, map its motion, and tally what was bought and at what price. No one is quite sure why counterclockwise shoppers buy more. Paco Underhill, CEO of Envirosell, mentions one popular guess, that North Americans see shopping carts as "cars" to be driven on the right. "If you want to get my attention," Underhill said, "it better be to my right." By this theory, the right-handed majority finds it easier to make impulse purchases when the wall or shelf is to the right. Sorensen's findings have been widely adopted, with markets putting their main entrance on the right of the store's layout to encourage counterclockwise shopping.

One of Richard Thaler's best-known thought experiments concerns a grocery store. You're lying on a beach on a hot day and desperately want a cold beer. A friend offers to go get a beer from the only place nearby, a small run-down grocery store. He warns it might be expensive, so he asks how much you're willing to pay. He'll buy the beer only if the store's price is no greater than your limit.

When Thaler sprang this riddle on executives in the early 1980s, the average reserve price was $1.50. Another group heard the same story, except that the place selling the beer was said to be the bar of a fancy resort hotel. For this group, the average price was $2.65.

Both versions of the story made it clear that the friend was buying a bottle of your favorite brand of beer. It was the same product no matter where it was purchased. The ambience of the hotel was irrelevant because the beer was to be consumed back on the beach. Nevertheless, the average executive was willing to pay $2 for a bottle of beer from the fancy hotel, but not for the same bottle from the run-down grocery. The hotel bar that charged $2 was understood to be offering a fair price; for a run-down grocery, that $2 was price gouging.

Thaler considered what his imaginary grocer could do to boost beer sales. He advised "investing in seemingly superfluous luxury or installing a bar." This would raise expectations about what the proper price of beer would be, resulting in more purchases.

Another suggestion was that the owner of the shabby grocery sell beer in unusually large containers, maybe 16 ounces instead of the usual 12. Consumers remember what a 12-ounce bottle of beer sells for. They may not know what 16 ounces should go for. (They could figure it, but most won't.) Also, it's easier to sneak extra profit onto a bigger quantity of beer than a smaller one.

Both of Thaler's ideas can be observed in today's supermarket industry. Upscale markets like Whole Foods make the most of "superfluous luxury." This allows them to charge prices that wouldn't be tolerated otherwise. Every Whole Foods store features a spectacularly styled produce department. "How cute are these?" asked a folksy sign next to Russian Banana fingerling potatoes in Manhattan's Time Warner Center store. *Cuter than your basic spuds,* apparently—and don't you dare go comparing prices.

Warehouse stores like Costco and Sam's Club sell gallon drums of blue cheese salad dressing and thirty-roll packs of toilet paper. You are supposed to think you're getting a good deal by buying in bulk. Sometimes you are . . . Other times, the deal isn't so good as you think. It's hard to tell. Not many shoppers know what a six-pound can of pineapple chunks ought to cost.

The "organic" and "green" designations have been windfalls for markets upscale and downscale. Whatever those terms mean, they also mean that the premium price doesn't seem like such a rip-off.


Another beer problem: Joe Sixpack is reaching for a brew on the market shelf. There's a premium beer that costs $2.60, and a bargain brand that's only $1.80. The premium beer is "better" (whatever that means). Connoisseurs have rated the premium brand 70 out of 100 in quality, while the bargain brand is only a 50. Which should Joe buy?

Joel Huber and Christopher Puto, then a professor and grad student at Duke University's school of business, posed this dilemma to a group of business undergraduates. The students preferred the premium beer by a 2-to-1 margin.

Another group choose among three beers, the two above and a third with a rock-bottom price of $1.60 and a quality rating in the basement (40). Not a single student wanted the super-cheap beer. Yet it affected what they did choose. The proportion of students choosing the original bargain beer rose to 47 percent, up from 33 percent. The existence of the super-cheap beer legitimized the bargain beer.

In another set of trials, the three choices were the original bargain and premium beers, and a super-premium beer. Like many upscale products, this was much more expensive ($3.40) and only a little better in quality (rated 75). Ten percent of the students said they'd choose the super-premium beer. An astonishing 90 percent chose the premium beer. Now nobody wanted the bargain beer.

It was like pulling the strings on a marionette. Huber and Puto found they could make the students want one beer or the other, just by adding a third choice *that few or no one wanted*.

Choosing an American beer *ought* to be simple. A profusion of blind taste tests claim that avid drinkers can't tell Budweiser from Miller from Coors. Since all mass-market beers taste pretty much alike, the one trade-off is between price and quality (and you have to wonder whether "quality" is an illusion of marketing).

Look at the chart on the previous page. The ideal beer would be both cheap *and* high quality, falling in the upper left-hand corner. I don't have to tell you, that's not the way beer or life works. There is usually a correlation, however loose, between price and quality. That means that brands tend to fall in a diagonal line from lower left to upper right.

In order to raise the market share of the bargain brand A, Huber and Puto found, you need only offer a cheaper option C. C becomes a "decoy." It probably won't get much of the market itself, but it will exert an attraction effect, shifting consumer choices downscale to the original bargain brand A. Likewise, adding a high-priced decoy D (instead of C) pulls consumers upscale, augmenting the market share of the premium brand B.

After the choosers had stated their choices, Huber and Puto asked them why they had chosen as they did. The answers made a certain amount of sense. Those who had chosen the middle-priced option of three described their decision as "safe," a "compromise" choice. The cheapest beer might taste terrible, and the most expensive might be a rip-off, but one in the middle of the pack ought to be okay.

Huber and Puto's paper, published in a 1983 issue of *The Journal of Consumer Research*, is now a foundation of contemporary marketing. They remarked, however, that businesses had already intuited these ideas. Anheuser-Busch's Budweiser was the nation's best-selling premium beer when that company began an aggressive promotion of a super-premium brand, Michelob, in the 1960s. Were it true that beer drinkers know exactly what they want and how much to pay, Michelob would have cannibalized the market for Budweiser. Instead, the total of Budweiser and Michelob sales increased. Huber and Puto argue that Michelob made Budweiser appear "less extreme, less expensive, and less elite." Some Budweiser drinkers switched upscale to Michelob, but this was balanced by buyers of cheaper beers switching up to Bud. In other words, Michelob ads made some Miller people switch to Budweiser. Overall, Anheuser-Busch came out ahead.

The attraction effect has been used dynamically. In 1961 Procter & Gamble introduced Pampers, a brand of disposable diapers. Originally, Pampers' competition was cloth diapers. The disposables were seen as being more convenient and far more expensive. In 1978 Procter & Gamble rolled out a higher-priced brand of disposable diapers, Luvs. Besides capturing whatever market existed for upscale disposable diapers, Luvs presented a contrast, convincing cloth diaper users that Pampers was not such a pricey indulgence after all. By the mid-1990s, times had changed again. Parents had switched to disposable diapers, except for a minority of the environmentally sensitive. Procter & Gamble decided it could use a downscale decoy more than an upscale one. Starting in 1994, Luvs was respositioned as a bargain brand.

# Twenty-six

# Shilling for Prada

The one psychophysics term on the lips of Prada store managers is "anchor." In the luxury trade, that describes an obscenely high-priced article displayed mainly to manipulate consumers. The anchor is for sale—but it's okay if no one buys it. It's really there for contrast. It makes everything else look affordable by comparison. "This has been a strategy that goes back to the seventeenth century," Paco Underhill said recently. "You sold one thing to the king, but everyone in court had to have a lesser one. There's the $500 bag in the window, and what you walk away with is the T-shirt."

Today the strategy can mean five-figure handbags and seven-figure watches. In the midst of the grimmest recession since the 1930s, Ralph Lauren was hawking a "Ricky" alligator bag for $14,000. Hermès has a watch for $330,000, and an even million will buy Hublot's One Million $ Black Caviar Big Bang watch "with 322 black diamonds invisibly set to conceal any sign of metal." (The metal being concealed is 18K white gold.) Who would pay $1 million for a watch? That is exactly what you're supposed to ask yourself. The follow-up question is how much *would* you pay for a really nice watch? These are similar to the questions posed in anchoring experiments and probably have the same result.

An anchor price tag is like the dazzling white ring in S. S. Stevens's experiment. It makes the drabber shades of shopaholic gray look like a bargain. High prices also work like shills. They convince shoppers that *somebody* must be paying that kind of money (otherwise why would they have it on display?). This is not necessarily a correct conclusion. Hublot made only one million-dollar watch (and cagily identifies it as a special order). Hermès made two of its $330,000 watches, and ultra-expensive handbags are often one to a flagship store. The illusion of an authentic supply-and-demand market for such things is aided and abetted by the *Robb Report* and the celebrity press. Eva Longoria was photographed carrying a Coach "Miranda" bag in hot blue python skin! Whether she paid list for it is beside the point.

Even in the best economic times, luxury stores are Potemkin villages, existing to convince aspiring materialists of a world richer, more spend-thrift than it actually is. Marketing consultant Dan Hill of Sensory Logic said that successful stores use high-priced items to create "a mixture of anger and happiness." Upper-middle-class consumers are *angry* because they can't afford the gear featured in the store and worn by celebrities. The knee-jerk reaction is to get *happy* by buying something else.

One of the key insights of behavioral pricing is that items that don't sell can change what does. Amos Tversky liked to tell this story. The Williams-Sonoma chain, known for high quality and prices to match, once offered a fancy breadmaker for $279. They later added a somewhat bigger model, pricing it at $429. Guess what happened?

The $429 model was a flop. Unless you're running a boarding school, who needs a bigger breadmaker? But sales of the $279 model nearly doubled. Clearly, there were people charmed by the idea of a quality bread-maker from Williams-Sonoma. The only thing that stopped them from buying was the price. It seemed high at $279. Once the store added the $429 model, the $279 machine was no longer seen as such an extrava-gance. It could be rationalized as a useful product that did nearly every-thing the $429 model did, at a bargain price. Adding another price point, even though hardly anyone chose it, increased the price consumers were willing to pay for a breadmaker.

As far as Tversky could tell, Williams-Sonoma didn't plan things this way. Since then, retailers have gotten wise to contrast effects in prices. Extending the work of Huber and Puto, a 1992 paper by Tversky and Ita-mar Simonson laid down two commandments of manipulative retail. One is *extremeness aversion*. They showed through surveys (involving Minolta cameras, Cross pens, microwave ovens, tires, computers, and paper towels) that when consumers are uncertain, they shy away from the most expensive item offered or the least expensive; the highest quality or the lowest quality; the biggest or the smallest. Most favor something in the middle. Ergo, the way to sell a lot of $800 shoes is to display some $1,200 shoes next to them.

"Contrast effects are ubiquitous in perception and judgment," Simonson and Tversky wrote. "The same circle appears large when surrounded by small circles and small when surrounded by large ones. Similarly, the same product may appear attractive on a background of less attractive alternatives and unattractive on a background of more attractive alternatives. We propose that the effect of contrast applies not only to single attributes, such as size or attractiveness, but also to the trade-offs between attributes."

This leads to their second principle, *trade-off contrast*. Go into a leather goods store and there will be dozens of handbags, none of them indisputably the best by anyone's standards. One bag is more practical, one is more stylish, another is a more interesting color, and still another is 40 percent off. The customer, being loss averse, is uncomfortable with this cornucopia of choice. She fears she will pick bag A and then decide she should have picked B . . .

The trade-off contrast rule says that when item X is clearly better than an inferior choice Y, consumers tend to buy X—even when there are many other choices and it's impossible to say whether X is the best choice of all. Just the fact that X is better than Y is a selling point, and it carries more weight than it reasonably should. Apparently the shopper tries to reduce anxiety by choosing an item that can be justified (to herself, to a friend, to a spouse cross-examining her on the credit card bill). She is able to talk herself into X because it's so much better than Y.

Trade-off contrast is particularly important in the luxury trade, where brands have flagship stores selling their own goods exclusively. On top of that, retailers with strong brands have great flexibility on prices (a shopper who *must* have a Jimmy Choo pump doesn't care so much what other brands are selling for). Simon-Kucher's consultants often find themselves in the position of scolding clients for setting their prices too low. "Luxury goods prices are not directly linked to any type of costs," one SKP marketing report drily lectures. "The art of luxury pricing lies in quantifying the value-to-consumer regardless of cost, competitor or market prices."

Coach allots only one or two ultra-expensive bags to each of its flagship stores. They are displayed beautifully, with the price in as large and legible a typeface as decency permits. Coach does not sell many of these bags and would probably be happy to sell none at all. To give one example, they have a $7,000 alligator handbag and a rather similar bag, in ostrich leather, for $2,000. Most shoppers would be hard put to guess which is the $7,000 bag and which is the $2,000 bag. Some will think ostrich more exclusive than alligator, anyway.

For trade-off contrast to work, one choice must be "inferior." Since nearly everyone, even a Coach customer, *does* care about price, anything that appears to be gratuitously overpriced is an "inferior" choice in one important respect. A $7,000 bag makes a similar $2,000 bag more desirable. (It's so much less expensive, and it's still got the designer label!) This results in increased sales for the $2,000 ostrich bags—which might otherwise have been rejected as too expensive, too willfully over-the-top.

The realities of fashion fit well into Simonson and Tversky's two rules. Serious style has always been expensive, uncomfortable, shocking, out there. A select few, of flawless body and bank account, can carry it off. Everyone else settles for something a bit more comfortable, pricewise and otherwise. A handful of near-unattainable items can manipulate the great mass of consumers.

Prada believes in engineering the context. It paid over $1,700 per square foot for its Rem Koolhaas–designed store in SoHo and is forking over equally stratospheric rents. It would not devote floor space to goods that hardly ever sell unless there was a reason for it. Trade-off contrast is part of the cost of doing business, like advertising or window displays or "starchitect" designs. It's not unusual to find items similar to the high-priced anchor selling for a tenth as much. Anyone who can't swing that can always try the $300 sunglasses. Or the $110 mobile phone charm. The British Prada website hints at where the money is (online, at any rate). It offers 10 makes of women's shoes, 23 handbags, and 54 "gifts"— trinkets like keychains, bracelet charms, and golf tee holders. At £60 for a bracelet charm, the profit margin must be staggering.

# Twenty-seven

# Menu Psych

"Daniel Boulud has a restaurant that serves a truffle and Kobe steak hamburger for $100," restaurant consultant Brandon O'Dell said. "Maybe once a week somebody will go in there and blow $100 on a hamburger. But the point of the hamburger isn't to make a lot of money selling hamburgers. It's to make everything else on the menu look cheap by comparison. Someone sees a $100 hamburger on the menu, and they can look at a $50 steak and see it's a bargain."

Boulud is credited with starting the pre-recession trend of ridiculously expensive items on Manhattan menus. In 2001 Boulud's db bistro moderne began selling a burger (stuffed with braised short ribs and foie gras) for a then unthinkable $28. It got a lot of press and a lot of imitators. Boulud raised the ante with a version containing 20 grams of black truffles (in season) for $150. One of his imitators, the Wall Street Burger Shoppe, offers a $175 Kobe burger with 25 grams of truffles and gold flakes.

Hotel restaurants have taken to this idea, perhaps on the theory that anyone who can afford a hotel in Manhattan has money to burn. There is a $1,000 caviar and lobster omelet on the menu at Norma's in the Parker Meridien, and a $1,000 truffle and goji berry *bagel* at the Westin Hotel. Having these prices on the menu costs the restaurant very little. If and when an order comes in, it's the chef's lucky day. But mainly, thousand-dollar bagels exist to bewitch customers into spending more than they would have. The effect is unconscious but no less real for it.

•　•　•

"Places like Chili's and Applebee's make a science out of it," said the restaurateur-turned-menu-consultant Jim Laube. "Go to those places and take notice of what they do to draw attention to those items they want to sell. And believe me, they know exactly what they want to sell."

Sizzler, Hooters, TGI Friday's, Olive Garden: whatever their culinary limitations, this is the cutting edge of menu science. The goal of psychological menu design is to draw attention to the profitable (as in "overpriced") items. Industry convention divides menu items into *stars*, *puzzles*, *plowhorses*, and *dogs*. A star is a popular, high-profit item—in other words, an item for which customers are willing to pay a good deal more than it costs to make. A puzzle is high-profit but unpopular; a plowhorse is the opposite, popular yet unprofitable. A dog is unpopular and unprofitable. Consultants try to turn puzzles into stars, nudge customers away from plowhorses, and convince everyone that the prices on the menu are more reasonable than they look.

One common trick is "bracketing." Expensive items like steak are offered in two sizes. The customer isn't told how much smaller the small portion is, but no matter. He assumes the smaller size is attractively priced because, um, it costs less. In reality, the "small size" is the steak they wanted to sell all along, and the "lower price" is what they intended to charge for it. "If you do this with three menu items," the consultant Tepper Kalmar said, "it really adds up."

"Bundling" is the practice of selling several items for a supposed bargain price. It describes fast-food "combo meals" and tony prix fixe selections. As everyone understands, the bundle dangles an incentive to order something extra. The burger plus fries plus soda combination costs just pennies more than burger plus soda à la carte. You might as well get the fries. "By discounting the third item a small amount, the overall gross profit goes up," Kalmar said.

There is another reason for the effectiveness of bundling. It fosters confusion. A restaurant's prix fixe pricing prevents diners from getting upset about paying $13 for two scallops (an example Richard Thaler found in a San Francisco Zagat guide). It's hard to be sure what costs what and whether it's too much.

The bundling effect wears off as repeat customers become familiar with the prices of their favorite combos. For this reason, chain menus are an ever-changing caloric kaleidoscope. New entrées are offered, and old ones change or vanish. Combos can be super-sized. Do you want curly fries? You can't buy exactly the same thing you did last time; neither can you compare prices, exactly.

When all else fails, Kalmar tells restaurateurs to exploit "opportunity" price increases. This adopts the fairness research finding that sellers should blame someone else for any price increases. When necessary, Kalmar suggests that restaurants post signs explaining that gas prices or energy costs or crop failure (whatever) have forced them to pass on their extra costs in a "temporary" price increase.

Manipulative menu design is often a matter of typography. Above is a sample of the menu of Pastis, and on page 162 is one from the Union Square Café, both popular New York eateries. By the thinking of menu consultants, Pastis has done almost everything wrong, and Union Square Café has done just about everything right. The most common menu mistake of all, according to Brandon O'Dell, is listing prices in a column, as Pastis has done. "The menu turns into a price list. They go down and choose from the cheapest items, instead of choosing what they want and *then* deciding whether it's worth it."

The Pastis menu also uses leader dots. The purpose of leader dots is

## Main Courses

Pan-Roasted Cod with Aromatic Vegetables, Blood Orange-Lobster Broth and Black Olive Oil    30

Grilled Wild Striped Bass, Gigante Beans, Roasted Onions and Romesco Sauce    31

Seared Sea Scallops, Brussels Sprout-Bacon *Farrotto* and Black Trumpet Mushrooms    31

Pan-Roasted Giannone Chicken, Anson Mills Polenta, Root Vegetables & Swiss Chard Pesto    27

Crispy Duck Confit, Fingerling Potatoes, Cipollini, Bitter Greens & Huckleberry *Marmellata*    29

Grilled Lamb Chops *Scotta Dita*, Potato-Gruyère Gratin and Wilted *Insalata Tricolore*    35

Grilled Smoked Cedar River Shell Steak, Vin Cotto-Glazed Grilled Radicchio and Whipped Potatoes    35

Winter Vegetables – Fennel *Parmigiano*, Grilled Radicchio, Lentil Farrotto, Fried Polenta and
Pesto Root Vegetables    26

to draw the diner's gaze from the items to the prices—and they do just that. But that's not what restaurants should want. A diner who orders based on price is not a profitable diner. To minimize price sensitivity, Seattle consultant Gregg Rapp tells clients to scrap the leader dots and omit dollar signs, decimal points, and cents. Union Square Café has done all of this. The centered justification of its menu keeps the prices from forming a neat column. It's not that customers *can't* check prices, but most will follow whatever subtle cues are provided. The cues here say "Pay attention to the food, not the prices."

On page 163 is a page of a recent menu for Balthazar restaurant, New York. Though it has too many prices in columns, the Balthazar menu uses some sophisticated tricks of menu psychology.

The typical diner opens the menu and looks first at the upper right-hand page. Balthazar isn't taking any chances about that: it's got a picture at upper right, another way to draw the eye. From there the gaze usually moves down to the center of the right page. Menu consultants use these prime menu spaces for high-profit items and price anchors. In this case, the anchor is the Le Balthazar seafood plate, for $110. Psychophysics says that the contrast effect is strongest in the immediate vicinity of a stimulus. It's anyone's guess whether this applies to prices on menus, but consultants seem to believe it does. They recommend putting high-profit items immediately adjacent to the high-priced anchor. The real agenda of the $110 price is probably to induce customers to spring for the $65 Le Grand plate just to the left of it or the more modest seafood orders below it.

## LE BAR A HUÎTRES

### PLATEAUX DE FRUITS DE MER

**LE GRAND**
*65.00*

**LE BALTHAZAR**
*110.00*

| OYSTERS | | SHELLFISH | |
|---|---|---|---|
| Malpeque | *1/2 dozen* 19.00 | Little Neck Clams | 11.00 |
| West Coast | P/A | 1/2 Crab Mayonnaise | 19.50 |
| Oysters du Jour | P/A | 1/2 Lobster | 21.00 |

*Shrimp Cocktail 15.00*

| | | |
|---|---|---|
| BALTHAZAR SALAD *with haricots verts, asparagus, fennel, ricotta salata and truffle vinaigrette* | | 14.00 |
| ESCARGOTS *in garlic butter* | | 14.00 |
| SHRIMP RISOTTO *with celery root and rosemary* | | 14.00/21.00 |
| BRANDADE DE MORUE | | 11.00 |

A box around a menu item draws attention and, usually, orders. Is $15 such an indulgence for a shrimp cocktail? Not next to a $110 extravaganza! A really fancy box is better yet. The *fromages* at bottom are probably high-profit puzzles.

Other ways of promoting profitable items are text descriptions and photographs. Photographs of food are among the most powerful motivators and also one of the most inflexible menu taboos. Extensively used in the Chili's and Applebee's type of chains, photographs are considered death to any place with foodie pretensions. Even the Red Lobster chain felt it had to drop photos from the menu when it recently upgraded its image. Balthazar's tasteful drawing of a seafood plate is about as far as a restaurant of this caliber can go, and it's used to draw attention to the two most expensive orders.

Rapp doesn't see his mission as eliminating the unprofitable entrée.

"We don't want to take it off the menu because we might lose that customer," he explained. Instead, an item can be "minimized" by reversing the above advice—removing boxes or copy and exiling it to menu Siberia. Balthazar has done this with its easy-to-miss burgers and the mysteriously unannotated *brandade de morue*.

# Twenty-eight

# The Price of a Super Bowl Ticket

Each year the NFL sells 500 pairs of Super Bowl tickets at "face value." Currently, that's around $400 a ticket ($800 a pair), and for the uninitiated, that's *cheap*. Resale websites list Super Bowl tickets for $2,000 to over $6,000.

The chances of getting a face-value ticket are remote, and you have to jump through hoops. Requests must be "typed" (they have heard of computers, right?) and sent by certified or registered mail to the NFL's New York office between February 1 and June 1 of each year. In October they hold a random drawing. In recent years, about 36,000 fans have applied for tickets, meaning that the chance of winning is around 1 in 70. Some scratcher lottery tickets offer better odds. Why the charade? In the words of NFL vice president for public relations Greg Aiello, the purpose of the lottery is to set a "fair, reasonable price."

This isn't as disingenuous as it sounds. The NFL system fits in perfectly with the fairness research showing that lotteries and lines are judged fairer than sky-high free-market prices. At those market prices, only the wealthy would be able to afford Super Bowl tickets. A Simon-Kucher & Partners report found that sports ticketing "virtually screams for non-linear pricing structures" in which different people pay different prices for the same ticket.

The Princeton economist Alan Krueger scored tickets for Super Bowl XXXV and managed to do a quick survey of the fans. He found something astonishing: that about 40 percent of those surveyed had gotten in for *free*. Only 20 percent had paid more than the tickets' face value.

How is this possible? The NFL says that about 75 percent of Super Bowl tickets are distributed to the league's teams, mostly to the two teams playing. The teams are allowed to dispose of the tickets as they see fit. Most hold their own ticket lotteries, typically restricting them to season ticket holders. The other 25 percent of tickets are distributed by the NFL itself. Most are given to VIPs, the media, and charities. The NFL can afford to be generous. About 60 percent of the league's revenue comes from TV licensing.

Krueger's most remarkable finding was that practically no one was willing to buy *or* sell a Super Bowl ticket at its market price. Karen McClearn, a Baltimore Ravens season ticket holder, told Krueger that she and her husband had come because they won tickets in a lottery, paying a way-below-market price. Krueger asked whether she'd have been willing to sell her tickets for $4,000 each. *No way,* McClearn insisted. When the Ravens took a 17–0 lead over the New York Giants, McClearn amended that: she wouldn't sell for $5,000 each.

In a more formal poll of fans who had paid face value for their tickets (then $325), Krueger asked whether they would have sold their ticket for $3,000. Ninety-three percent said no. The ticket was apparently worth more than that. Given a choice between the $3,000 and the ticket, they'd choose the ticket. Krueger also asked the fans to imagine that they had lost their face-value ticket: Would they have paid $3,000 to replace it? The fans overwhelmingly said no. Put this way, the ticket *wasn't* worth the market price. A Super Bowl ticket is in some strong sense priceless: no single, one-dimensional dollar valuation can account for the fans' responses to Krueger's questions.


The NFL has experience in distributing too-scarce tickets to too-enthusiastic fans. Compare that to the free-for-all accompanying the 2007 Hannah Montana tour. A feeding frenzy of tweener parents snatched and clawed for every possible Hannah Montana ticket through-out the show's 55-stop tour. In every city, tickets, priced at about $25 to $65, sold out in minutes through official channels. A large fraction went to scalpers, amateur or professional. Tenfold markups weren't uncommon. Members of the Miley Cyrus Fan Club filed a lawsuit, claiming they had been told their $29.95 annual memberships would give them access to tickets, but they couldn't get them. An online poster had this take on the lawsuit: "Mommy get me tickets or I'll hold my breath forever!" Radio stations offered tickets as contest prizes. One woman won an essay contest for tickets by claiming her daughter's father had been killed by a roadside bomb in Iraq. (He hadn't.) Given the markups, the scalpers must have collectively made more from the tour than Cyrus and Disney did. But what was a ticket worth? Nowhere near the eBay prices (according to parents who didn't have tickets). Priceless (felt lucky families who did).

Ticket sellers break the rules of fairness at their peril. During Bruce Springsteen's 2009 tour, the Ticketmaster website began redirecting fans to TicketsNow, a resale site that just happened to be a wholly owned subsidiary of Ticketmaster. The "sold out" Springsteen tickets were readily available on TicketsNow—for as much as $1,600. One fan, Diane La Rue, said she signed on to the Ticketmaster site from two computers the instant the tickets went on sale and was immediately directed to the scalper site. Springsteen was furious, forcing a weaselly apology from a Ticketmaster spokesman and a promise never, ever to do it again. The New Jersey attorney general promised an investigation. It was odd, though—fans were more worked up about the high prices (that they had no intention of paying) than about missing the show.

This paradox is not unique to entertainment tickets. Think of the hotel minibar. It's stocked to overflowing with yummy treats *at prices you'd have to be insane to pay*. Were prices one-dimensional, you'd just ignore the minibar. ("It's too expensive and that's that.") The thing is, sometimes you end the day tired and hungry in a strange city, and there's nothing you'd like better than a big chocolate chip cookie. The one in the minibar will set you back $8 plus tax. You are likely to experience conflicting gut reactions. One, you want that cookie, no matter the cost, and, two, there should be a law against charging $8 for one cookie.

A wise friend would say, *Buy the damn cookie already*. Thrift becomes stinginess when it prevents you from having something you want and can easily afford. Even erstwhile spendthrifts find it hard to follow this advice. *It's the principle of the thing . . .*

Richard Thaler explains this with the concept of "transaction utility."

When the consumer believes an item's true value is more than its selling price, the purchase has positive transaction utility. In plain language, it's a bargain, and everybody loves a bargain. When the perceived value is less than the price, it's a rip-off, and the transaction utility is negative. Thaler's point is that buying decisions depend on transaction utility as well as on the traditional trade-off of price versus desire.

Transaction utility has two consequences, both familiar. Sometimes the perception of a sweet deal causes consumers to buy completely useless junk. Infomercials, factory outlets, riot racks, going-out-of-business sales, and duty-free shops thrive on this psychology. The flip side of the coin is the dilemma of minibars and Super Bowl tickets. Sometimes consumers deprive themselves of things they want and can afford because of an inner voice telling them it's a rip-off. Either that, or they complain about prices they're not going to pay anyway. You can say all you want about free markets—that's hollow logic, and this is emotion.

In Thaler's model, the consumer is of two minds. Lately there's been evidence that this is almost literally true. It involves some ingenious brain-scanning studies of the ultimatum game. A responder faced with a low offer experiences the Super Bowl–minibar dilemma. Let the offer be $1 out of $10. On the one hand, that $1 is found money. We've all been trained from birth to grab on to any money pushed our way. On the other hand, one lousy dollar out of ten is a raw deal. For most Westerners, the raw deal trumps the found-money argument, and they'll veto.

In a 2003 experiment by Alan Sanfey and colleagues, plucky volunteers played the game while their heads were immobilized within an MRI scanner. This revealed that fair offers ($5 or $4 out of $10) activated different parts of the brain than grossly unfair offers ($1 or $2). The unfair offers activated the insula cortex, which is otherwise triggered by pain and foul odors, and the dorsolateral prefrontal cortex, a region involved in planning and decision making. This appears to represent an inner conflict between a visceral rejection of a low offer and a desire to keep free money. As one survey article said of this study, "The fact that unfair offers activate [the] insula means that a verbal statement like 'I am so disgusted about being treated this way' is literal, not metaphorical— they really *do* feel disgusted."

# Twenty-nine

# Don't Wrap All the
# Christmas Presents in One Box

In 1978 adman Arthur Schiff took on the unpromising assignment of devising a commercial for a cheap knife made in Fremont, Ohio. Schiff concocted the faux-Asian name "Ginsu" and wrote a two-minute TV spot that set the template for future infomercials. Schiff's leap of imagination was that you don't just sell the product, you sell a bunch of extra stuff for "free." "How much would you pay for a knife like this?" the announcer of the Ginsu commercial asked. "Before you answer, listen: it even comes with a matching fork to make carving a pleasure. Wait, there's much, much more . . ." Soon the announcer was throwing in a "six-in-one kitchen tool," a set of steak knives, and a "unique spiral slicer." "At the end of the offer," said one of the Ginsu partners, Ed Valenti, "you don't know what you're getting, but you know it doesn't cost a lot."

At the original price of $9.95 for the Ginsu—plus all that other stuff for free—the commercial had pared away the uncertainties of buying from a TV ad to a bare nub. Valenti even claims the Ginsu commercial coined the term "toll-free" for its order lines. His company posted $50 million in sales before it was bought by Warren Buffett's Berkshire Hathaway in 1984.

Infomercials are as stylized as a Kabuki drama. There is a reason for that. The infomercials that succeed are those best at pushing consumers' buttons. However different the products, human nature is pretty much the same. Central to the infomercial industry is a principle that Richard Thaler calls "Don't wrap all the Christmas presents in one box." In a 1985 paper in the journal *Marketing Science*, "Mental Accounting and

Consumer Choice," Thaler presented an original view of how consumers decide what's worth buying and at what price.

Thaler applied prospect theory to typical transactions, in which one
side surrenders a price (a loss) to acquire something of value (a gain).
There are diminishing returns to both gains and losses. A $30,000 bonus
is nice, but it's not three times as nice as a $10,000 bonus. There is thus
more pleasure in receiving three separate $10,000 bonuses (all unantici-
pated, and spread out a little in time) than in receiving one lump sum of
$30,000. With three bonuses, you'd get to rejoice three times. The actual
dollar amount of those windfalls isn't so important, or so additive, as you
might think.

Thaler tested this principle with Cornell students. He asked them
who was happier, a Mr. A who won $50 and $25 in two lotteries, or a
Mr. B who won $75. Most felt that Mr. A was happier. He won twice.

From this Thaler deduced that marketers should devote less energy to
promoting how absolutely wonderful their product is, and more to break-
ing it down, feature by feature, or selling several products in one bundle.
Infomercials were already doing this in the 1980s, and they still do. The
one thing you can't buy in an infomercial is *one thing* (of anything).

"Buy one Snuggie with FREE Book Light for $19.95 + $7.95 P&H
and receive a second set free" runs the pitch for Snuggie, the "blanket
with sleeves." What if you want just one Snuggie? Sorry, it doesn't work
that way. One Snuggie is like the sound of one hand clapping (in a
cheap fleece sleeve).

For one seen-on-TV adhesive, the minimum is about three and a half
bottles: "Normally 1 Bottle of Mighty Mendit is only $19.99 and just
$8.95 S&H, but order today and we'll triple your order to 3 Large bottles
of Mighty Mendit. And as a special bonus, you'll receive a travel size bottle of Mighty Mendit, 1 bottle of Mighty Gemit, and a money saving idea
guide for FREE!"

The Magic Bullet—a blender shaped like live ammo—has one of the
most fulsome applications of Thaler's rule. "What You Get . . . High
Torque Power Base . . . Cross Blade and Flat Blade . . . Tall and Short
Bullet Cups . . ." They go on to list 21 parts and attachments, as if each
one is a separate and worthwhile product. For good measure they throw
in "Four Party Mugs with Comfort Lip Rings [to] turn your Magic Bullet
into the Ultimate Party Machine . . . The Magic Bullet '10 Second

Recipe' Book" and—"Bonus Items!"—the "Magic Bullet Blender and Lid . . . Magic Bullet Juicer . . ." Then, just when you think it's possible that they're selling a singleton: "Get two complete 21 piece MAGIC BULLET systems for the price of 1! . . . 30 DAY SUPPLY FAT BURN-ING BOOST FREE WITH YOUR ORDER!"

Clearly, it's not about the value so much as it is about the staccato rhythm of the pitch. Every feature, freebie, or three-for-one offer is another hedonic rush. Willingness to pay surges with every bullet point until the price—whatever the price—seems just about right.

# Thirty

# Who's Afraid of the Phone Bill?

Prices are more annoying than ever. When the Apple iPhone came out in 2007, customers were astonished at the size of their bills—the *physical* size of their bills. Pittsburgh blogger Justine Ezarik's August bill came in a box. It was three hundred pages, and she made a viral YouTube video about it. Ezarik was being billed for data usage every single time her iPhone connected to the Internet. The data usage was free. The bill had thousands of items saying data usage $0.00.

In the past generation, most of us have come to accept that we will never fully understand our phone bills, cable bills, Internet bills (or bundles of all three); airline fares, car rental rates, hotel rates; premiums for health insurance, car insurance, life insurance; dues for health clubs and country clubs; credit card bills and adjustable mortgages. Prices have been replaced with algorithms. If you can get a simple price at all, it'll cost you.

Simon-Kucher & Partners deserves at least some of the credit, or blame, for the complexity of phone bills. They have advised T-Mobile, Vodafone, Deutsche Telekom, Swisscom, and others on pricing. The complexity of today's phone bills is part of an elaborate philosophy grounded in the precepts of prospect theory. In the usual business school thinking, a price is just a number. Sales go up as prices go down, and there is a certain price X at which profits are at a maximum. Solve for X . . . SKP's consultants are trained to think in terms of price structures. Instead of one price, there's a formula telling what each act of consumption costs.

The customer usually gets to choose the formula ("billing plan"). Taken at face value, price structures are generous. "If you're paying too much for phone minutes, here's a plan with unlimited minutes." More options means freedom of choice, and common sense tells us that's a good thing. Actually, the consumer is both hammer and anvil. Given that preferences are constructed from the choices presented, extra options can be manipulative. Offering an additional billing plan may cause the consumer to be willing to pay a higher price—or buy more— or both—than he would without the option.

"Optimizing" pricing generally means making it more complicated. Hermann Simon tells of a successful promotion used by Deutsche Bahn, the German railroad. They introduced the BahnCard, a discount card costing 400 euros. This BahnCard entitles customers to a 50 percent reduction on all rail tickets in the course of a year. Otherwise, it's worthless. You can't redeem the BahnCard itself for travel.

Is the card worth 400 euros? It all depends. The only thing that's certain is that frequent travelers can save a lot of money. "With more than 3 million customers every year, the BahnCard has been a huge success," Simon wrote. "But only a few customers know where the break-even point compared to the normal fare is."

Not knowing the break-even point is becoming the postmodern condition. An SKP publication says that the key to pricing lies in managing the consumer's limited attention:

> Companies need to answer several questions: What pricing elements matter most in the perception of the customer? Where will the customer's eye be drawn when he or she examines the offer? Would they pay more attention to one-off charges, a monthly fee, or a price per download, a hardware subsidy, or some other element?
>
> Those elements which are in the customer's focus will require attractive prices to draw them in, while those outside the customer's main focus can be maintained at higher, less attractive levels. The colorful mix of pricing elements in mobile telephony—which range from one-off installation charges to monthly fees to per minute charges (peak, off-peak, weekend) to billing intervals (full minutes, 10 seconds), etc.—shows how many degrees of freedom such a complex pricing challenge can present.

With complex billing plans, it is difficult to comparison shop (every plan is different) and nearly impossible to predict what a plan will cost. Choosing a phone plan becomes a judgment under uncertainty, mediated by loss aversion and heuristics.

One of the most powerful tools of psychological pricing is the flat-rate bias. Consumers like flat rates, even when they cost more. A 2009 study by the Utility Consumers' Action Network claimed that cell phone users in the San Diego area paid an average of $3.02 a minute for calls. That's the price when you divide the aggregate amount paid by the number of minutes used. The per-minute tab is surprisingly large because many customers who don't talk much nevertheless choose flat-rate plans.

Richard Thaler has explained this as a consequence of prospect theory. Just as infomercials slice and dice the product into many little bonuses, an opposite rule says that you should sweep losses into one big pile. A $90 parking ticket is not three times as bad as a $30 ticket. It is better to get one $90 ticket than three $30 tickets on three separate days.

Since the cost of any product is a loss, costs are less painful as flat rates. You pay once (per billing cycle) and don't have to worry about it. "Free" food is an unaccountably big draw for cruise ships. Vacationers know they paid for the food with their fare, and that it wasn't exactly cheap . . . but it *feels* free. You don't have to count the cost of every rumaki. The flat-rate bias helps define the American middle class. Americans love owning their homes and cars and hate renting or taking public transportation. It isn't that owning is cheaper than renting, necessarily. It's just that with renting the cost is more apparent. ("All you'll end up with is a pile of rent receipts!") Many urbanites would find it cheaper to sell their SUVs and take taxis everywhere. But the thought of paying $15 in cab fare to go to the supermarket is unconscionable. No one likes to hear the taxi meter running.

Many believe that the success of the video rental service Netflix is largely the result of pricing. It offers DVD rentals by mail, with an assortment of plans currently ranging from $4.99 to $47.99 a month. All but the cheapest plan have unlimited rentals. Had Netflix charged per rental, it would have been competing on price with the video stores. A reasonable customer contemplating a Netflix subscription must estimate how many movies he or she will watch a month. Academic studies have shown that consumers have a tendency to grossly overestimate their usage of various services. At that, the Netflix customer normally expects her household's viewing habits to change. With "free" DVDs and easy return in a postage-paid mailer, everyone watches more movies, or thinks they will. The movie lover is likely to conclude that Netflix is reasonably priced almost regardless of what that price is. With willingness to pay so vaguely defined, Netflix has scope to price aggressively, as the video store does not.

Another of Simon's favorite examples is a movie chain that gave customers free loyalty cards. The cards recorded the number of visits. The chain charged one price for the first visit each month, a lower price for the second visit within the month, a still lower price for the third visit. These prices subtly encouraged customers to "save" money—by attending more movies. But the customers didn't save money. The number of tickets sold increased 22 percent under this scheme, *and* the average ticket price paid went up 11 percent. The chain's profits were up 37 percent. "Such improvements are not possible through one-dimensional price increases or decreases," Simon wrote, "but only through new price structures that have been carefully researched."

To hear today's price consultants tell it, the goal is to devise price structures that extract the maximum willingness to pay from each consumer. Capitalism takes on a weirdly Marxist twist: every customer pays according to his ability. This is a discomfiting idea, like the Firesign Theatre bit advertising the bicycle seat that fits you like a glove. In the digital age, this is where we're heading—to price plans morphing to the soft contours of consumer desire.

# Thirty-one

# Breakage and Slippage

Rebates make no sense. Instead of buying something and getting a rebate, why not just pay a lower price in the first place? Practical-minded consumers have been asking this question for years. Businesses and most everyone else have paid little attention. Rebates are more pervasive than ever. About a third of all computer gear comes with rebates, and over 20 percent of LCD TVs and digital cameras do. Fly your favorite airline and get frequent flyer miles for free trips and first-class upgrades. Use a credit card and get cash back, or more of those airline miles. Cars have "dealer incentives," and some real estate developments offer free cars to buyers. You do not need the savvy of a coupon queen to cop a rebate trifecta at any checkout line: use a manufacturer's coupon, swipe your loyalty card for another discount, and then pay with a credit card that gives back a few percent vigorish.

Rebates have been big business at least since the early twentieth century. In 1896 Thomas Sperry and Shelly Hutchinson founded a company issuing S&H Green Stamps. Sperry and Hutchinson sold the stamps to markets and gas stations, who gave them away free with purchases. Consumers were supposed to save the stamps, paste them in free "books," and redeem the books for merchandise. This created what was euphemistically called loyalty. Customers didn't want to switch markets because they needed more stamps to get a toaster or a bathroom scale. Green Stamps peaked in popularity in the 1960s, when Sperry and Hutchinson was printing three times as many stamps as the U.S. Postal Service, worth some $825 million. The company operated a chain of "redemption centers," mini–department stores that didn't accept money—only Green Stamps. The business took a downturn in the 1970s and was supplanted by the rise of modern rebate programs like frequent flyer miles and supermarket loyalty cards in the 1980s. Sperry and Hutchinson still runs a "GreenPoints" program for Internet purchases, a rather insignificant part of today's rebate picture.

One thing Sperry and Hutchinson bequeathed to today's rebaters is the "Green Stamps Syndrome." It was a lot of *work* to paste stamps into books. Americans had drawers full of stamps and never got around to redeeming them. The unredeemed stamps were pure profit for Sperry and Hutchinson.

Two independent companies, Young America and Parago, handle much of the nation's rebate paying. In consumer circles, their reputation is little better than the average dogfight promoter's. "Breakage" is the industry term for rebates that never get sent in, and "slippage" refers to checks that are sent out but somehow never get cashed. Both are big drivers of profit. "The game is obviously that anything less than 100 percent redemption is free money," the consultant Paula Rosenblum told *BusinessWeek*.

In theory, rebate processors do not profit from unredeemed rebates. Their clients do. But one processor, TCA Fulfillment Services, bragged about the low, low percentage of rebate checks it cut and that got cashed—as little as 10 percent for a $10 rebate. "If you are using another fulfillment company, add 20% to these redemption rates," said a TCA promotional brochure. (TCA sold its customer list to Parago, which has disavowed this claim.)

By industry convention, rebates require a store receipt with the price circled; a UPC code cut from the box (making the item unreturnable); and a completely and correctly filled out form. Minor omissions mandate "further research," requests for more paperwork, and transferring the case to a "special team." This is defended as necessary to prevent fraud, but it also has the effect of causing many a consumer to give up. One of the industry's tricks for increasing slippage is to mail the check in an unmarked envelope that looks and feels like junk mail. Guess where the checks end up?

Comical as this may sound, rebates are a big business. By one recent estimate, about 400 million rebates are offered per year, with a face value of $6 billion. Anything that shaves a few percent off that is worth nine figures. About 40 percent of all rebates are believed to go uncollected.

This says something about why rebate programs appeal to the companies that offer them. The tougher question is, Why are rebates so entrancing to consumers? Both experiments and practice confirm that rebates cast a magic spell. People are more inclined to buy a $200 printer with a $25 rebate than a similar printer for $175.

Richard Thaler explains rebates as psychophysical arbitrage. The $200 does not seem that much higher than $175, first of all. But there's a big psychological difference between getting a rebate and not getting a rebate. Most prefer the rebate. Thaler calls this the "silver lining" principle. He demonstrated it with this survey question:

> Mr. A's car was damaged in a parking lot. He had to spend $200 to repair the damage. The same day the car was damaged, he won $25 in the office football pool.
> Mr. B's car was damaged in a parking lot. He had to spend $175 to repair the damage. Who was more upset?

A large majority of Cornell students felt that Mr. B was more upset. Though no worse off financially than Mr. A, he missed out on the $25 windfall.

The commonsense dismissal of rebates is right about one thing: there's no free lunch. Every product that offers a rebate has to be more expensive because of it. This need not dampen sales. Since consumer price sense is vague at best, shoppers take a cue from the posted price. A $200 printer is assumed to be better than a $175 printer, no matter that the only extra "feature" is the rebate.

# Thirty-two

# Paying for Air

For about $2,400, any gas station operator can buy a machine that pulls two of the most audacious grifts ever conceived. One side of the machine sells *air*. The other side sells *vacuum*.

The air-vacuum machines are "long life and low maintenance" to "send more dollars to your bottom line," according to one manufacturer's website. The price of air and vacuum apparently has little to do with the amortized cost of the machine and everything to do with psychology. We pay for air because we've come to accept that you have to pay for it. The price is whatever is. That kind of uncontemplative consumption is a marketer's nirvana.

In many ways, we all end up paying for air. Take batteries. What you're buying is battery life: how many pictures you can take in a camera, how often you have to replace the smoke detector battery, how long a flashlight lasts in an outage. But battery life isn't disclosed anywhere on the label. Instead, batteries are labeled by voltage, a measure of limited relevance to the consumer. It's as if you had to buy gasoline from pumps that told you the octane rating and not how many gallons you were getting.

This would be okay if battery life was the same across brands. It's not. A 2008 *Consumer Reports* piece tested the life of 13 brands of single-use AA batteries in digital cameras. The best battery was good for 637 photos, the worst for 95. Some batteries pack a lot more juice than others, and consumers are left to guess which ones they are.

The chart on page 180 shows how 12 tested batteries compare. (I've excluded the single lithium battery that *Consumer Reports* tested. It was

Batteries: You Don't Get What You Pay For

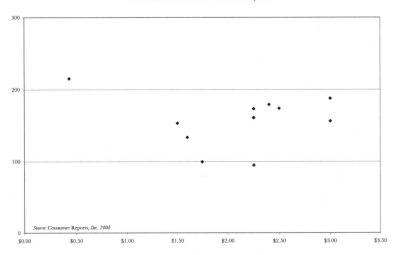

Source: Consumer Reports, Dec. 2008

much more expensive and offered about four times the life of regular batteries). The price for two batteries is on the bottom, and the number of photos a pair of batteries is good for is on the left axis. If you got exactly what you paid for, the dots would form a diagonal line from lower left to upper right. Instead, the dots are a formless cloud better fitting a horizontal line. All the tested batteries were good for somewhere around 150 photos, and price didn't matter. The cheapest battery (Kirkland Signature, a house brand sold by Costco) performed the longest.

Okay: There's a rack of batteries in front of you, and you haven't memorized *Consumer Reports*. How do you choose one? Well, I tell myself I can't judge battery life but I can judge price. I tend to choose the cheapest battery. But I'm also a sucker for discounts. I'll see a Duracell or Energizer marked down *almost* to my usual bargain-basement level. I'll buy it, just to feel like a regular American buying a real brand advertised on TV. I justify this by telling myself that there must be a grain of truth to those Energizer bunny commercials, so I'm not really paying any more than with my no-name brands. That's exactly how the Energizer and Duracell people want me to think.

Batteries aren't the only product where it's hard to judge what you're getting. Liquid laundry detergent is, by definition, "watered down" to greater or lesser degree. You know how much *water* you're buying, not how much soap. Lately, manufacturers have started claiming that their liquid detergent is twice as concentrated. They don't say relative to what.

The same goes for perfume, the liquor in bar drinks, and anything that comes in a spray can. The situation is almost as bad with infrequently purchased durables. It's hard for a consumer to know how well a refrigerator or water heater or fax machine will perform or how long it will last. We buy only a few in our lifetime, and each time, brands and models and features have changed. A conscientious consumer willing to pay a premium for green appliances is even more at a loss. A 2008 Consumer Electronics Association survey found that 89 percent of consumers planned to consider energy efficiency in choosing their next TV—while more than half confessed to being clueless about what energy efficiency labels mean.

Possibly the greatest ongoing con job of American capitalism is text messages. The so-called market price of a text message has nothing to do with bandwidth or any technological reality. It is determined by how much consumers (or their parents) can be persuaded to pay.

A text message is a very, *very* small package of bandwidth. It is limited to 160 characters, each requiring a byte. Compare that to a multimedia message (MMS) or e-mail, which can include pictures running into the megabytes. A Simon-Kucher & Partners survey found that consumers believed an MMS was worth 3.5 times as much as a text message. Measured by data, a typical MMS is about a million times bigger.

For cell phone users paying à la carte, the retail price of transmitted data is around $1 a megabyte. At that rate, the price of a 10-character message ought to be about about 1/1,000 of a cent. Rounded to the nearest cent: free.

Even the 1/1,000-cent figure arguably overstates the true cost of a text. Unlike e-mail, Internet, and voice data, text messages are piggybacked onto the cellular network. They occupy otherwise unused space in a control channel used for network maintenance. So as far as text messages are concerned, the cell phone companies are like the mean clique in high school who sold elevator passes (and there's no elevator).

Given that consumers have little sense of what texts ought to cost, they take their cues from the phone companies. The text message business plan has been a huge success. From 2005 to 2008, the price American carriers charged for text messages doubled, from about 10 cents to 20 cents. In that time, the volume of text messages grew about tenfold.

# Thirty-three

# Cheap and Cheaper

The word "cheap" appears forty-five times on the CheapTickets home page (according to my browser's text search, and not including three more times in the window title and URL display). I can personally testify to the hypnotic power of the CheapTickets trademark. Did I ever actually believe they have cheaper fares? Naw . . . uh, *maybe*?

Airlines were one of the first to pioneer differential pricing—charging different prices to different customers based on willingness to pay. Robert Crandall, formerly the CEO of American Airlines, once said, "If I have 2,000 customers on a given route and 400 different prices, I'm obviously short 1,600 prices." The Internet was supposed to make things easier on the traveler by enabling quick, easy price comparisons. It hasn't worked out that way, and a good example is CheapTickets. Its site doesn't show fares for bargain airlines like Southwest or JetBlue. Since these airlines have a reputation for the lowest fares, the promise of "CheapTickets" rings hollow. You're getting the cheapest fares—of the more expensive airlines?

It's little wonder that many go directly to the Southwest or JetBlue sites. I just now checked fares for a trip from Los Angeles to Phoenix, one of Southwest's busiest routes. The lowest round-trip on the Southwest site is $98 plus taxes and fees. On CheapTickets, United and US Airways offer the same trip for the same price, $98.

The bargain carriers' fares truly are cheaper . . . except when they're not. Sometimes they're more expensive than the regular airlines' lowest fares. Those more expensive fares are important to the bargain carriers' bottom lines. Southwest and JetBlue are able to charge some higher fares, ironically, because they've forged a reputation for the lowest fares. Cheap is relative, and it depends on context. This is one important reason why Southwest and JetBlue aren't on the major travel sites. They'd rather their customers didn't compare.

Actually, *all* airlines feel that way. It's a funny business: most discretionary travelers choose a flight based on price, period. (Imagine what the hotel business would be like if travelers refused to pay a penny more than Motel 6's rates.) Airfare price sensitivity has led to the practice of *unbundling*: charging for checked luggage, pillows, meals, coffee, phone reservations, paper tickets, seat selection, and all the other amenities that used to be free. "Three or four years ago, airlines got fed up with their tickets being priced like bushels of wheat on a commodities exchange, so they set out a strategy for how to make prices less transparent," said Rick Seaney, CEO of FareCompare.com. It was European carriers that pioneered unbundling. In the United States, it took hold with a vengeance in May 2008, when American Airlines started charging $15 for the first checked bag. Indignant travelers promptly vowed never to fly American again. That resolve didn't last. It crumbled as other airlines added their own baggage fees and started charging for previously free amenities.

Consumers equate unbundling with nickel-and-diming and imagine that the fees are pure profit. That's not really true, at least not on competitive routes. The real purpose of unbundling is the same as for bundling—to make it harder to compare prices. The tacked-on fees vary greatly. One airline will be cheapest for checked luggage, another has a good deal on pillows and soft drinks, and still another will let you make a phone reservation for free. There are now too many amenity charges to compare the true price of a trip without a spreadsheet (some websites help with this). But most travelers do as the airlines intend: they shrug off the fees and choose a flight based on something, *anything*, other than the lowest price.

# Thirty-four

# Mysteries of the 99-Cent Store

"I'll tell you what brilliance in advertising is," Roger Sterling says on an episode of *Mad Men*. "99 cents." Surveys assert that anywhere from 30 percent to 65 percent of all retail prices end in the digit 9. This holds through many orders of magnitude. Sometimes the 9 is thousands of dollars, sometimes it's pennies, and in the case of gasoline, it's tenths of a cent. Apple's Steve Jobs was hailed as a genius for insisting on 99-cent pricing for the first iPod downloads ($1.99 for videos). In 2009 Apple relented only to the extent of adding prices of $0.69 and $1.29 for music.

The apotheosis of this phenomenon is the 99-cent store. In the 1960s, David Gold ran a liquor store in Los Angeles and wanted to get rid of some slow-moving cheap wine. He tried putting up a banner saying "Wine of the World. Your Choice: 99 Cents." It worked; customers bought almost anything at the 99-cent price.

The funny thing was, the wine had previously been marked at prices ranging from 79 cents to $1.49. "The 79 cents sold better at 99, the 89 cents sold better at 99, and of course the $1.49 sold better at 99," Gold said. The 99-cent effect was so amazing that Gold joked he ought to open a whole store selling merchandise at that price. The joke became reality in 1982, when Gold opened the first 99 Cents Only store. The chain now has about 277 stores and has inspired similarly named outlets ("knockoffs" is not quite the right word) from coast to coast. To anyone who failed to read the sign, the typical 99-cent store would be an enigma. It stocks ramen noodles, tube socks, playing cards, detergent, Halloween costumes, feminine hygiene products, tinsel, and marshmallows. Nothing relates to anything else, and everything is vaguely suspect.

A 2008 *New York Times* piece surveyed the flourishing state of 99-cent stores in New York (none of them affiliated with Gold's 99 Cents Only chain). Frederick Douglass Boulevard, the busy commercial strip in Harlem, has the New Futa 99¢ Plus Store and the rival Bab's 98-cent Plus Discount Store. The power of 9 spills over liberally. Signs promise merchandise for 99 cents, 98 cents, or a whole flurry of 9-ish prices. Brooklyn's Ditmas Avenue boasts "59¢ 79¢ 99¢ and Up" and "69¢ 89¢ 99¢ & Up" stores.

Among the imitators, rules are hard to discern and ever-shifting. "The 99-cent promise is becoming more and more of an empty one," concluded the *Times*. "The stores have fallen back on a bait-and-switch trick, luring customers with the sign, only to reveal, amid more expensive items, a grim 99-cent row of little-girl barrettes, shiny stickers and single rolls of toilet paper perhaps best suited for sanding furniture."

It's no secret that inflation is constantly assailing the business model. What was 99 cents in 1982 dollars would cost over $2 now. For the 99 Cents Only chain, the future arrived in 2008. After years of work-arounds like half-dozen cartons of eggs and ever-shrinking containers of milk, it bit the bullet and raised its top price to $99.99. For president Jeff Gold, it was almost like a death in the family. "The number 99 is a magic number—deviating from that is something we absolutely are not taking lightly," he said. "I find significant discomfort emotionally about considering making the change."


A price that is a little below a round number is known as a "charm price." That usually means a price ending in 9 or 99, but 98 and 95 are considered charm prices too. No one knows when, where, or why the practice began. One theory mentions British coinage. Up until the Civil War, American pennies were scarce, and British shillings and sixpence circulated in the United States. New York stores often quoted prices in both British and American money. The conversion from shillings usually produced an odd number of pennies. According to legend, odd-penny prices became associated with British imports, which were considered superior to American goods. Shrewd shopkeepers began putting odd-number prices on domestic goods to lend a touch of anglophile class.

A marginally more believable story credits the cash register. James Ritty, a Dayton saloon keeper, invented the first cash register in 1879. Ritty knew it was almost impossible to check a saloon's liquid inventory against cash receipts and suspected the worst of his bartenders. He therefore created a machine requiring employees to punch in a price in order to open the change drawer. When the employees did so, a bell rang to alert the owner. An owner could expect to hear steady ringing during the lunch hour and could investigate a suspicious lull. Ritty's machine also kept a record of the amounts entered, and it was relatively simple to check the record against the cash. Macy's was one of the first big stores to adopt cash registers. Since Macy's prices were often even dollar amounts, they began using odd-numbered prices to compel employees to punch in prices and make change. Indeed, as shown on page 187, Macy's ads from the 1880s show charm prices.

Neither the British money nor the cash register tale truly accounts for the magic number 9. A shilling was valued at 1/8 of a dollar, resulting in prices like 12 1/2 cents, 25 cents, 37 1/2 cents . . . none of them ending in 9. As far as the cash register explanation goes, any price that's not an even dollar amount would require making change.

However they started, charm prices are widely used, not just in America, not just by marketing pros, and not just for cheap things. Prices ending in 9 are omnipresent on eBay, and FSBO listings price three-bedroom colonials at $599,000. Other than real estate, the most expensive charm price I came across was for a diamond-encrusted watch in Louis Vuitton's Rodeo Drive store: $149,000. Do they really think it sells better at that price rather than $150,000? (It was the most expensive and prominent bauble in a wall display. Oddly, the cheaper LV watches—one a mere $7,450—were not charm priced.)

In addition to prices ending in 9 (plus zeros), there are prices with a nonzero digit to the right of the 9: $197,000 or $3.95. Prices like the latter are a pet peeve for restaurant consultant Brandon O'Dell. "They could be pricing at $3.99," he said. "There's absolutely no difference in value for the consumer, but it's four cents." In the restaurant business, four cents an order adds up.

Charm prices are now so identified with fast food that they are the stuff of self-satirizing marketing campaigns. In 2008 Taco Bell president Greg Creed wrote an open letter to rapper 50 Cent, asking him to

A Macy's ad from the November 2, 1890, *New York Times*. About 60 percent of the prices end in 9.

change his name to "79 Cent," "89 Cent," or "99 Cent" to promote the chain's low prices. The rapper responded with a lawsuit for the uncharming figure of $4 million—resulting in ample free publicity for both parties.


Charm prices inaugurated the study of psychological pricing. In 1936 Columbia University's Eli Ginzberg published a one-page note on what he called "customary prices." "For many years, retail prices in this country have been quoted at one or two cents below the decimal unit—$.49, $.79, $.98, $1.49, $1.98, tell the tale." Ginzberg reported on the informal experiment of an unnamed large retailer. The firm was curious enough to print multiple versions of its catalog, some with the already customary 9-ending prices and others with the corresponding round amounts.

To Ginzberg the results were "as interesting as they were perplexing." Some products sold better with charm prices, and some sold worse. His brief article did not supply statistical detail. "The vice-president in charge of merchandising ventured the guess that the losses were balanced by the gains. He realized full well that a repetition of the experiment might . . . permit more definite conclusions." With money on the line, "the experimental zeal, even of a daring business man, was . . . held in check."

For nearly half a century, much informed opinion held that charm prices were a harmless superstition. This didn't keep retailers from using them. By the 1980s, the Kahneman-Tversky revolution had revived interest in psychological pricing. In eight studies published from 1987 to 2004, charm prices were reported to boost sales by an average of 24 percent relative to nearby prices.

Don't take that quotable figure too seriously. The increase in sales varied from insignificant to over 80 percent. Take an experiment done by Eric Anderson of the University of Chicago and Duncan Simester of MIT. They found a mail order house willing to print up different versions of its catalog. The company sold moderately priced women's clothing and normally used whole-dollar prices ending in 9. One of the items tested went for $39. In experimental versions of the catalog, the company offered the same item for $34 and $44. Each catalog was sent to an identically sized random sample of the company's mailing list.

| Price | Number Sold |
|-------|-------------|
| $34   | 16          |
| $39   | 21          |
| $44   | 17          |

There were more sales at the charm price of $39 than at either of the other prices. The key finding was that more people bought at $39 than at $34. At the charm price there was greater volume *and* greater profit per sale.

This fits in with what's known of the balance sheets. In 2002 *Forbes* magazine concluded that the 99 Cents Only chain's gross margin was an astonishing 40 percent, twice that of Wal-Mart. On average the chain was paying only about 60 cents for the items it sold for 99 cents. A typical coup: David Gold bought a Fruit of the Loom closeout lot of 700,000 packs of *Star Wars: The Phantom Menace* underwear and sold them when the next *Star Wars* movie came out. Discerning shoppers might have wondered why they were selling *Phantom Menace* and not *Attack of the Clones* underwear—but the 99-cent price answered any questions.

Why do charm prices work? You may feel the answer is obvious. Shoppers must round numbers down, or at any rate focus their attention on the first significant digit. A price like $29.99 registers mentally as twenty-something dollars, while a price of $30.00 or more gets pegged as thirty-something. Twenty-something seems so much less than thirty-something.

This explanation has been widely debated in the marketing and psychological literature. Charm prices actually raise some intriguing questions about how the mind works. Numbers are arbitrary mileposts on the endless highway of magnitude. Does the brain have a deep understanding of quantities signified, or does it manipulate numbers in only superficial ways?

There is a body of psychological research implying that people, even young children, have a decent grasp of magnitudes. They understand that 29 is only a little less than 30. Anchoring experiments have also shown that magnitudes (not just numbers per se) influence estimates and decisions.

Mental rounding alone can't explain results like Anderson and

Simester's. If shoppers paid attention to the first digit only, you'd expect that both $34 and $39 would be understood as thirty-something dollars. Sales at both price points would be about the same. Instead, buyers were more likely to buy at the higher price of $39. Nine truly is a magic number.

An alternate theory says that charm prices convey the message that the price has been discounted. Once upon a time, a small-town gas station charged 20 cents a gallon. A new station went up across the street, undercutting the price by a penny: 19 cents. The first station retaliated by charging 18 cents . . . The cultural memory of long-ago price wars has perhaps led us to associate numbers like 19 with competitive pricing and round numbers like 20 with monopolies and poorer values. Unquestionably, something like this is going on even now. Harlem's 98-cent Plus store was named to undercut the 99¢ Plus store, and it briefly had competition from a 97 Cent store.

Charm prices are informative to any astute shopper. A good way of judging the ambitions of a restaurant or hotel, and sometimes the quality, is whether the prices are in whole dollars or end in .99 or .95. Nordstrom's department store makes a point of not using charm prices. They mean to say, "We're not Wal-Mart, come here for quality and expect to pay for it." This may be why charm prices sometimes don't work. Price consultant Frank Luby tells of an automaker that thought it wanted to sell a car for $19,999. His research showed the car would sell just as well at $20,000+. Possibly the car's buyers didn't want to feel they were buying a "cheap" car. Some retailers, such as Eddie Bauer and J. Crew, have adopted 99-cent endings only for reduced items. Costco uses 97-cent endings to signal that an item is discontinued or slow-moving. To someone who knows this code, the charm prices speak loudly. Of course, customers don't have to be aware of any explicit rule to respond unconsciously.

In Anderson and Simester's experiment, there was no significant difference in sales when a garment was priced at $44 or $34. This is further proof that buyers don't have a strong innate sense of value. It was the $39 price that boosted sales. One hypothesis is that charm prices seem cheap in mental comparison to the round price.

The catalog company was in the habit of putting items on sale and marking them with old and new prices: "Reg $X SALE $Y." The researchers had them print up some catalogs with the sale prices but without any indication that they were discounted. As you'd expect, they saw higher sales when the sale prices were highlighted as such. Buyers didn't know that $Y was a bargain price unless the catalog told them it was.

Sale price markers were more powerful motivators than charm prices. Consumers were more likely to buy an item marked with the sale price on the left than with the charm price on the right.

**Reg $48**

$^{$}$**40**

**SALE**

$^{$}$**39**

Anderson and Simester tried both gimmicks together, using sale-marked charm prices like "Reg $48 SALE $39." This had the strongest effect of all. The effect was not additive, though. It boosted sales only a little more than the sale price alone did. This could mean that sale prices and charm prices exploit the same mental principle. Standing on its own, a charm price implies a discount that's not there. It's like a mime faking a glass wall. The price's audience reacts to the virtual discount in much the way they react to an actual one.

Supporting this interpretation is the fact that the charm prices had a bigger effect on new items that the catalog had not carried before. Customers would have had the weakest notion of value with new items and depended more on price cues.

There's nothing crazy about liking bargains (when the bargain *is* a bargain). A price of $19.99 means what—marked down from $20.00? Gee, thanks. Even that old standby, 99 cents, is only a 1 percent discount from a round dollar (see page 192). By reasonable standards, that should be too trivial to affect behavior much. Yet this fits in with studies of con-

Reg $1.00

99¢  =  99¢

SALE

sumer choice and trade-off contrast. When there are many hard-to-evaluate options, attention wanders. It is drawn to easy comparisons, to options that are clearly superior to another, even if the difference is slight. The imagined round-number price becomes a foil for the 99-cent price, bathing it in an unaccountably alluring glow.

## Thirty-five

# Meaningless Zeros

The ultimate discount is to FREE!—as in FREE GIFT!! Beloved by marketers, the "price" of zero triggers some unique psychology. In one experiment by Dan Ariely, Nina Mazar, and Kristina Shampanier, they set up a chocolate stand offering Hershey Kisses and Lindt truffles. You don't have to be much of a chocophile to know that Hershey Kisses are about the lowest form of chocolate, and Lindt truffles are better. They offered the Hershey Kisses for 1 cent apiece, and the Lindt truffles for 15 cents. A prominent sign said ONE CHOCOLATE PER CUSTOMER.

Of the people who bought, 73 percent chose the Lindt truffle. With apologies to Hershey's, no mystery there. Then they reduced both candies' prices by 1 cent. They offered the Lindt truffles for 14 cents, and the Hershey Kisses for free (still with the one-to-a-customer rule). This reversed the preferences. Sixty-nine percent of customers took the free Hershey Kiss, and only 31 percent bought the Lindt truffle.

Ariely and company were selling the Lindt truffles for about half the wholesale price. Most customers were passing up a 14-cent discount in order to get a free candy they didn't especially like that might be worth about a cent.

Ariely believes this is largely due to the certainty effect. Any purchase carries a risk of buyer's regret. The chocolate I bought may not taste as good as I'd thought . . . I might find out I could have bought it cheaper somewhere else . . . what about my diet? . . . etc., etc. Free things are different. You can't regret spending your money on something free because you didn't spend any money. By overvaluing certainty, we overvalue anything that's free.

•    •    •

The magnitude scales of psychophysics are said to have meaningful zeros. On a scale of loudness, the "sound" of silence should be a zero. In practice, things aren't quite that simple. It can be a challenge to distinguish a barely audible sound from true silence. People tend to say they experienced something—or didn't—based on power of suggestion, and they feign consistency. (This is why Paul Hoffman had to go to all the trouble of building a fake optometrist's office in Oregon.)

Much the same applies to the price scale. Consumers do not recognize true worthlessness when they see it. Among items of low value, there is a largish zone of confusion in which it's unclear what is worth paying for and what is not. This was demonstrated in an already famous 2006 paper by Dan Ariely, George Loewenstein, and Drazen Prelec, "Tom Sawyer and the Construction of Value."

The title alludes to the classic preference reversal of American literature. Mark Twain's trickster-hero Tom Sawyer is given the irksome chore of whitewashing a fence. Tom would much prefer to let someone else do it. To achieve that, he pretends to enjoy the job so much that his friends want some of the fun. They beg Tom to let them help, to paint a few strokes at least. Tom refuses, then finally gives in—on the condition that his friends pay him for the privilege of painting the fence. Mark Twain's mordant point is that there are no absolutes in life, and those who say otherwise are as big a fraud as Tom was.

In one of the 2006 "Tom Sawyer" experiments, the researchers tried to interest marketing students in a poetry reading (Walt Whitman's *Leaves of Grass*) that Ariely was supposedly going to give on the Berkeley campus. One group was asked whether they would be willing to pay $2 to hear Dan Ariely recite poetry. The answer was a pretty firm no. A scant 3 percent said they'd be willing to pay.

After the answers were all collected, the students were informed that in fact Ariely's reading was going to be free. They were asked to indicate whether they wanted to be notified by e-mail of the time and location. Now 35 percent said yes, they wanted to be informed.

That's as you'd expect. More were open to attending an event, provided it was free. A second group of students was asked a different question: Would you be willing to listen to Ariely recite poetry if we paid you

$2? This time 59 percent said yes. Then these students, like the first group, were told that the reading was going to be free (forget about that $2 payment). When asked whether they wanted to be informed of the specifics, only 8 percent indicated they were still interested.

Up to 35 percent of the first group thought the free recital was worth attending—a positive experience with greater-than-zero value. Only 8 percent of the second group thought that way. The only difference was that the first group had been led to think the recital was worth money, and the second had been told it was a chore meriting pay.

In another variation, the researchers asked two groups of MIT students whether they would pay/demand to be paid $10 to hear Ariely recite poetry for 10 minutes. They then asked the same students to name prices for 6, 3, and 1 minutes of poetry reading. As with the annoying-sound experiments, the average prices were scaled to the duration. But this time, one group was assigning *positive* prices (money they were willing to pay for the pleasure of hearing Ariely's vocal interpretations) and the other was naming *negative* prices (wages, to put up with the recital). On the whole, the MIT students had no conviction as to whether they should be paying or be paid.

The Tom Sawyer experiments refute the common sense that every experience can be sorted as a positive or a negative. Yes, there are dreadful experiences and glorious ones. Most experiences are distinctly mixed. Is a trip to Paris a good thing? Well, sure, everyone immediately says yes. That's because everyone *else* says yes, and not incidentally because *it costs a lot of money*. Suppose trips to Paris were free, and would always be free from now on. Would you go there this weekend? How about the weekend after that?

Tom Sawyer's innocent con game has become the first big business model of the twenty-first century. It's called Web 2.0. Google, YouTube, Facebook, and Twitter have become multimillion-dollar businesses with what is respectfully called user-generated content. All are founded on the premise that users will do worthwhile "work" (journalism, filmmaking, political commentary) for free. Someone is making a lot of money—someone, but not the folks whitewashing the Internet's fences.

# Thirty-six

# Reality Constraint

One of Margaret Neale's most famous experiments infuriated real estate agents and even her own mother. Neale wanted to see whether anchoring would work in the real estate market.

She arrived at the University of Arizona in 1982, with an interest in the psychology of bargaining. "Negotiation at the time was relatively moribund," she said. Psychologists and economists "weren't speaking to each other." Neale immersed herself in the work of Kahneman and Tversky, Hillel Einhorn, and Robin Hogarth. She realized that the psychology of decision making could be a powerful tool for negotiators. "The argument that we were making at the time was there's not a lot to be changed in negotiation," she explained. "You're faced with the situation as it exists. We know people behave differently when there's a future" (when they know they will have further dealings with a bargaining partner). "But when you get in a negotiation, you don't get to choose whether there's a future. You don't get to choose the personality of your counterpart. It's already there, it's already set. What you can change is the cognitive perspective that you take."

"Maggie and I used to have lunch together every day," said colleague Gregory Northcraft. "We sat down, and we'd start seeing connections between what was going on in our lives and what was going on in our research." One connection involved anchoring and home prices. Northcraft and Neale were each buying their first house. "We both had the experience that when we were looking at houses, it was hard to know what to think of a house until we saw the listing price," said Northcraft.

"When the price was higher, we tended to focus on the things that made it a higher priced house, and if it was lower, we tended to focus on the things that explained why the price was lower."

They recognized this as anchoring. They also knew that economists had doubted whether Tversky and Kahneman's findings would apply to major financial decisions. Market forces would mandate reasonable prices, it was claimed.

"There's really two ways of looking at this," Northcraft told me. "One is that heuristics and biases make a huge impact when there's very little information. If you don't have any other information, you go to your bag of tricks and pull out something. But a lot of people were saying, yeah, when you get into a rich, real-world setting, then there's lots of other things to pay attention to, and you don't need the shortcuts.

"The flip side of that is that when you get into a sufficiently rich setting, the amount of information available can become overwhelming. That provides a secondary route for heuristics and biases to come into play. When you have too much information, they're there to sort that information out."

Northcraft and Neale applied to the National Science Foundation for a grant to test heuristics and biases in the real world. They sketched three likely domains of research: real estate, business negotiations, and legal judgments. They got the grant and started with real estate.

Their goal was to see whether anchoring could affect the perceived value of actual houses on the market in Tucson. To do that, they needed a real estate agent to lend them a house to use in the experiment. Neale asked her mother, a real estate broker, for advice. She advised playing up the networking possibilities. Agents would welcome the chance to make some connections with the faculty, she said. Agent Katherine Martin of Tucson Realty and Trust agreed to let them use one of her listings.

The experimental subjects were 54 junior and senior undergraduate business students and 47 local real estate agents. For those real estate professionals, the Tucson market was their bread and butter. On average, they bought or sold 16 properties a year and had been selling real estate in Tucson for more than eight years.

Northcraft drove the participants to the home, and all were free to inspect it, to "kick the tires," just like a buyer. The subjects were given all the information a buyer would normally have, including a list of comps for nearby houses that had recently sold and a packet containing Multiple Listing Service sheets for the house and for all the nearby houses then on sale. The subjects were then asked to estimate what the home was worth. The one experimental variable was the listing price. Each of four groups was told a different price.

"Science is often portrayed as this very systematic, clean, sterile process," said Northcraft, "and this study proved that good science is often nothing of the sort." Just as Northcraft was driving the subjects to the house, a desert cloudburst began. It was as though someone were heaving buckets of water at the windows. The subjects refused to get out of the van. On the drive back, the streets were flooding to hubcap level.

They tried again on a sunny day, but the home sold before they had all the data they wanted. They had to get permission to use a second house. The results for both homes were similar. I'll describe the second house, as they collected more data for it. This home had been appraised at $135,000 the previous year and was listed at $134,900. No one in the experiment saw this price, though. The subjects heard one of four fictitious prices: $119,900, $129,900, $139,900, and $149,900.

Both the real estate experts and the student amateurs were asked to price the home in four distinct ways. They were to play home appraiser and give a fair appraisal value; to pretend they were a listing agent and suggest a proper listing price; to assume the role of buyer and name a reasonable price to pay; and finally, to play seller and give the lowest offer that they would be willing to accept. All four measures showed similar anchoring. I'll give the estimates for buyer's reasonable purchase price.

*Estimated Purchase Price (average)*

| Listing Price | Amateurs | Experts |
| --- | --- | --- |
| $119,900 | $107,916 | $111,454 |
| $129,900 | $120,457 | $123,209 |
| $139,900 | $123,785 | $124,653 |
| $149,900 | $138,885 | $127,318 |

Now remember, all these figures apply to the same house. For the student amateurs, raising the listing price $30,000 (from $119,900 to $149,900) increased their average estimate of the home's value by nearly $31,000. They understood that the purchase price would be less than the listing price. But every dollar added to the listing price added a dollar to what they thought the house was worth.

Those who cherish faith in licensed professionals will be pleased to learn that the pros were less influenced by the fake listing prices. For the pros, raising the listing price by $30,000 raised their estimate by "only" $16,000. *Listing prices shouldn't make any difference at all to a professional.* Agents are the first to say that the market, not the seller, determines value. The seller is usually a nonexpert who may have completely unrealistic expectations. Part of an agent's job is to know the market price and (as buyer's agent) to steer clients away from overpriced properties.

How could working real estate agents be so fallible? "I think there are a lot of areas where people who have experience think they're experts," Northcraft said. "But the difference is that experts have predictive models, and people who have experience have models that aren't necessarily predictive."

Experience is useful only to the extent that there is feedback. An agent who sells a home at a price that is a little too high or low will rarely be confronted with wiggle-proof evidence that she mispriced the property. "For these judgments," Northcraft and Neale wrote, "expertise may amount to little more than knowledge of relevant accepted conventions, and feedback may correct descriptions of the judgment process (so that the descriptions conform to convention) rather than the accuracy of the judgments themselves. For such judgment tasks, we might expect experts to talk a better game than amateurs, but to produce (on average) similar judgments."

There was one telling difference between the experts and the amateurs. Thirty-seven percent of amateurs admitted that they considered the listing price. Only 19 percent of the experts said they did. "It remains an open question," Northcraft and Neale archly observed, "whether experts' denial of the use of listing price as a consideration in valuing property reflects a lack of awareness of their use of listing price as a consideration, or simply an unwillingness to acknowledge publicly their dependence on an admittedly inappropriate piece of evidence."

Before the experiment began, a consulting group of agents had told Northcraft and Neale that there is a "zone of credibility." Any listing price that differed from the appraisal value by more than 5 percent would stand out as "obviously deviant."

The experiment's two middle prices ($129,900 and $139,900 in the table above) were just within the zone. Each was about 4 percent off the appraised price. The two more extreme prices were 12 percent off and should have raised a red flag.

Only they didn't. The agents thought the house was worth nearly $3,000 more when listed at the deviant price of $149,900 rather than the more credible $139,000. The amateurs thought the house was worth $15,000 more at the higher price.

"At issue here is just how malleable decision processes might be, and whether there is some reality constraint on the extent to which such processes can be influenced," Northcraft and Neale wrote. "For instance, can just any listing price really influence the perceived value of a piece of real estate, or does the listing price need to be credible to be considered, and therefore to influence value estimates? This study provided only limited support for a reality constraint . . ."

This experiment, published in a 1987 issue of *Organizational Behavior and Human Decision Processes*, brought intense reaction. "Back in those days, the economists weren't doing much reading of the organizational literature," said Neale. That was to change, at least for this paper. It supplied needed evidence of the practical reality of anchoring, resulting in more than two hundred citations in scholarly papers.

Least impressed were real estate agents. When the researchers presented their results to a group of the agents who participated, "they absolutely rejected the findings," Neale recalled. "Their counterpoint was, 'You can do anything with statistics. It isn't true.' My mother wasn't real impressed, either. Over the years, I finally convinced her—but this was not something she got right away."

It would be wrong to go away with the idea that real estate agents are charlatans. The agents were indeed less susceptible to anchoring than students who lacked their expertise. This experiment was really about the way the human mind generates numbers from the world's rich and immersive data. It speaks not just of real estate agents but of all of us. (When I reminded Northcraft of some of the acerbic comments about agents in his 1987 article, he remarked, "I guess I would say there's no shame in being human.")

The Arizona experiment made the important claim that anchoring by listing price is powerful *even for something with a market value*. Northcraft concludes that the zone of credible prices is broader than most agents believe. Furthermore, there is no reason to think that 12 percent over appraisal was any sort of limit to strategic anchoring. It was simply the highest figure they dared to try in this experiment.

Neale jokes that her colleagues read the paper for advice on how to sell their own houses. It is not a complete blueprint. As everyone knows, there is a trade-off between asking price and the time on the market. The benefits of a higher listing price have to be weighed against the costs of taking a longer time to find a buyer. (Real estate agents are not shy about pointing out *that* fact of life.)

"One of the things we've worked on since is, 'At what point does my offer become silly?' " Neale said. In the psych lab, silliness doesn't necessarily matter. Anchoring works with numbers understood to be absurd. Home buyers, however, are unlikely to look at a home that's priced outside their range. "The adage 'You can always come down' does not work in this market," explained New York agent Diane Saatchi, speaking of the 2008 real estate slump. When reasonably priced homes sit for months without an offer, there is not much scope for pricing well above market value. Or is there?

# Thirty-seven

# Selling Warhol's Beach House

In 2000, Paul Morrissey, the film director and business partner of Andy Warhol, listed his Montauk estate for sale. He and Warhol had bought a 22-acre property, called Eothen, for $225,000 in 1971. Warhol never spent much time there—the ocean breezes kept blowing his wig off. In its heyday, Eothen played host to everyone from Jackie Onassis to the Rolling Stones. After Warhol's 1987 death, his foundation donated three-quarters of the open land to the Nature Conservancy as a preserve. Morrissey was selling the remainder, 5.6 acres occupied by five homes, a three-car garage, a stable, and 600 feet of Atlantic oceanfront.

By East End real estate standards, Eothen was the unique property from hell. Built in 1931 as a sportsmen's lodge for an Arm & Hammer baking soda heir, Eothen had stuffed deer heads and mounted fish on its weathered wood walls. Warhol and Morrissey never changed the outré décor. The small, never-updated rooms—characterized as "hobbit huts"—were unlikely to appeal to anyone who could possibly afford to buy it.

There was another way of looking at things. Conceivably the Warhol provenance was the place's greatest asset. Hamptons buyers were the same people paying record prices for Warhol paintings. Morrissey spoke wistfully of finding a buyer who would preserve the place.

The mix of positives and negatives made it incredibly difficult to gauge Eothen's market value. Morrissey set an asking price of $50 million. The real estate community felt that was way out of the ballpark. The East End buyer wants "satin sheets and ice makers and Sub-Zero refrigerators and flat-screen TV's, built-in pools," Realtor Paul Brennan told *The New York Times*. "If he would sell it for $25 million, I could sell it for him."

Going by that, Morrissey was asking about twice a realistic asking price. That's a much higher anchor than those used in Northcraft and Neale's experiment. Morrissey wasn't impatient. He kept Eothen on the market for seven long years—a time study no psychologist could afford. Morrissey wasn't in a hurry because he had the use of Eothen each summer, renting out some of the houses to defray expenses. Over time, he cut the price to $45 million, and then to $40 million. It apparently wasn't until the latter reduction, in the summer of 2006, that he started to get serious nibbles. The $40 million price was still outside any zone of credibility (being 60 percent over Brennan's suggested listing price), but it was no longer such a deterrent to lookers. On January 9, 2007, Morrissey closed a deal with Mickey Drexler, CEO of J. Crew. The sale price was $27.5 million. "He seems to be a great guy who understood it immediately," Morrissey said of Drexler. "His intention is to keep it exactly like it is."

The real estate agent's nightmare is the client who wants to keep a property on the market to get a good price. Agents are not paid by the hour, and they would rather sell sooner than later. They have evolved several scare stories to justify this predilection to buyers. One says that an overpriced property becomes damaged goods. When it does sell, it's sure to sell for less, not more.

Some would say that Morrissey was foolish to set such a high price; that the all-powerful and wise market brought an unrealistic seller down to earth. The marketing of Eothen seems equally consistent with experiments like Northcraft and Neale's, saying that a high listing price raises perceptions of value. Eothen's sale price was 8 percent more than the agent Brennan's suggested $25 million list price (quoted just four months before the sale). Figure that a $25 million asking price might signal a willingness to sell for, say, $23 million. Then Morrissey got about $4.5 million (20 percent) more by anchoring with a ridiculously high price.

Most sellers who set too-high prices do so in the hopes of getting those prices. They are destined for disappointment. Anchoring does not mean "You get whatever you ask for." It means "The more you ask for, the more you get." To use anchoring successfully, a seller must set a high price and *not* expect to get it.

Not many home sellers are in a position to wait seven years—or to alienate their hard-working agents. There is a way to have your cake and eat it too. It's to use the trick known in other contexts as *advertised reference pricing* (ARP).

Discount stores have long used ads and price tags comparing their store's price to a higher "reference price" charged at another place or another time. The higher price acts as an anchor, increasing the product's perceived value and presenting a favorable contrast. For the same reason, stores leave old price tags visible when they discount items for clearance sales.

"This past summer, I went out to purchase a tennis racket," explained Donald Lichtenstein (no relation to Sarah), a University of Colorado marketing researcher specializing in psychological pricing. "I went to the sporting goods store and looked at the vast array of rackets they had, about half (thirty-five or so) of which were on sale. When comparing the prices, I paid as much attention to the ARP as the purchase price. I knew better, but I just couldn't help myself."

That's why reference prices are so insidious. Everyone knows they can't possibly work! As Lichtenstein remarked in a 2004 speech,

> ARPs work, a lot of research shows they do, and retailer practice and returns show that they do. This is nothing new—it is widely known. If I advertise a sale price of, say, $29.95 and accompany it with an ARP of, say, $39.95, in most contexts, sales will increase relative to a no ARP present situation. Sales will likely increase as I increase my ARP to $49.95, to $59.95, and to $69.95. But what if the ARP is set at a level of $129.95? What about $329.95? And just to add some interest, what about $5,000?

Lichtenstein and others have done experiments on how far reference prices can be pushed. One 1988 study reported that the relationship between the reference price and perceived value for consumer goods is almost linear, even when the reference price is as much as 2.86 times the usual market value. That would correspond to a $279 item being advertised as selling for $799 elsewhere. As Lichtenstein put it, "your idea of what an item should cost is influenced by advertised prices even when they are totally unbelievable."

For seven years, Eothen was notorious. Montauk cocktail parties and open houses were abuzz with talk of the $50 million white elephant. When Morrissey cut the price to $40 million, the $50 million price did not vanish into thin air. You can bet that every buyer was told that the property had originally been listed for $50 million. Intentional or not, it was tantamount to an advertised reference price. That original price still pulled estimates of value upward. Buyer Mickey Drexler obviously knew the $50 million and $40 million prices were hot air. But if he's anything like experimental subjects, he must have felt he was getting a good deal. In the real estate market, just as at J. Crew, it's hard for anyone to ignore a 45 percent discount.

One gimmick of home flippers is to list a property for a short time at a very high price, then cut it to a more reasonable asking price, consistent with the seller's and agent's patience. Thereafter the listing can "honestly" mention the original price (REDUCED FROM $X). This tactic adds only a few days to the time the house is on the market, yet it likely gets most of the benefit of the anchor price.

I will leave it to you to decide the ethics of such things. A somewhat more devious trick is for seller A to put his house on the market and persuade neighbor B to post her house as an FSBO (for sale by owner) on some websites. B doesn't really want to sell; she lists at an absurdly high price (which she'd be glad to accept!). The point is to make A's house look like a deal.

The Zillow website has a "make me move" feature whereby homeowners can post fantasy prices for their property, even though it's not for sale. Anyone who uses Zillow knows that these "make me move" prices are ridiculous. Yet the "make me move" prices show up on the same maps and lists that buyers see when they search for homes that are for sale. One has to wonder whether they have a contrast effect, helping sell the nearby properties.

Not many home sellers use anchoring or reference pricing because they're sure buyers are too smart to fall for it. Donald Lichtenstein compares the reference price effect to certain urban legends. A rumor once went around that McDonald's used ground earthworms in its hamburgers. Sales plummeted as much as much as 30 percent in some areas. Practically nobody believed the rumor. Certainly 30 percent of the public did not believe that a big corporation would risk its billion-dollar brand in order to save a few dollars on beef. The point is, things no one believes still affect behavior.

# Thirty-eight

# Groundhog Day

"Anchoring is not a curiosity," Daniel Kahneman said. It "works quite well in negotiations, where getting in your number first gives an advantage." For bargainers, this simple rule may be the most important and easily applied finding of the psychology of price. The first figure named in a negotiation silently shifts the other side's expectations of what it will have to pay or accept. The evidence for this claim includes both field studies and lab experiments. Decision psychologists seem to have little doubt of its real-world applicability. Yet this rule has been extraordinarily difficult to communicate to businesspeople. The problem, according to Margaret Neale, is that executives no more believe in anchoring than in the tooth fairy.

After all, business negotiators give more thought to prices than does the shopper buying peanut butter. Before they sit down to bargain, they think long and hard about what their reserve price is. They try to estimate the other side's reserve price and the surplus that supposedly lies sandwiched between those two prices. This thinking promotes the idea that reserve prices are real and solid.

That's not necessarily the case. A famous hard bargainer, Samuel Gompers, was once asked what the labor movement wanted. His reply was "More." The one universal conviction of bargainers is that they want as much as they can possibly get. Prices are not a unilateral expression of what someone wants; they are about what someone thinks he can get. That's necessarily a guesstimate. There is abundant evidence that such guesses can be manipulated.

Neale, now a professor at Stanford's Graduate School of Business, consults with Fortune 500 companies and governments on negotiation techniques. "We spend a lot of time talking to real folks making real decisions about the power of these anchors," Neale said. "People are resistant. They say, it's not possible that I'm influenced by that; I've done a lot of things and I *know*. And I say, you don't know. Look, what our research is capable of doing, which you are not, is that I can put Maggie in this situation without an anchor, and then I can put Maggie in that exact same situation with an anchor. And I can then compare the differences in her behavior. There are differences, and they are systematic, and they are powerful effects."

The invention of the microscope provoked a strong emotional reaction. Anton van Leeuwenhoek revealed wriggling monstrosities within a drop of the pure lake water that would refresh a thirsty traveler. He discovered the corpuscles of blood, the tadpoles that are sperm cells, and a gruesome zoo within the human mouth. Everyone knew this couldn't be true. Any Dutch burgher of good eyesight could hold his hand in front of his face and see all there was to see there. No one ever saw bacteria.

Behavioral decision theorists are showing us something we could not learn any other way. There is no replay button to life. Never is there a chance to hit rewind, to see how we might have decided differently, or what price we might have agreed to, had the situation been just a little different. That takes an experiment.

The results of those experiments often challenge the notion of free will. By their nature, executives are strong-willed people. When you tell them that something like who names a number first can exert an unconscious influence on them, an influence affecting their company's bottom line, they can get indignant (as in "I'm too strong-willed to be hypnotized!"). They are sure they would have learned from experience what works and doesn't work in negotiation.

Colin Camerer calls this the *Groundhog Day* argument. In the 1993 movie, Bill Murray plays a man who wakes up each morning to find it's February 2 (again) and he has the day to live over. Murray is able to conduct a succession of "decision experiments": romancing women, driving drunk, even committing suicide with impunity. After many disastrous attempts, he finally he gets his life in order. The difference between that and real life, says Camerer, is that people never learn. Life rarely grants them the opportunity to match a complex cause to a complex effect.

Ilana Ritov of Ben-Gurion University in Be'er Sheva, Israel, did an experiment in which 148 managerial and engineering students engaged in a simulation of bargaining. Half the participants were given badges identifying themselves as buyers, the other half as sellers. The goal of the game was to make as much profit as possible by negotiating deals for the sale of an imaginary commodity. Each deal had to specify a price, delivery terms, and a discount level. The players consulted a profit schedule to determine how much they would earn under any particular agreement. In an attempt at realism, the two sides were not simply splitting an $8,000 pie. Depending on how the deal was structured, buyer and seller could gain as much as $5,200 apiece. It generally took a bit of back-and-forth to arrive at that win-win solution.

There are no rules to real-world bargaining, so Ritov didn't impose any. Anyone could partner with anyone they liked, as long the pair included a buyer and a seller. Either could make the first offer. They could offer any justification they liked for their offers, and use any negotiating strategies. Anyone who felt they were spinning their wheels could walk away and find another bargaining partner. Once a deal was made, both players could approach other partners and keep making deals, until the assigned time ran out. Players could try to maximize profit on every deal or "make it up in volume."

Ritov found that her sellers were usually the ones to approach a buyer. In a way, this was surprising because the game was so abstract. There was no physical merchandise to lug around and hand over; no fundamental difference between the two groups aside from the name tags. They might just as well have been called "skins" and "shirts."

Words can frame behavior, though, and the players fell readily into the familiar roles of buyer and seller. Normally a seller sets an asking price, and the buyer responds with a counteroffer. For the most part, that's what happened.

We often miss the forest for the trees. Ritov's experiment was able to reveal something that was not apparent to the bargainers themselves: the power of getting your number in first. On average, those who made the first offer made more money, and the higher the initial offer, the more money was made.

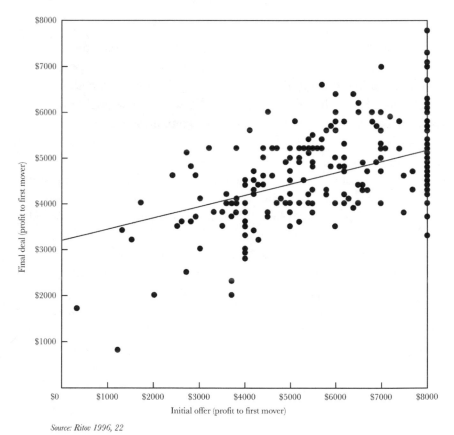

Source: Ritov 1996, 22

This is readily visible in a chart from Ritov's 1996 paper in *Organizational Behavior and Human Decision Processes*. This chart (above) plots initial offers on the horizontal axis versus final agreements on the vertical. In both cases, the offers are expressed as the profit to the initiator. Each point is a finalized deal. The important thing is not the individual "trees" but the shape of the "forest." The swarm of points roughly follows an upward-sloping line. In other words, *the more you ask for, the more you get.*

The maximum profit, to any one player in any one deal, was $8,000. The minimum was zero. Quite a few initiators started by asking for the kitchen sink—their maximum $8,000. The dense cluster of points sitting on the chart's right border represents this. That "greedy" opening left little or no profit for the partner.

Yet there was no evident downside to asking for the kitchen sink. While nobody ended up with an $8,000 profit, the people who made that their first offer did as well as or better than those who asked for less.

Another finding was more surprising yet. A chart of profit to non-initiators looked much the same. The better the initial offer was for the other guy, the more the other guy ended up with. This underscored how the initiator determined the fates of *both* parties.

In real estate, the seller sets an asking price. There's not much a buyer can do about that. In many other situations, the first-mover advantage is up for grabs. This is often true of salary negotiations.

Most employees negotiating a salary rightly feel at a disadvantage. A big company interviews thousands of applicants a year. It makes hundreds of salary offers and sees how many of them are accepted. This gives the employer a good feel for current market conditions. The average job seeker interviews sporadically and is left guessing at his or her current market value. Ask for a too-low number and you cheat yourself; ask for a too-high amount and you look foolish (and may miss out on a job you'd like). It's no wonder that many job seekers fall back on this strategy:

(a)  Let the employer make the first offer
(b)  Whatever it is, say it's not enough
(c)  Demand 20 percent more
(d)  Settle for 10 percent more [or fill in your own percentages]

Should you follow this to the letter, you'd end up settling for the employer's initial offer plus 10 percent, *no matter what the initial offer was*. That would mean you'd be even more a slave to the anchor than typical experimental subjects are.

The person who names a number first creates the strongest anchor. No one should willingly cede that opportunity. Fortunately, it's easier than ever for job seekers to research their current worth. Sites such as Salary.com ask a few questions (job title, education, experience, zip code) and generate a bell curve of likely salaries. You can learn, for instance, that 90 percent of comparable workers make less than $73,415. Answer the site's questions honestly, and that 90th percentile figure is a decent anchor/first offer. You won't likely get that much, but neither will they laugh you out of the office.

One of the worst things that can happen in a negotiation is for the other side to open with a wholly unacceptable number. In such situations, Max Bazerman and Margaret Neale believe it's necessary to "re-anchor"—to demand a fresh start. In their *Negotiating Rationally* (1992), a popular text in MBA courses, they warn, "Responding to an initial offer with suggested adjustments gives the anchor some measure of credibility . . . Threatening to walk away from the table is better than agreeing to an unacceptable starting point."

# Thirty-nine

# Anchoring for Dummies

Possibly the commonest objection to the idea of price anchoring is that it must be for dummies. *I'm too smart to fall for it, and so are the people I deal with.*

In 2008 Jörg Oechssler, Andreas Roider, and Patrick W. Schmitz of the German Institute for the Study of Labor tested this notion. They had a group of 1,250 volunteers answer the three-question Cognitive Reflection Test (CRT), a sort of mini-IQ test. The questions are classic brain-teasers. You're welcome to try them. Answer all three before reading on.

(1) A bat and a ball together cost 110 cents. The bat costs 100 cents more than the ball. How much does the ball cost? _____

(2) If it takes 5 machines 5 minutes to make 5 widgets, how long would it take 100 machines to make 100 widgets? _____

(3) In a lake, there is a patch of lily pads. Every day, the patch doubles in size. If it takes 48 days for the patch to cover the entire lake, how long would it take for the patch to cover half the lake? _____

The CRT doesn't purport to measure intelligence in any meaningful sense. It's better described as a test of willingness to *think things through* and *check your answer*. All three items are "gotcha" questions to which the first answer that occurs to just about everyone is wrong.

Oechssler's team split their subjects into two groups. Anyone who got two or three questions right was in the "reflective" group, and anyone who got zero or one right was in the "impulsive" group. (Just so you know where you'd fit in, the correct answers are (1) 5 cents; (2) 5 minutes; (3) 47 days.)

Both groups also answered questions involving anchoring. There was no difference between the impulsive and reflective thinkers in susceptibility to anchoring. In fact, they found slightly more of an anchoring effect with the reflective people, though it wasn't statistically significant.

For bright, reflective people, a number or hypothetical question triggers a rich network of associations. The longer and harder someone thinks about an answer, the more extended the exposure to these primed thoughts. This appears to counteract whatever accuracy advantages might have come from additional thought.

# Forty

# Attention Deficit

"When I build something for somebody," Donald Trump once confided, "I always add $50 million or $60 million onto the price. My guys come in, they say it's going to cost $75 million. I say it's going to cost $125 million, and I build it for $100 million. Basically I did a lousy job. But they think I did a great job."

Trump is hardly the only deal maker to appreciate the power of *two* numbers. Consider a novel ultimatum game devised by Max Bazerman, Sally Blount White, and George Loewenstein. One group of responders was simply asked to indicate the minimum offer they would accept out of $10. The average answer was $4, and that's typical.

A second group of responders was presented with two offers rather than the usual one (say, $3 and $2). These responders could accept either offer—or veto both.

This changed behavior greatly. Responders given a choice were more likely to accept the higher offer ($3) than to veto. Remember, the majority of people in the first group indicated that they would veto a $3 offer (or any offer under $4). The implication is that people who happily accepted $3, *when a $2 offer was also on the table*, would have vetoed that same $3, had it been the *only* offer.

Bazerman's team tested various pairs of offers. They found that the minimum offer accepted, when it was the higher of two, averaged $2.33. In this context, that's a big effect. Responders were willing to accept about 40 percent less just because it was presented as the better of two offers.

Why? It's apparently a matter of contrast and misdirection. In the standard ultimatum game, a responder offered $3 can compare it only to the $7 the proposer wants to keep for himself. The $7 makes the $3 look small and triggers feelings of unfairness, even anger. When there are two offers on the table, attention is diverted to the fact that one is better than the other. There is less mental machinery available to contemplate how the offers compare with what the proposer would be getting. At the moment of choice, deciders settle for the executive summary: which will it be, $3 or $2 or nothing?

"Automatic processes—whether cognitive or affective—are the default mode of brain operation," Colin Camerer, George Loewenstein, and Drazen Prelec wrote recently. "They whir along all the time, even when we dream, constituting most of the electro-chemical activity in the brain . . . Attention, for example, is largely controlled by automatic processes, and attention in turn determines what information we absorb." You can be doing your taxes when a baseball crashes through the window. You don't "decide" to look up and see what made the noise. It's automatic.

Neuroscience is starting to sketch in the details. There's a nubbin of gray meat at the base of the brain called the amygdala. One of its roles is to act as watchdog, detecting possible threats even when the focus of attention is elsewhere. In lab studies, the amygdala "sees" objects in peripheral vision that are invisible to the more deliberative parts of the brain.

Magicians have long exploited the unconscious machinery directing the roving gaze of attention. They know that their audience will quickly adapt to what they see and hear, and then react mostly to contrasts or changes. In the lore of magic, misdirection is best accomplished with objects that are moving rather than still; alive rather than inanimate; newly appeared rather than previously onstage; odd rather than familiar. The sudden appearance of a gorgeous assistant in a puff of smoke allows the magician cover to slip the rabbit into his hat. One of the canons of magic is "a big move covers a small move." To deflect attention from a little suspicious action, do something *big* and suspicious. The small move seems less suspicious by comparison and is ignored. This simple ruse works because the mind is always joining vagrant perceptions into the illusion of a perfect, seamless, real-time map of the surrounding world—somewhat the way that Google Maps fabricates a world map from thousands of satellite photos taken on sunny days. Google's cloud-less globe is an illusion, as is the universal conviction of seeing every-thing before our eyes.

Magic trades on the illusion of free will. Because the audience is unaware of the psychological manipulations that caused them to pay attention to A, B, and C rather than X, Y, and Z, they believe they saw everything of importance, or at any rate *could have* seen everything had they chosen not to look at the assistant's cleavage. Today's behavioral decision theorists are inclined to see bargaining and price setting in somewhat the same terms. The people who are successful at it are good at exploiting their partners' limited attention and bounded rationality.

The two-offer ultimatum game resembles such venerable techniques as "dead dog on the table" and "good cop, bad cop." A sharp bargainer will sometimes make an offer he knows will never be accepted (the "dead dog"). He sticks to it awhile, then reconsiders, making a second offer much more favorable to the other side. The new offer seems so good in comparison that the other side jumps for it. *Gotcha!* The new offer is what the sharpie wanted all along—something the other side wouldn't have accepted otherwise.

Alternatively, one member of a bargaining team (the "bad cop") makes the dead-dog offer. When he goes to the bathroom, his partner, the "good cop," expresses sympathy to the other side and floats the possibility of more generous terms. When the bad cop returns, he and the good cop disagree. Eventually the good cop wins the dispute. The other side is delighted to accept his offer (and that's what both "cops" wanted all along).

Bazerman's group found similar effects with these choices. Which would you rather have:

(a)  $400 for yourself and $400 for the other party, or
(b)  $500 for yourself and $700 for the other party?

When these options were presented singly, the group that saw (a) rated it acceptable, and the group that saw (b) judged it not so good. The fact that the other party does better in (b) was a deal breaker.

But when the two options were presented together, as (a) or (b), take your pick, an overwhelming majority (78 percent) chose (b). The direct comparison drove home the point that anyone choosing (a) is penalizing himself $100. Option (b) is more profitable for *both* parties.

In this abstract situation, the participants had no way of judging how "acceptable" an offer was except by comparing it to something else. Adding a second option changed what they paid attention to.

Bazerman asked some of his MBA students at Northwestern's Kellogg Graduate School of Management to rate hypothetical job offers (in mid-1990s dollars):

> *Job A*: The offer is from Company 4 for $75,000 a year. It is widely known that this firm pays all starting MBAs from top schools $75,000 . . .
>
> *Job B*: The offer is from Company 9 for $85,000 a year. It is widely known that this firm is paying some other graduating Kellogg students $95,000 a year . . .

Job B is an affront to an ambitious MBA's ego. When the offers were presented sequentially, most future execs rejected B in favor of A. When they were shown the two offers as a pair, they favored B. Whatever the value of equity, it wasn't worth passing up an extra $10,000 a year.

This finding is worth mulling because few of us have any choice but to evaluate job offers in sequence. Offers trickle in one by one. If and when you get one, you've got a few days to decide: *Is this salary good enough? Do I say no and keep looking?* The decisions we make under such circumstances are not necessarily those we would make, were it possible to stockpile job offers and choose among them, two or more a time.

Bazerman, White, and Loewenstein argue that there can be a dark side to so-called fairness. "Together, our studies suggest that when evaluating outcomes in isolation, people tend to be more concerned with interpersonal comparison of outcomes than with maximizing personal outcomes," they wrote. "These results imply that if people make policy decisions on a case-by-case basis, they may have a tendency to base these decisions on perceptions of fairness that are suboptimal for themselves and for society as a whole."

# Forty-one

# Drinking and Deal Making

The Duc de Richelieu remarked that the fate of empires was often changed by an extra bottle of Johannisberg. American businesses evidently agree. They spend roughly $20 billion each year wining and liquoring clients and business partners. That's about 12 percent of the retail alcohol market. It's not largesse. The liquor is expected to pay its own way, by causing customers and suppliers to make deals they wouldn't, and quote better prices than they would, when sober. The anchors known as trial balloons are often broached over drinks, and occasionally the outline of a deal is sketched on a cocktail napkin. The IRS allows businesses and individuals to write off alcoholic "entertainment" as long as it is "ordinary and necessary." Nobody seems to doubt that it's both.

When the economy goes south, alcohol-lubricated deal making is one of the last things to be cut. As the New York real estate market tanked in 2008, Prudential Douglas Elliman was offering high-net-worth customers condo tours awash in free Talisker and Lagavulin whiskey—which sell for $60 and $77 a bottle. "A little bourbon" could be good for sales, suggested one broker, who sounded confident that the liquor budget would be recouped and then some. Real estate journalist Christine Haughney wrote, "Just as a few drinks may coax timid traders onto a dance floor, it could help them muster the courage to buy multimillion-dollar apartments."

Are the prices people agree to under the influence different from those they'd accept fully sober? A British team at the University of Leeds and Oxford did an experiment in which social drinkers consumed alcohol or a placebo, then filled out a battery of psychological tests, including a series of choices between gambles. The experimental cocktail was a tangy blend of tonic water, Tabasco sauce, and alcohol—or, for the control group, a virgin counterpart. The amount of alcohol, scaled to body weight, was the equivalent of three strong drinks. (Yes, it's hard to believe that the subjects couldn't determine whether they were in the alcohol group or the control group. The perennial problem with alcohol experiments is that it's impossible to devise a credible placebo.)

In folk wisdom, alcohol promotes risk taking. You have to wrestle the keys from a drunk friend who's sure he can drive; "free" liquor in casinos encourages customers to bet more recklessly. Yet in many respects, there wasn't much difference between the intoxicated and placebo groups in the British experiment. Alcohol did not wash away prospect theory. Both drinkers and nondrinkers were loss-averse with gains, risk-seeking with losses. Both groups reliably favored "P bets," those with the better chance of winning.

The one significant difference that the British team found was a very specific one. It occurred when participants were presented with "difficult" Lichtenstein-Slovic-type choices involving large losses.

If you want to try the experiment yourself, you'll need to make three drinks. For each, carefully measure 3.6 ounces of 80-proof vodka into a highball glass and top off with tonic to make 10 ounces of beverage. (The 3.6 ounces applies to a 150-pound person. Scale the alcohol amounts accordingly.) You have fifteen minutes to consume all three drinks. Then wait ten minutes and answer these two questions (in both, I've converted the British psychologists' "points" into dollars):

*Question 1.* Which would you rather have?
(a) a 50 percent chance of winning $10; otherwise you lose $10
    —*or*—
(b) a 66 percent chance of winning $20; otherwise you lose $80.

*Question 2.* The choice is
(a) a 50 percent chance of winning $10; otherwise you lose $10
    —*or*—
(b) a 66 percent chance of winning $80; otherwise you lose $80.

Write your answers here: 1. ___ and here: 2. ___. Now for the most important part of the instructions: Do not drive, ride a bike, operate machinery, or do anything stupid for at least two hours.

By design, both questions present difficult choices. No answer is indisputably better. Option (a), identical for both questions, is a fair coin flip. Because losses are regretted more than gains are valued, that's subjectively a losing bet for almost everyone.

The two (b) gambles are P bets, and we know that everyone likes P bets. Choose (b), and you will probably walk away with some quick cash. (As Guy Grand asks in *The Magic Christian*, "How 'bout it, pal—got a taste for the easy green?")

Hold on, there's a catch. Both of the (b) bets carry a worrisome penalty of $80. That makes these bets less attractive. With the first and possibly the second question, participants are forced to choose the lesser of two evils.

There is only one difference between Questions 1 and 2. It is the amount of the win in option (b). It's $20 in the first question, and a more generous $80 in the second. Logically, you would expect more people to choose (b) in Question 2 than in Question 1.

That is indeed what happened. Most subjects (sober or intoxicated) picked (a) in Question 1 and (b) in Question 2. However, the shift was larger with the sober group. They were more responsive to the change in win amount than the alcohol group was.

The British team's overall conclusion was this nuanced one. When weighing the prospect of large losses, drinkers had a diminished capacity to factor in the amount of gains. When the gain in (b) was raised from $20 to $80, many drinkers didn't change their choice. It was as if they didn't notice.

Alcohol narrows an already limited scope of attention, a phenomenon that's been dubbed *alcohol myopia*. This places yet tighter bounds on rationality. Both questions 1 and 2 make competing demands on the chooser's attention. Since subjects had been asked to choose (rather than name a price), they would have focused attention on the probabilities of winning (50 versus 66 percent). Second, they had to worry about the downside risk. The biggest loss possible was $80, and this is so much more than the $10 loss in (a) that the $80 loss commanded the attention. Much like a magician's "big move," the $80 loss created misdirection. The subjects were preoccupied with weighing how bad a 1-in-3 chance of an $80 penalty is, and whether that should overturn an innate preference for a P bet.

Buzzed or sober, this left few cognitive resources for giving the (b) option gains the consideration they deserved. There were just too many numbers to juggle. The intoxicated subjects were especially overwhelmed. They ended up not paying much attention to gains. This sometimes led to decisions that appear risky, and other times to choices that were anomalously conservative.

There are many counterparts in business. Quoting a price to a potential client is a gamble. It can never be known exactly how much work will be involved, how demanding the client will be, what can go wrong with the job, and what the relevant chances are. A three-martini lunch converts complex problems into deceptively simple ones. Any prices quoted are apt to be "wrong" in the sense of not reflecting all the relevant information. A vendor may lose profitable business by pricing himself too high and saddle himself with ruinous contracts by pricing too low.

One bit of singles bar wisdom might help you to remember this rule. Going home with a stranger is a gamble (posing small chances of date rape, an STD, and/or a bad marriage followed by a messy divorce), but normally a favorable one. Drinkers forfeit the ability to discriminate between the worthwhile risks and the bum bets. After a few drinks, they all look good.

# Forty-two

# An Octillion Doesn't Buy What It Used To

A billion Zimbabwean dollars doesn't buy what it used to. In July 2008 Robert Mugabe's government released a Z$100 billion bill. It became an instant collector's item, which is just as well. As money, it was nearly worthless in a few weeks. In January 2009 the Reserve Bank of Zimbabwe introduced a new Z$100 trillion bill. It had a picture of a buffalo and Victoria Falls on it, and was said to be worth about $30 American. By then hardly anyone was using Zimbabwe's money. The inflation of the Zimbabwean dollar peaked at a reported rate of 500 billion percent a year. Besides printing up ever larger denominations, the government periodically lopped off zeros, thirteen by the end of 2008. Strictly speaking, that Z$100 trillion bill was really Z$1 octillion (1,000,000,000,000,000,000,000,000,000) in the old money of just a few years previous. Somehow Zimbabwe's currency designers resisted the scientific notation taboo.

How had Zimbabweans managed? The world was left asking that question, and journalists in Zimbabwe found it difficult to give outsiders a straight answer. Zimbabwe's economy was a shambles, with 80 percent unemployment and rampant starvation. Inflation was the least of the average Zimbabwean's problems. Those lucky enough to have jobs coped with the money, though. They stoically accepted that their nation's dollar was about as perishable as milk, with a similar expiration date. Day to day, the ratios of prices remained reasonably steady, even as absolute prices changed.

The first great scholar of hyperinflation psychology was Irving Fisher

(1867–1947), an economist currently experiencing a revival of interest. No less a figure than Richard Thaler has hailed Fisher as a pioneer of behavioral economics. One of Amos Tversky's last papers treated Fisher's concept of a "money illusion," a cognitive trick that comes into play during times of inflation.

Fisher was an unlikely hero-before-the-fact to this crowd. In his 1892 dissertation, Fisher complained of Gustav Fechner's baleful influence on the profession of economics. "The foisting of Psychology on Economics seems to me *in*appropriate and vicious," he wrote. For several decades in the twentieth century, Fisher was probably America's most famous economist. The public first knew him as the author of a bestselling self-help book with the earnest title *How to Live*. A successful inventor, Fisher devised an index card system, a precursor of the Rolodex, and came into a fortune when his index card company merged into Remington Rand (a typewriter company that eventually became the early computer company Sperry Rand). From his perch at Yale, Fisher pontificated on the issues of the day. He was for vegetarianism, prohibition, eugenics, and just about every nutty health regimen under the sun. His daughter Margaret died in 1919 after he allowed a quack to remove parts of her colon in a misguided attempt to cure schizophrenia.

Fisher's brilliant career came screeching to a halt in 1929. Days before Black Monday, Fisher tried to calm the jangled nerves of investors. The market's recent volatility, he said, was only a "shaking out of the lunatic fringe." With the lunatics out of the market, prices were sure to rocket *higher*. "Stock prices have reached what looks like a permanently high plateau." They hadn't, and that statement trashed Fisher's reputation just as the market decimated his index card fortune.

Fisher believed it ought to be possible to predict prices with the rigor of a physicist. He must have been encouraged in this by his doctoral advisor, the reclusive physicist Josiah Willard Gibbs. Just as the volume of a gas can be computed from its pressure and temperature, Fisher aspired to predict prices from supply and demand. His thesis described how to do that, and Fisher went so far as to build a price-generating machine (see page 225). It was a tank of water with a flotilla of half-flooded wooden "cisterns" connected by a system of levers. Adjustments to "stoppers" and levers fed in data on incomes, marginal utilities, and supplies; then prices could be read off scales. Gibbs must have been pleased. The device prefigured, if not parodied, the direction of twentieth-century economics. ("Press stopper I and raise III," read part of Fisher's instructions for the thing. "I, II, III now represent a wealthy middle class and poor man respectively . . .")

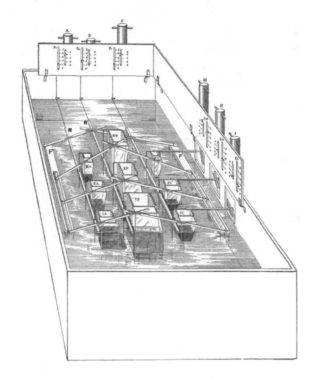

Unlike some of his contemporaries, Fisher was keenly interested in the anomalies that didn't fit the machine. Fisher's 1928 book, *The Money Illusion*, is a still unsurpassed epic rant on the subject of inflation. Fisher traveled to Weimar Germany in 1922 to see how average citizens were coping with the nation's raging inflation. German printing presses were churning out marks to pay its staggering war debts, and prices had increased by a factor of fifty since the war. In a Berlin shop, Fisher picked out a shirt and paid the shopkeeper her quoted price. "Fearing to be thought a profiteer, she said: 'That shirt I sold you will cost me just as much to replace as I am charging you.' Before I could ask her why, then, she sold it at such a low price, she continued: 'But I have made a profit on that shirt because I bought it for less.' "

Of course, the shopkeeper *wasn't* making a profit in any meaningful sense. She had paid so many marks for the shirt, back when those marks had a certain purchasing power. Between that time and the sale to Fisher, the purchasing power of the mark had decreased. She was charging a markup, but only in marked-down marks.

Fisher's point was that money is just a tool for getting stuff. When prices are stable, we can act as if money and purchasing power are one and the same. When the purchasing power of money varies, it's necessary to draw a distinction.

This is how economists think, at any rate. Regular folks, like the shopkeeper, tend to ignore inflation. The peak year of German hyperinflation was 1923, when prices were doubling every two days. A news photo showed a German woman shoveling marks into her furnace. By then, a pile of burning cash generated more heat than the shrinking pile of firewood it could buy. Fisher nonetheless found that Germans managed to live in partial denial. Their mind was on the prices, not on the stuff.


The money illusion is almost always introduced in the context of inflation. Actually, the shrinking dollar, American or Zimbabwean, need have nothing to do with it. The money illusion can occur whenever prices change. Its basis is that consumers pay too much attention to prices and not enough to the buying power that those prices represent. The signifier becomes more important than the signified.

You have just opened a bottle of good Bordeaux for a dinner with friends. The bottle comes from a case you bought on the futures market (before harvest) for the price of $20 a bottle. It turned out to be a very good year. You happen to know (and can't resist informing your guests) that the very same wine is now selling for about $75 a bottle. How much do you feel the bottle is really costing you to serve tonight?

  (a) Nothing (since you paid for it years ago and might not even
        remember the price)
  (b) $20 (since that's what it cost originally)
  (c) $20 plus interest
  (d) $75 (since that's what it would cost to replace it today)

(e) *Negative* $55 (since you're getting a $75 bottle of wine for only $20)

In 1996 Richard Thaler and Eldar Shafir posed this question to a group of wine collectors subscribing to a wine newsletter. Many must have encountered this kind of situation before. There were no "right" or "wrong" answers, of course. Thaler and Shafir were only asking how much it *feels* as if the wine costs. The exact wording: "Which of the following best captures your feeling of the cost to you of drinking this bottle?"

Economists almost invariably side with answer (d). Wine you drink right now costs whatever it would take to replace it right now. How much you paid for it way back when is a nice story to tell over dinner . . . but price history is bunk.

Option (b) might be natural to an accountant. FIFO and LIFO methods of valuing inventory use the price paid. This makes sense because a retailer knows the price paid. She doesn't necessarily know the current market value, and it may not be worth the effort to determine it.

Answer (a) says that price history is not only irrelevant but possibly forgotten, and (e) turns the history-is-bunk argument on its head, resulting in a *negative* cost for perfectly good wine! Both economists and accountants would throw their hands up at that. Yet (a) and (e) were the most popular answers, garnering 30 and 25 percent of the responses. Only 20 percent of the wine lovers chose the economists' answer, (d). The vast majority were haunted by the ghost of prices past.

One reason that nominal-dollar amounts are so hard to deny is that we're bombarded with them. "Common discourse and newspaper reports often manifest money illusion, even in familiar contexts and among people who, at some level, know better," Eldar Shafir, Peter Diamond, and Amos Tversky wrote. Try thumbing through the *Guinness Book of World Records*. It's full of money records—the highest-paid athlete, the record auction price, the most expensive meal, etc., etc. Few of the entries attempt to adjust for inflation. Yes, Andre Agassi earns more simoleons than Arnold Palmer ever did. You still have to wonder who was wealthier, *really*.

The *Guinness* editors are hardly worse than *The New York Times* or

CNN. Look at almost any news chart of money values over time. Not many adjust for inflation, even in the smartest media. Perhaps the press-release affection for superlatives has something to do with it. "The largest donation to veterinary medicine programs ever" makes a snappier lead than "the eighth largest donation, in real terms."

What causes the money illusion? The simplest answer is that it's too much trouble to do the math. That can't be the whole story, though. Researchers have grilled math-savvy students with "easy" questions in which the relevance of inflation or changing prices is made bonehead-obvious and is readily computed. By and large, those students still fall victim to the money illusion.

Shafir, Diamond, and Tversky surveyed a diverse group at Newark International Airport and two northern New Jersey malls. One trio of questions concerned "Ann" and "Barbara," two employees of publishing firms. One year, during a time of no inflation, Ann got a 2 percent raise. Another year, during a time of 4 percent inflation, Barbara got a 5 per-cent raise.

One group was asked who was doing better "in economic terms" after their raise, Ann or Barbara? The majority picked Ann. This is the "right" answer. The raise increased Ann's buying power by 2 percent. Barbara's raise was only about 1 percent in real terms because of inflation.

Now for the interesting part. A second group, randomly chosen from the same population of New Jersey travelers and shoppers, was asked who was *happier* after the raise. Most chose Barbara. A third group was asked who was more likely to leave her job. They favored Ann (meaning that Barbara was more likely to stay). The overall theme was that $$$ = happiness = actual dollars *not adjusted for inflation*.

The answers to the first question indicate that the participants were able to allow for inflation. They tended to do so when prompted by the phrase "in economic terms" but not otherwise. The authors attributed this to "multiple representations." There are two ways of mentally repre-senting money, one based on actual dollars and another based on buying power. Practically everyone knows that the first way is "wrong" whenever there's inflation. But both representations command attention and both affect decisions, sometimes unconsciously. This suggests that the money illusion may be a form of anchoring. The nominal dollar amount is an anchor, and adjustments (for inflation) are usually insufficient.

Average folks are the true victims of the money illusion. Their employers use inflation to cut their wages and call it a "raise." Labor negotiators pat themselves on the back for the "victory." They put their savings in savings accounts, real estate, bonds, and annuities that have little or no real return. The government taxes "profits" on their houses and savings that aren't profits at all.

Not that the money illusion is always bad. A 2008 *Los Angeles Times* piece observed that "California's run-up in housing prices after 2000 actually helped open the real estate market for minorities by diminishing fears that their arrival in a neighborhood meant home values would decline." In any event, the money illusion must be reinforced by lifelong conditioning. All too often, our society is a crazy Pavlov's dog experiment in which money is the bell. After much repetition, we salivate over the hollow symbol, not the meat.

## Forty-three

# Selling the Money Illusion

My dog is worried about the economy because Alpo is up to 99 cents a can. That's almost $7.00 in dog money.                                                        —Joe Weinstein

Put yourself in the place of the head of a computer company's Singapore division. It's 1991, and you're negotiating a contract to sell computers to a local (Singapore) company for delivery two years hence. You currently sell the computers for $1,000. By the time of delivery in 1993, prices in Singapore are expected to be 20 percent higher. Of course, that's a guess. There are two ways of structuring the deal.

> Contract A: You agree to sell the computer systems (in 1993) at $1,200 apiece, no matter what the price of computer systems is at the time.
> Contract B: You agree to sell the computer systems at 1993's prices.

Which contract do you prefer? Shafir, Diamond, and Tversky offered these choices in a survey. They found that their survey group was split between the two options, with 46 percent choosing A and 54 percent choosing B. The psychologists also found that they could change the responses drastically just by changing the way they described the two contracts—a finding that "could have significant consequences for bargaining and negotiation."

The descriptions above were worded to be as neutral as possible. Another group received the same problem with the contracts framed in "real" (inflation-adjusted) terms:

> Contract A: You agree to sell the computer systems (in 1993) at $1,200 apiece, no matter what the price of computer systems is at the time. Thus, if inflation is below 20% you will be getting more than the 1993 price; whereas, if inflation exceeds 20% you will be getting less than the 1993 price. Because you have agreed on a fixed price, your profit level will depend on the rate of inflation.
> Contract B: You agree to sell the computer systems at 1993's price. Thus, if inflation exceeds 20%, you will be paid more than $1,200, and if inflation is below 20%, you will be paid less than $1,200. Because both production costs and prices are tied to the rate of inflation, your "real" profit will remain essentially the same regardless of the rate of inflation.

When things were put this way, the group overwhelmingly (81 percent) preferred B. This version makes the case that B guarantees a real profit, while A is a gamble.

Still another group got the same contracts described in dollar-value terms—so as to promote the money illusion:

> Contract A: You agree to sell the computer systems (in 1993) at $1,200 apiece, no matter what the price of computer systems is at the time.
> Contract B: You agree to sell the computer systems at 1993's price. Thus, instead of selling at $1,200 for sure, you will be paid more if inflation exceeds 20%, and less if inflation is below 20%.

This wording paints A as a sure thing and makes B look like a gamble. Here, 59 percent favored B. According to Shafir's group, this implies two things. One is that people "naturally" look at things in dollar-amount terms. The reaction to the "neutral" question was not much different from that to the version slanted in favor of the money illusion.

The other conclusion is that choices are remarkably fluid. Loss aversion is a powerful motivator. People will pay more to avoid risk and (so the experiment suggests) will also pay more for mere *words* that down-play risk.

Shafir, Diamond, and Tversky argued that people tend to accept whatever framing they're given. Union leaders wanting to sell a contract to the rank and file—or management wanting to sell a proposal to the union—should think carefully about how they describe the offer. The trick is to present the contract as minimizing risk. This is possible regardless of what the contract actually says.

- If the contract calls for a wage increase to $20 an hour, the pitch should be that it *guarantees* $20 an hour. An adjustable wage would carry the risk of making less than $20 an hour, or even a cut in wages.
- If it calls for a 3 percent yearly raise, say it *guarantees* that raise. Wages are certain to go up, and you don't have to worry about deflation, which would cause wages to decrease with an indexed contract.
- And if the contract indexes wages to the cost of living, as Irving Fisher thought all sensible contracts should, then you can say it *guarantees* the only thing that really matters, purchasing power. Ironically, it's most important to hammer this point with the indexed contract. The survey indicates that people don't adopt this frame unless it's presented to them.

Marketers exploit the power of inflation all the time. Internet marketing guru Marlene Jensen advises clients to use this cleverly larcenous tactic. Say you've got a $100 product. You don't sell it for $100, goodness no. It's $149 discounted to $99. As time goes by, inflation nibbles at your profit and you have to raise the price. Jensen advises, *Don't raise the price—lower the discount.*

The official price, which nobody pays, remains $149. But now you discount it to $119. For a lot of things, like newsletter subscriptions, many customers won't notice. They won't remember the old price, and they haven't a clue what the product should be selling for. Instead, they'll fall for the lure of getting a $149 product for "only" $119.

That's half of Jensen's scheme. More time passes, and inflation never sleeps. You tell your customers that, in view of increased costs, it will be necessary to raise prices, from $149 to $179. *But* for selected customers (meaning basically everyone), you're increasing the discount so that they pay not a penny more than they did before, $119. Nobody can object to this. The price paid remains the same.

This lays the groundwork for the next ratchet upward. Eventually, you go back to the customers and decrease the discount—while holding the line on the official price. Repeat as needed.

# Forty-four

# Neutron Jane

Jane Beasley Welch picked up the extension phone and heard a lot more than she wanted to hear. Her husband, Jack Welch, the recently retired CEO of General Electric, was talking to a strange woman. Jane quietly put down the phone. She confirmed her suspicions by reading messages on Jack's BlackBerry. The biggest shock came when Jane confronted her husband. He didn't deny an affair or softpedal it. He had fallen in love with Suzy Wetlaufer, forty-two, with the looks and bearing of a model. Wetlaufer was editor of the *Harvard Business Review*. The magazine had asked to do a profile of Jack and he consented. Welch had no idea that he was walking into "the most expensive tryst in history."

Two teams of divorce attorneys were soon bickering over quite different estimates of the Welches' net worth. Jane's lawyers put it at $800 million (and wanted half); Jack's team said it was only $456 million (and were offering Jane less than 30 percent). As negotiations dragged on, Jack was giving Jane a temporary allowance of $35,000 a month. To a woman with Jane's sense of entitlement, that didn't go far. It was time for Jane to play the ultimatum game.

The summer of 2002 was abuzz with talk of greedy, grabby CEOs. Scandals were unfolding simultaneously at Enron, WorldCom, Tyco, and Adelphia. On June 14, corrupt Tyco CEO Dennis Kozlowski threw a fortieth birthday bash for his wife, Karen. Guests were flown to Sardinia for a "Roman orgy" featuring toga-clad waiters, a cake in the shape of a nude woman, and an ice sculpture of Michelangelo's *David* urinating a never-ending stream of Stolichnaya vodka. Kozlowski called the party a shareholders meeting and used that pretext to bill Tyco for one-half of the $2 million cost. Within weeks, this and other scandals had made Kozlowski a pariah who had little choice but to resign. The irony was that Kozlowski had often been likened to Welch—at the time, about the highest praise one could bestow on a chief executive officer. To those who skimmed the business section, Jack Welch was the last unscathed CEO left, the one man whose probity and plainspoken candor were still unquestioned.

Jane Welch had the power to change that. She knew that Jack was receiving an astonishing array of perks from GE, unknown to shareholders or the press. For instance, GE had agreed to supply Jack with an $80,000-a-month Trump Tower apartment throughout his working life *and* retirement. Jane's attorneys told her she could demand use of the apartment, just as if it were an asset of Jack's. Jack had a lot of perks like that. Her attorneys grilled Jane on them and compiled an affidavit with multicolored charts.

This became a crucial bargaining chip. In that year of corporate scandals, release of the information would knock Welch off his pedestal (at the very least) and might compel him to relinquish the perks. The demand was, *Give me a fair share of the perks or nobody gets them.*

Jack Welch was very much part of the GE tradition of ultimatum bargaining. He had acquired the nickname "Neutron Jack" for his practice of firing the 10 percent of worst-performing managers. Jack destroyed humans while leaving the building standing. But if he thought that Jane was bluffing, he was wrong.

Jane's attorneys filed the affidavit on September 5. Its details were all over the next morning's *New York Times.* The story was no longer an A-list divorce but the polymorphous perversity of Welch's compensation package. Welch's GE pension, some $8 million a year, was about double what his top salary had been. This was for doing absolutely nothing. Welch was also consulting for GE, and for that he received an $86,000-a-year salary in perpetuity.

The salary was a bagatelle next to the perks that Welch retained for life. These included free use of a corporate Boeing 737 complete with free pilot and free fuel. GE sprang for prime seats at Red Sox, Yankees, and Knicks games; paid Welch's tab at restaurants; paid for cars, cell phones, fresh flowers, dry cleaning, wine, and vitamins. The real mystery was how Welch would spend his $8-million-a-year pension. "It appeared that he had negotiated a retirement plan," *The New York Times*'s Joseph Nocera wrote, "that would cause him to never take cash out of pocket to pay for anything."

Jack, furious over the disclosure, was soon being compared to Dennis Kozlowski—and this was not a compliment. Barely ten days after Jane's exposé hit the news, Jack caved in to the torrent of criticism. He announced that he was relinquishing all his GE retirement perks. By one calculation, Jane's ultimatum had cost the couple $2.5 million a year for the rest of their lives.

It was a T-shirt that sparked Sara Solnick's interest in gender and bargaining. As a young economics student she signed up for a summer institute sponsored by Daniel Kahneman and Richard Thaler. There she came across T-shirts asking "Does *Homo Economicus* Exist?" "They critiqued the existing models of economic man, but they still thought it was a *man*," Solnick recalled. "I said, this person's identity also makes a difference."

Solnick had studied labor economics and knew that one of the field's puzzles was the gender gap. It had long been known that women earn less than similarly qualified men, even after allowing for every obvious factor that might distort the results. After Solnick learned about the ultimatum game, she reasoned that it could address the role of gender from a new angle. She wondered whether there would be gender differences even in the game's minimalistic simulation of price setting. Solnick's advisor told her it was a good research topic because it would be interesting whichever way it turned out. She applied for a $5,000 grant and set to work.

In Solnick's clever design, proposers and responders sat on opposite sides of a partition and could not see each other. A control group of players learned only the code number of their unseen partners. Another group learned the first name of their partner. Everyone in the second group must have been aware of their partner's gender, yet nobody knew the experiment was "about" gender. (A few subjects had gender-neutral names like "Casey" or "Jordan." Their results were not counted.)

The proposers who didn't know the gender of their partner offered an average of $4.68 out of $10. But for the proposers who knew their partner was a man, the average offer was $4.89. When they knew they were dealing with a woman, the average was only $4.37.

One conceivable explanation is that everyone expects men to be vindictive jerks and women to be doormats. In any case, the gender gap was even greater when the proposers were women. Females offered male responders an average of $5.13—more than a fifty-fifty split—yet stiffed female responders with an average of $4.31. Either the women were more generous with men, or more afraid of making them mad. One female proposer gave the full $10 to her male partner, something that almost never happens, even in New Guinea. Her explanation: "I want at least one of us to get something."

Solnick had her responders state the minimum offer they would accept. This minimum was higher when they knew the proposer was female. Women got the short end of the stick no matter which role they played.

Terms like "sexism" are probably misleading here. Solnick's subjects were students at the University of Pennsylvania, too young to remember a prefeminist past. Though they might have consciously rejected a double standard (just as anchoring subjects deny being influenced by random numbers), gender made a difference. The mere mention of a name triggered an unconscious pattern of gender behavior, measurable in dollars.

Overall, the male proposers in Solnick's study made about 14 percent more money than female proposers did. That is close to reported figures for the gender gap in real-world wages. Salaries are negotiated, Solnick noted, and "women may end up with a smaller share of the portion of wages that is up for grabs."

These are disturbing findings for our would-be egalitarian society. "Equal pay for equal work" can be a tricky concept when individuals negotiate their salaries. What is to be done if employers, male and female, unconsciously quote lower salaries to women—and women accept them? Solnick has found that many employers are remarkably unconcerned. One common reaction to her research from employers is: "If women take our first offer, too bad for them. The men bargain and got a better starting salary."

There is of course a difference between equality of opportunity and equality of outcome. Everyone's for equality of opportunity. In the main, we prefer to think that equality of opportunity leads naturally to equality of outcome. Solnick's research challenges this hopeful thinking. "If you really want to be fair," Solnick said, "you can't just assume that you are fair. You have to have procedures in place."

It's important for women to learn that they can and should negotiate more, Solnick suggested. They should start with a strong anchor, consider offers critically, and accept that there will be difficult moments in a negotiation. It's not the woman's unique responsibility to make everyone feel comfortable at all times.

Contentious divorces are one example of an ultimatum game complicated by gender. The Welch divorce was not atypical of its kind. The spouse with greater earning power played proposer, demanding more than a 50 percent share. The other side's power rested largely in its ability to veto any proposal (and keep the attorney meter running). What Jane Welch did was conceivably the most effective thing she could have done. By sacrificing perks worth millions a year to *both* the Welches, Jane became Neutron Jane. She demonstrated her willingness to reject unfair offers, overriding any preconceptions that Jack or his legal team might have had. It may have worked. Just before an October 2002 hearing on the temporary alimony, Jack said, "Let's talk." They came to an agreement within hours. According to *The Wall Street Journal*, "both sides say the amount is far more than the $35,000 a month Mrs. Welch has been receiving."

# Forty-five

# The Beauty Premium

Hotties, male and female, get all the breaks. Economists have been slow to sneak up on what everyone else already knew. In recent years, labor economists have determined that better-looking employees are paid more. This seems to be true regardless of occupation—whether they're a model on a runway or a coder in a cubicle. There is a "beauty premium" for the congenitally fabulous. For everyone else, there's a plainness penalty.

Sara Solnick thought the ultimatum game might be a way to investigate the effects of physical appearance on prices and salaries. This is normally a complicated matter, because there are many reasons an employer might pay attractive people more. In sales or waiting tables, appearance is part of the total package. An employer can reason that the public likes an attractive face. The ultimatum game eliminates at least some of these factors. "There are no productivity issues, no expectations, and no contact between subjects," Solnick and collaborator Maurice Schweitzer wrote. If looks matter even in the ultimatum game, they probably matter whenever people set a price or negotiate a salary.

In Solnick and Schweitzer's experiment, seventy student volunteers agreed to be photographed. To spare the subjects' feelings, the photographs were sent to another university where a jury of complete strangers rated each photo on an 11-point category scale ranging from −5 (very unattractive) to +5 (very attractive). Solnick and Schweitzer took the six most and six least attractive people of each gender. The resulting twenty-four photos were compiled into an album.

A group at the second university played the ultimatum game. Each was shown a picture from the album and told that that person was their partner. There was no meaningful difference in how the attractive and unattractive people played. The difference was in how *other* people reacted to them.

Proposers offered attractive people slightly more money than they did unattractive people ($4.72 vs. $4.61). Responders, however, demanded more *from* attractive people. The average minimum demand was $3.53 when the partner was in the most attractive group, and $3.32 when he or she was in the least attractive set. Because most offers are accepted, the latter disadvantage was less important than the former advantage. Overall, attractive people made more money.

This experiment might modestly support the value of looks in occupations that involve soliciting prices from the public (real estate agents, car dealers, auctioneers, salespeople). But Solnick and Schweitzer also looked at gender and found it mattered more than looks did. For the purposes of this experiment, it was more profitable to be a man than to be very attractive. Both genders offered men more and expected less of them. The men thereby earned 15 percent more than the women. Being very attractive was a double-edged sword. Overall the most attractive group earned 10 percent more than the least attractive group. The latter figure exaggerates the effect of looks, though. It contrasts only the best- and worst-looking groups, leaving out the average Joes and Janes.

## Forty-six

# Search for Suckers

The belief that women are poor bargainers can be a self-fulfilling prophecy. This idea appears to be rampant among car dealers. Former car salesman Darrell Parrish recalled,

> Salesmen . . . categorize people into "typical" buyer categories. During my time as a salesman I termed the most common of these the "typical uninformed buyer" . . . As a rule they were indecisive, wary, impulsive, and, as a result, were easily misled. Now take a guess as to which gender of the species placed at the top of this "typically easy to mislead" category? You guessed it—women.

The argot of car dealers has a revealingly sexual term for a woman who pays sticker price: a "lay-down."

The best-known experiment on gender, ethnicity, and car prices may still be a controversial 1991–1995 study conducted by Ian Ayres of the Yale Law School and Peter Siegelman of the American Bar Foundation. They sent a small army of 38 volunteers to some 153 randomly selected car dealerships in the Chicago area. The volunteers were all between twenty-eight and thirty-two years old, with three or four years of college education. They were instructed on how to dress: for men, polo or button-down shirts, slacks, and loafers; for women, little makeup, blouses, straight skirts, and flats. All arrived at the dealerships in rented cars, waited for a dealer to approach them, and began to negotiate for a new car.

Like a candidate preparing for a big debate, each volunteer had been coached on a negotiation "script" for two days. Each was to wait five minutes for the dealer to make an initial offer; should none be forthcoming, the volunteer was to prompt the dealer to make one. The volunteer was to respond with a counteroffer equaling the dealer's marginal cost (options included), computed from *Consumer Reports* Auto Price Service and *Edmund's New Car Prices*.

They then followed a rote negotiation strategy. One was "split the difference." Whatever the dealer offered, the volunteer raised his previous offer by half the difference between the dealer's new offer and the volunteer's previous offer. This was continued until the dealer accepted or refused to negotiate any further. In the former event, the volunteer said he or she wanted to think about it, and in both cases, the volunteer left without buying.

The experiment found striking evidence of racial bias. On average the final offer quoted to black men was $1,100 more than for white men. This was for the same model, at the same dealership, at nearly the same time. In fact, in about 44 percent of the cases, the white males got an initial offer that was lower than the final negotiated price achieved by female or black counterparts.

The women volunteers required a high tolerance for being called "honey" and "cutie." "You are a pretty girl, so I'll give you a great deal," said one dealer who didn't. Despite that, the evidence for gender bias was inconclusive. White women paid a bit more than men, but this wasn't statistically significant. Black women cut slightly better deals than black men.

In designing a field experiment like this, the devil is in the details. There are so many subtle things that can bias the results (even when the experiment is *about* bias). Ayres and Siegelman's experiment was compelling because of its many well-thought-out safeguards. It was a true double-blind experiment in that neither the dealers nor the volunteers knew what was going on. Ayres and Siegelman had told the volunteers nothing about gender or race, only that they were "studying how sellers negotiate car sales." Each volunteer was part of a pair (though they didn't know it). One member of the pair was a white man, and the other was black or female or both. It was arranged that both members of a pair visited the same dealership within a few days of each other, to bargain for the same model of car.

Ayres and Siegelman's results occasioned much indignation in the media. Evidence of price discrimination is a complicated thing, though, difficult to reduce to a sound bite. As Ayres pointed out, his results did not necessarily imply what many were assuming—that dealers were prejudiced and wanted to exploit blacks and women. The dealers often steered the volunteers to salespeople of their own race and gender "who then proceeded to give them the worst deals." Blacks actually got better deals from white dealers, and women got better deals from men.

In 1996 Pinelopi Koujianou Goldberg published another price discrimination study that appeared to overturn any conclusions drawn from Ayres and Siegelman. Instead of doing an experiment, Goldberg used the Consumer Expenditure Survey to check what buyers nationwide had paid for new cars from 1983 to 1987. Goldberg found no statistically significant price differences between blacks and whites, or between men and women. This had liberals pointing to Ayres-Siegelman as proof of the continuing burden of discrimination, conservatives pointing to Goldberg as demonstration that things aren't so bad, and mainly a lot of people scratching their heads at yet another case of dueling scientific studies.

Goldberg argued that the contradiction can be reconciled. It is necessary, first of all, to understand why car dealers bargain in the first place. Cars are interchangeable, mass-produced products with factory warranties. There's no reason one new car should sell for a different price than the identical one parked next to it. The vast majority of American buyers insist they hate bargaining. One popular make, Scion, caters to that distaste with no-haggle pricing.

According to a dealer quoted by Ayres, the reason for bargaining is simple. Car selling is a "search for suckers." Some customers will pay full sticker price, out of ignorance or neurotic aversion to bargaining. There aren't many customers like this, but they account for a disproportionate share of a dealership's profits. Ayres reported that some dealerships earn half their profit on 10 percent of their sales.

Earlier this year, I asked a car dealer during an interview whether the bulk of his profits are concentrated in a few sales. He told me that his dealership made a substantial number of "sucker" and "non-sucker" sales. He added, "My cousin, however, owns a dealership in a black neighborhood. He doesn't sell nearly as many [cars], but he hits an awful lot of home runs. You know, sometimes it seems like the people who can least afford it have to pay the most."

Goldberg found more variance in the prices paid by blacks and women. There were more outliers paying high prices among these groups than among white men, even though the average sales price was nearly the same for all groups. This could account for the difference between the two studies. In Ayres and Siegelman's experiment, everyone was required to use the same negotiation strategy. This was intended to reveal whether dealers treated minorities differently, and it did. But the experiment wasn't designed to test whether black and female buyers bargain differently than white males.

One plausible guess is that many dealers believed in the "sucker theory." Therefore, they quoted many high initial prices to minorities (in Ayres-Siegelman). Buyers quoted a high initial price tended to bargain longer and harder than buyers quoted a good price. This erased most of the evidence of racial and gender bias (in Goldberg).

If nothing else, this shows how complex price discrimination can be. It's possible that some dealers weren't even aware of a sucker theory. Their price quotes may have been statistically biased by race and gender without any conscious intention.

Ayres found that one bit of information was worth $319 to buyers across genders and races. Volunteers who said they had already taken a test drive paid an average of $319 less than those who didn't, and this was statistically significant. It's not hard to understand why this makes dealers anxious to close a deal.

**Forty-seven**

# Pricing Gender

A group including Sendhil Mullainathan and Eldar Shafir conducted a particularly ambitious experiment in the fall of 2003. They got permission from a large consumer lender in South Africa to test a grab bag of psychological tricks in its junk-mail pitches for loans. The lender was offering the equivalent of American payday loans—short-term cash for the working poor, at loan shark rates.

The lender sent letters offering a special interest rate to 53,194 past customers. Among other factors, Mullainathan and Shafir's team tested the effect of having a photograph in the mailing. They found stock photos of pleasant, smiling faces and put them in the lower right corner of the letter, near the signature. This implicitly suggested that the person depicted was a bank employee, maybe the one who had written the letter.

Half the photos were of men, and half were of women. Some recipients got a photo of someone of their own gender and some of the opposite gender. Since race affects everything in South African society, they tested that too. They used photos of blacks, whites, Indians, and mixed-race people.

An economist would say that a photograph should have no bearing on a reasonable person's decision to take out a costly loan. An advertiser or a con artist would differ, insisting on the value of a pretty face or an ethnic shill. Mullainathan and Shafir were interested in putting an exact value on any effect the photos had. In order to do that, each letter offered a randomly assigned interest rate. In South Africa's consumer loan business, it is customary to quote a monthly rate of simple (not compounded) interest. The tested rates ranged from 3.25 to 11.75 percent a month. For these customers, the 3.25 percent was a true bargain, less than half the company's usual minimum. The 11.75 percent was the customary maximum rate offered to the least creditworthy borrowers.

As you'd expect, customers were more likely to take up low-interest offers than high ones. By tracking the response to specific letters, the researchers were able to tell which factors had motivated customers to apply for loans. They found that gender mattered and race didn't. The gender effect was strictly a guy thing. At a given interest rate, male customers were much more likely to take out a loan when the letter had a female photo. For female customers, the photo didn't matter.

There is such a tradition of selling with sex, of bikini models draped over the tractor-trailer, that you may get the wrong idea about this experiment. The photos were simply black-and-white headshots of businesslike young women. The men who received letters with these generic female photos were more likely to apply for loans than those who received a letter with a male photo or none at all. There was no meaningful difference in response rates between the male-photo and no-photo letters. That indicates it was the female gender that mattered and not simply "putting a human face on an impersonal corporation."

Here's the really incredible thing. Mullainathan and Shafir's group calculated that adding a female photo to letters addressed to men generated the same volume of additional loan applications as lowering the interest rate 4.5 percentage points. That's a difference of 4.5 percentage points *a month*. It would be 54 percent more a year.

"Why?" is the toughest question in psychology. South Africans are exposed to Calvin Klein ads, *The Family Guy*, and hard-core porn. It is safe to assume that the customers weren't making a rationalization along the lines of "I'll get to meet this hot babe, and that'll be worth paying a killer interest rate." They couldn't have been conscious of basing financial decisions on the photos at all.

Whether to toss junk mail or read it is normally a split-second decision. One possible explanation is that men simply like pictures of women, and this caused a few more to read the letter rather than trash it. Pictures of men don't have the same effect on women, or so it would seem.

Another hypothesis (not mutually exclusive) is that the photos primed automatic patterns of gender behavior. Men believe women to be weak bargainers (or act as if they do—this may all be unconscious). Putting a woman's face next to a given interest rate identifies it as a good deal. It's almost as if the woman is a human reference price, saying "This rate is cheaper than what you'd get from a man." This doesn't exhaust the possible psychosexual explanations. In many a social context and experiment, men are competitive with other men, less so with women. Seeing the woman's picture may relax the usual anxiety about getting the best possible interest rate.

A little photo = massive incremental profits. There's got to be a catch. Shafir's group combed the data for evidence that something, *anything*, was not as it appeared. They wondered, for instance, whether it was possible that the customers who "fell" for the pictures were poorer credit risks. Their reaction to the photos could be symptomatic of bad financial decision making generally. This could erase any hoped-for extra profit.

The researchers found no statistical evidence that the customers susceptible to the female photos differed in income level, education, or payback rates of the loans taken out. On the contrary, the photos were more effective at raising profit than simply raising the interest rate. A loan company that charges a higher rate will have fewer customers, for one thing, and those customers paying the higher rate are normally more likely to default. The photos allowed the company to attract more customers at high rates *without* increasing the default risk. Such is the power of gender.

# Forty-eight

# It's All About Testosterone

Terence Burnham of Harvard's Program for Evolutionary Dynamics conducted a much-discussed experiment on testosterone and bargaining. It was an ultimatum game in which the proposers each had $40 to split. They were required to choose between keeping $15 for themselves (leaving $25 for the responder) and keeping $35 ($5 for the responder). This forced the proposer either to be more generous than he probably wanted to be, or to be dangerously stingy, inviting a veto. The other novelty was that all the players were male, and they submitted saliva samples to be tested for testosterone content. This allowed Burnham to analyze the game behavior by testosterone level.

Of seven responders classed as high testosterone, five rejected the insultingly low $5 offer. Of nineteen other men, of average or low hormone level, only one rejected the $5 offer. A high-testosterone minority did 80 percent of the vetoing.

This is provocative because the veto is the emotional core of the ultimatum game. Everything else follows from it by mere logic. Proposers are "generous" to insure themselves against a veto. Gender differences in game play may reflect a common belief that women are less likely to veto. Similar behavior operates whenever people set a price. The vetoing responder exemplifies the bargainer who storms away from the table; the angry guy down the block who cancels his cable TV because they raised his rates; the tax protester who'd sooner bankrupt himself with attorney fees than pay his taxes. He's the ultimate price-sensitive consumer, the one willing to reject a too-high price even at a ruinous cost to himself. He's usually a man.

Burnham believes that responders veto to avoid appearing submissive. Concepts like money and logic and fairness came late in human evolution. The emotional behavior seen in the ultimatum game and in real-world price setting is presumably grounded in more basic and biological motives. In market societies, money is a medium of social dominance, a way for alpha males to impress potential mates by ritually emasculating rivals. It is no coincidence that a man who pays too high a price "gets screwed."

The threat of a veto has a deterrent effect out of proportion to how often it's exercised. Everyone is less inclined to make unfair offers and set unfair prices because they know they might not get away with it. In that sense, the high-testosterone minority helps create our world of prices.

Testosterone is responsible for male sexual development and for libido in both genders. It plays an important role in social dominance behaviors. The expression "testosterone poisoning" evinces the common belief that too much male hormone leads to impulsive, unprovoked aggression. Nearly as old as this idea is skepticism about it. Most of the experiments have been done on animals, and human research is occasionally embroiled in gender politics. Some worry that a testosterone-aggressiveness link would "excuse" men for inexcusable behavior. (Another view is that it would supply scientific proof that men are pigs.)

Under the best of circumstances, it is a challenge to isolate the effects of a hormone on human behavior. It is known that testosterone levels affect behavior *and* vice versa. After Brazilian soccer fans watched their team beat Italy for the 1994 World Cup, the Brazilians' testosterone levels went up, one study claimed, while those of the Italians went down. Similar results have been reported for successful and unsuccessful London financial traders.

In animals and humans, there seems to be a stronger case linking testosterone to aggressive *responses* (to another's provocation) than to initiating conflicts. A Swedish study in the 1980s failed to find evidence that high-testosterone youths were more likely to pick fights with other boys. It did find that they were more likely to talk back to teachers.

There have been ultimatum game experiments in which subjects were dosed with testosterone. "We essentially create alpha males in the study," Claremont Graduate University neuroeconomist Paul Zak said of one. In the ultimatum game, administered testosterone has about the same effect as the naturally occurring kind, rendering responders more likely to veto low offers.

Harvard psychologist Elena Kouri and colleagues devised a game in which each player sat isolated in front of a button. They were told that by pushing the button, they could reduce the amount of money paid to an unseen partner. The partner had a similar button and could retaliate, reducing the subject's payoff. The game was thus like a nuclear standoff. Nobody should be the first to push the button.

Just to make things interesting, Kouri's group told the subjects that their partner *had* pushed the button. The subjects who had been given testosterone were more inclined to retaliate massively with repeated button pushes. However, the testosterone group was not more likely than the placebo group to be the *first* to push the button.

Social dominance is a relative thing. The alpha male is the one who has more (females, money, power) than any other male around. Absolute numbers don't matter so much. When two stags fight over a female, the goal is not a win-win solution. It is to do better than the other male does. Put that in the context of the ultimatum game: It doesn't help to win a nickel when a rival gets 95 cents. Better that neither should get anything. This is the perspective that testosterone promotes.

It's like the joke about a hunter in the north woods who puts on a pair of expensive Nikes. "Hey, why the running shoes?" his buddy asked.

"That's in case we meet up with a grizzly bear," the man said.

"You think you can run faster than a bear?"

"I don't have to run faster than a bear," the man explained. "I just have to run faster than you."

So, okay, you're negotiating a price and would like to know how aggressive you can be. It would be helpful to know the other guy's testosterone level, right? You might be able to get a clue just by looking at his ring finger.

1. *Look for a wedding ring.* Studies show that married men have lower testosterone levels than single men.

2. *Check out how long the ring finger is relative to the index finger.* The ratio of the ring finger to the index finger is determined by prenatal

exposure to the androgens that determine gender. A number of recent studies have reported that men with long ring fingers (relative to the index) excel at competitive sports and deal making, and are more likely to reject low offers in the ultimatum game. A Cambridge University group headed by John Coates examined financial traders and found correlations between ring-to-index-finger ratio and trading success, and also between testosterone levels and trading success.

As a tentative rule, you may have the best luck driving a hard bargain with a man whose ring finger is short (compared to the index) and has a wedding ring on it.

# Forty-nine

# Liquid Trust

Many hormones come in yin and yang pairs. For price decisions, testosterone appears to have a complement in oxytocin. Isolated by Vincent du Vigneaud in 1953, oxytocin is released naturally during childbirth and breast-feeding. It helps foster an immediate emotional bond between mother and child. Both genders produce oxytocin, and like testosterone, it is both cause and effect of behavior. Oxytocin levels rise during sex and other forms of intimacy. When administered in the lab, oxytocin increases trusting behavior in money decisions.

Paul Zak is credited with coining the term "neuroeconomics." He has found that dosing ultimatum game players with oxytocin massively increases generosity. In a 2007 experiment conducted with Angela Stanton and Sheila Ahmadi, oxytocin boosted proposer offers 21 percent (from an average of $4.03 with a placebo to $4.86 with the oxytocin).

Oxytocin didn't affect the responder's minimum acceptable offers (as testosterone does). Zak's group also tried a dictator game and found no significant effect for oxytocin. Their conclusion was that oxytocin affects *strategic* money decisions, those in which someone has to consider how his or her actions will make another person feel. When oxytocin levels are high, proposers are more empathic, and this promotes generosity.

Zak's interest in price decisions dates to high school. He was working at a gas station outside Santa Barbara when a customer came in and said he'd found a string of pearls on the bathroom floor. Had anyone reported it lost? Soon the phone rang, and the caller said he'd lost the pearls, bought as a gift for his wife. Zak told him they had it. Great, the guy said, promising a $200 reward. He'd be there in thirty minutes. Meanwhile, the finder announced he had an important job interview and had to leave. He agreed to split the reward with Zak, fifty-fifty. Zak agreed, handing over $100 from the cash register in exchange for the pearls. Needless to say, the guy who "lost" the pearls still hasn't showed. The pearls were worth about $2. This "ultimatum game" is also known as the pigeon drop, and it's one of the oldest cons in the book.

That tale is worth keeping in mind when evaluating some of the products inspired by Zak's research. Internet retailers are now hawking oxytocin sprays to salespeople hoping to cut more and better deals. (Zak, of course, has nothing to do with the products.) One such spray, with the promising name Liquid Trust, runs $49.95 for a two-month sup-ply ("100% Money Back Guarantee!"). The website includes the usual gamut of testimonials, one from a bartender who claims the spray made his tips increase fivefold. It offers this advice:

HOW SALESPEOPLE USE LIQUID TRUST
Apply Liquid Trust every morning after showering.
Use it with your favorite cologne or perfume.
Throughout the day, a scentless mist of Oxytocin will be released from you.
Be yourself at sales meetings and discover how strongly prospects want to buy from you. Instead of feeling suspicious of you, they are now strangely attracted to you and your product.
Do you send thank you cards to prospects and clients? Spray some Liquid Trust on the envelope and see the magic happen. Even though they cannot smell it, Liquid Trust is there and working to increase trust in you.

The effect of oxytocin in the ultimatum game is so dramatic that, I suspect, few researchers doubt it could in principle affect business deci-sions. That part of the claim isn't necessarily crazy. What *is* crazy is the spray bottle. In Zak's experiments, 40 international units of oxytocin was sprayed directly into the nostrils. Good luck explaining that to the client from Buffalo. The Liquid Trust marketing implies that you can use it like a botanica's money-drawing spray. Well, not really. Oxytocin isn't volatile. Spritzing yourself or a thank-you note isn't going to have much effect on anyone else. Most of the recommended uses would expose the user more than the unsuspecting "victim." Even if the spray did work, the user would be the one willing to give away the farm.

# Fifty

# The Million-Dollar Club

In 1997 a General Electric subsidiary made an uncharacteristically generous wage offer. Jerry Seinfeld, star of NBC's hit sitcom, announced his intention to quit. He was making an unprecedented $1 million an episode. NBC responded with an offer of $5 million an episode if only Seinfeld would do one more season.

The offer penciled out. NBC was earning something like $200 million a year from *Seinfeld* advertising and syndication. That meant that each of a season's twenty-two episodes brought in about $9 million profit. Rather than forgo that windfall, the network was willing to be hyperfair—to surrender over half of its profit to the star.

Seinfeld passed. He stood firm on his intention to quit while his show was still funny. Inevitably, word of the NBC offer leaked out. It was soon all over the entertainment news. The network brass must have hoped that everyone would appreciate that *Seinfeld* was a special case and that a blue-sky $5 million offer did not set a precedent.

Actors at all levels of the TV food chain thought otherwise. Over the next few years, star—and sidekick—salary demands escalated as never before. In 2002, the leads of *Friends* collectively bargained their way to $1 million per episode. That was $1 million *each* for the six "friends." Ray Romano was making $800,000 an episode for *Everybody Loves Raymond*, and *Frasier's* Kelsey Grammer was the leader with $1.6 million an episode. James Gandolfini shut down *The Sopranos* after he found out he was only making as much money as the housekeeper on *Frasier*.

What is a TV star worth? For that matter, what's a construction foreman, ballplayer, or U.S. president worth? Labor economics treats salaries as the outcome of a reasoned trade-off between the supply of talent and the demand for it, or between the desire for leisure and the desire for money to buy things. More recently, behavioral economists have assembled a case that salaries can be as arbitrary as prices. "Wage earners, we suspect, do not have a good idea of what their time is worth when it comes to a trade-off between consumption and leisure, and do not even have a very accurate idea of what they could earn at other firms," wrote Dan Ariely, George Loewenstein, and Drazen Prelec. "In other words, workers care about changes in salary but are relatively insensitive to absolute levels or levels relative to what comparable workers make in other firms." They note that the coherent arbitrariness of salaries is tacitly recognized in an old one-liner: A wealthy man is one who earns $100 more than his wife's sister's husband.

The inflation-adjusted pay of top earners has varied fantastically. Consider CEOs. The Economic Policy Institute calculates a number of widely followed ratios. According to the institute, in 2005 America's top executives were earning about 1.8 times as much as their counterparts in the United Kingdom, and four times as much as Japanese CEOs. Another benchmark is the ratio of American CEO pay to that of an average worker (see below). In 2007, this stood at 275. It's changed a lot. It was around 50 in the Reagan era and 25 in the 1960s.

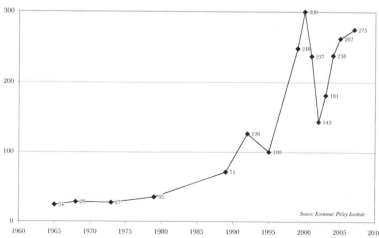

In the early 1990s, Senator Ted Kennedy led a chorus bemoaning the rise. Average workers had just about kept pace with inflation in the previous generation, while CEO pay had about doubled. The U.S. Congress responded with a 1993 law eliminating certain tax deductions above the million-dollar salary threshold.

Instead of reining in CEO salaries, the million-dollar threshold seems to have functioned as an anchor. The law broadcast to the more backward parts of the corporate world that seven-figure salaries were *possible* (so why not *me?*). In 1989, four years before the law, that ratio stood at 71. By 2000 it had surged to around 300. "In the hall of fame of unintended consequences," said Nell Minow of the Corporate Library, a management oversight group, "that has to rank right near the top."

The class war between labor and management has opened a new front, between management and shareholders. In response to shareholder concerns about allegedly insupportable CEO pay, the Securities and Exchange Commission issued new disclosure rules on executive compensation. "I absolutely thought [pay] would go down because the disclosures would be so embarrassing," recalled Graef Crystal, an architect of those disclosure rules. "But it turned out that when somebody is hauling in $200 million, he's not embarrassable."

As CEO of Apple Inc., Steve Jobs takes a salary of $1 a year. His real compensation comes mainly in the form of vested restricted stock. This came to $647 million in 2006, or about 11.6 percent of Apple's $5.60 billion profit. Apple was forking over a tenth of everything it made.

The "Lone Ranger theory" asserts that the CEO is primarily responsible for a company's stock market value. It is not too hard to believe that with Jobs and Apple; the two are almost synonymous in the public mind. In 2008 a succession of rumors, conference calls, and leaks about Jobs's allegedly failing health hammered Apple's stock value. Some statistical studies purport to find a strong correlation between chief executives and stock value, even for the garden-variety CEO less in the public eye than Jobs.

Accept the Lone Ranger theory, and almost any CEO paycheck becomes conceivable. The quintessential example is Jack Welch. In his twenty years at GE, the company's market value zoomed from $14 billion to $500 billion. "What's a CEO worth for such an achievement?" asked George Mason University economist Walter E. Williams recently. "If Welch was paid a measly one-half of a percent of GE's increase in value, his total compensation would have come to nearly $2.5 billion, instead of the few hundred million that he actually received."

The trouble with the Lone Ranger theory is that it's tough to say how much of the rise was due to Welch and how much to (for lack of a better word) luck. Inflation alone would have doubled GE's value from 1981 to 2001. Presumably Welch doesn't deserve credit for that. Nor does he deserve much (any?) credit for the bull market that increased S&P stocks ninefold in that time frame. Legacywise, Welch had the incredible fortune of retiring at just the right time, five days before 9/11. GE owned insurance companies that lost $600 million in World Trade Center claims and billions over the next few years. But that wasn't Welch's problem, nor were the miserable markets of the 2000s.

Under Welch's successor, Jeff Immelt, GE's market value has dwindled to about $96 billion. You might say Immelt is the Bizarro Jack Welch. On his watch, over 80 percent of stockholder wealth vanished into thin air. By the Lone Ranger theory, *it's all Immelt's fault.*

Now of course that's ridiculous. Immelt is a talented and hardworking manager, some say as good as Welch was. Immelt probably wouldn't have much patience with the proposition that he should be reimbursing GE shareholders for their losses rather than drawing a salary. He would insist the decline in GE's stock value was bad timing or bad luck. How much of Welch's success was good luck? Is there any way of telling?

Appearing on MSNBC's *Hardball* in 2006, Welch invoked the corporate world's favorite populist analogy. CEOs are like baseball players, Welch said. "Should there be a ratio with these people? Everybody is out with their checkbook and wallets trying to get somebody, and agents are having a ball. They've got three weeks. No different, Chris."

Host Chris Matthews helpfully recalled a famous Babe Ruth quip. Asked why he earned more money than the president, the Babe supposedly replied, "I've had a better year than he has."

Actually, baseball salaries are just as mystifying as CEOs'. In 1922 Babe Ruth became the first player to make $50,000 a year. That's about $640,000 in today's dollars. In 2000 Alex Rodriguez signed a ten-year

contract giving him over $25 million a year. When you adjust for infla-
tion, A-Rod is making 49 times what the Babe was. Why? It can't just be
the steroids. Neither Rodriguez nor baseball has nearly the pop culture
footprint that Babe and the game once had. Since the 1920s, the U.S.
population has increased (by a factor of about 3), and television has
broadened the baseball audience and ad revenues. Still, there's an awful
lot more ways to spend leisure time these days.

Suppose we take baseball salaries, adjust for inflation, and divide by
Babe Ruth's inflation-adjusted 1922 salary. Call the result the "Babe
Ruth ratio." The table shows that salaries have burgeoned even as baseball has become an ever smaller part of the sports and entertainment
universe.

| Year | Player | Salary (nominal dollars) | Babe Ruth ratio |
|------|--------|--------------------------|-----------------|
| 1922 | Babe Ruth | $50,000 | 1.00 |
| 1947 | Hank Greenberg | $100,000 | 1.49 |
| 1979 | Nolan Ryan | $1,000,000 | 4.63 |
| 1991 | Roger Clemens | $5,380,000 | 13.27 |
| 2000 | Alex Rodriguez | $25,200,000 | 49.17 |

There is great coherence in wage structures. Major leaguers make
more than minor leaguers, and Immelt makes more than his vice presi-
dents, who make more than the guy making lightbulbs on the assembly
line. It is less clear how arbitrary salaries are. We all like thinking that
pluck prevails over luck and that "star" talent can turn around a ball club
or a multinational corporation. But it's tough to prove that, much less to
put a price on it.

In practice, top salaries are left to the judgment of a few. The rest of
us shrug and figure that the numbers can't be too unreasonable. That's
not just supply and demand, it's anchoring and adjustment.

# Fifty-one

# The Mischievous Mr. Market

Late at night, you're flipping channels and see an infomercial for an amazing new product. It's a little black box that, exactly once a year, spews out a crisp new dollar bill. It's perfectly legal, the pitchman assures you, and you can spend the dollar any way you want. The box will produce a dollar this year, next year, the year after that, and so on—forever! How much would you pay for a product like that?

One way of evaluating the box's worth is to imagine how you could spend a dollar a year. You could tip someone you don't especially like for Christmas . . . supersize one fast-food order next summer . . . You will probably conclude that the box is worth paying at least a dollar for. You'll recoup that the first year, and then afterward it will all be gravy.

You might also reason that the box is worth less than your current life expectancy in dollars, since that limits how many dollar bills you can collect. (For the record, the box keeps working after the original owner's death, and you're allowed to bequeath it to anyone you like.)

Your price for the box should have something to do with your capacity for delayed gratification. That is, you're giving up some of your hard-earned money *now*, in the form of the purchase price, to enjoy a stream of earnings *later*. Someone who is focused on the present moment—the guy who's always maxing out his credit cards—might not be interested in the box at all. Someone who looks at the long term might be willing to pay a relatively high price.

One thing is clear. There is no indisputable right price. Were you to do an anchoring experiment, you would probably find that you could manipulate prices. Should the infomercial's studio audience clamor to buy the box for $2, most viewers would probably accept that as a reasonable price. Should the crowd decide it's worth $60, that would be reasonable too.

Benjamin Graham, the legendary founder of value investing, had a simple answer for the value of a $1-a-year black box: $8.50. Graham was actually speaking of stocks. A share of stock produces a stream of future earnings. Divide the share price by earnings per share, and you have the price-to-earnings (P/E) ratio. It tells how much buyers are paying for a dollar of future income. Since the black box produces an income of $1 a year, the price you pay for it, in dollars, would equal its P/E ratio. In Graham's analysis, the stock of a company with no earnings growth should sell at a price-to-earnings ratio of 8.5.

Graham caricatured the price psychology of investors in "Mr. Market." He's a well-meaning doofus who shows up at your door every weekday offering to buy or sell stock. Every day, Mr. Market's price is different. Though Mr. Market is persistent, you don't have to worry about offending him. Whether you accept his offer or not, Mr. Market is sure to be back tomorrow with a new price.

According to Graham, Mr. Market really doesn't know what stocks are worth. The smart investor can profit from this. One day Mr. Market will offer to buy your stock for more than it's worth. *You should sell!* Another day, Mr. Market will offer stock for less than it's worth. *You should buy!*

It worked for Graham and for a few of his disciples, like Warren Buffett. Following Graham's advice is easier said than done. During bull markets, less kindly known as bubbles, Mr. Market shows up every day quoting sky-high prices that only seem to go up. Most investors find it impossible to ignore the siren song. How could Mr. Market be so very wrong, day after day?

As early as 1982, Stanford economist Kenneth Arrow identified Tversky and Kahneman's work as a plausible explanation for stock market bubbles. Lawrence Summers took up this theme in a 1986 paper, "Does the

Stock Market Rationally Reflect Fundamental Values?" Summers (now head of the National Economic Council for the Obama administration) was the first to make an extended case for what might now be called the coherent arbitrariness of stock prices. From day to day the market reacts promptly to the latest economic news. The resulting "random walk" of prices has been cited as proof that the market knows true values. Because stock prices *already* reflect everything known about a company's future earnings, only the unpredictable stream of financial news, good and bad, can change prices.

Summers astutely pointed out that this "proof" doesn't hold water. The random walk is a *prediction* of the efficient market model, just as missing your train is a prediction of the Friday-the-13th-is-unlucky theory. You can't prove anything from that, as there could be other causes producing the same effect. Summers sketched one, a model in which stock prices have a strong arbitrary component yet adjust coherently to the day's financial news.

Summers's idea is a scary one. It proposes that stock prices could be a collective hallucination. Once investors stop believing, it all comes tumbling down. "Who would know what the value of the Dow Jones Industrial Average should be?" asked Yale's Robert Shiller in 1998. "Is it really 'worth' 6,000 today? Or 5,000 or 7,000? Or 2,000 or 10,000? There is no agreed-upon economic theory that would answer these questions."

**P/E Ratio of S&P Index**

Source: Robert J. Schiller

The chart on the previous page shows the history of the price-to-earnings ratio of the stocks in the S&P Index. The S&P is a broad index computed from 500 companies presently accounting for about three-quarters of American's total investment in domestic stocks. Like the price for a black box, the P/E ratio represents a capacity to defer gratification. You might think that this capacity would be a constant of human nature or else a slowly changing variable of American consumer culture. The chart tells a different story. The jittery line is the P/E ratio (using average earnings of the previous ten years, a measure Shiller uses). For reference, the thick gray line shows the historical average P/E ratio of about 16. In the past century, the S&P's P/E ratio has varied from less than 5 (in 1920) to over 44 (in 1999).

Some of that variation is reasonable. The market is trying to predict *future* earnings. When the outlook for earnings growth is good, the P/E ratio should be higher, and when the outlook is grim, it should be lower. Interest rates and tax rates should affect the ratio, too. But observers from Graham to Shiller have argued that much of the ratio's variability is due to investor mood swings. Were the P/E and sales volume figures scanner data, a price consultant would conclude that the "consumers" of corporate earnings have remarkably inelastic demand. This was roughly Graham's assessment. He believed that most investors made emotional decisions to plunge into or out of the market and didn't care much about the price.

There has been much experimental work on the psychology of market prices. Colin Camerer has used Caltech's Laboratory for Experimental Economics and Political Science to create super-simplified stock markets. The lab is the creation of Charles Plott, one of the economists who replicated preference reversal. It consists of a grid of cubicles, each with a computer. Every keystroke or mouse action is recorded and archived by software. At the end of an experiment, the researcher can play back everything that happened like a TiVo'd movie.

In one of Camerer's experiments, participants were given two shares of a virtual security and some real money. They were allowed to buy and sell the shares among themselves over a 75-minute period. All they had to do was type in buy or sell orders. The software matched buyers to sellers and executed deals. The students understood that they would be walking away with any money they retained or earned in the course of the experiment.

Since the security was imaginary, the participants could not look up its price. They had to assign their own bid and ask prices. Camerer made this as easy as possible. Each share paid a dividend of 24 cents like clockwork, every five minutes throughout the experiment. Therefore, anyone holding Camerer's stock throughout the experiment would collect exactly 15 dividends of 24 cents each, for a grand total of $3.60. By the standards of a strict value investor, the stock was worth $3.60 at the outset and shed 24 cents each time it threw off a dividend. A chart of the stock's value over time would look like a descending staircase.

Once the experiment began, the stock started trading at about $3. Ten minutes later, it had risen to around $3.50. It hovered around $3.50 for practically the whole experiment. Reality took hold only in the last ten minutes. With the end drawing near, prices crashed.

Camerer debriefed his subjects. "They'd say, sure I knew the prices were way too high, but I saw other people buying and selling at high prices. I figured I could buy, collect a dividend or two, and then sell at the same price to some other idiot. And, of course, some of them were right. As long as they got out before the crash, they earned a lot of money at the expense of the poor folks who were left holding the bag."

This is known as the "greater fool" theory. People bought tech stocks in the late 1990s, and real estate in the 2000s, not necessarily because they thought the prices were sensible but because they believed they could sell them at a profit to an even greater fool.

What about value investors (those rare souls who are nobody's fool)? In Camerer's experiment, they were left on the sidelines. Value investors would have sold their two shares early, after the "true" value dipped below $3.50. Thereafter they had no more stock to sell and no intention of buying at the prices sellers were demanding and getting. Value investors thus had no effect on the market price.

After many repetitions of this experiment, Camerer has learned how to turn bubbles on and off. The best way to create a bubble is through inflation. Camerer has run experiments in which he keeps pumping money into the virtual economy, much as the government does by printing money. With more money chasing the same number of stock shares, the prices rise. Camerer has found that he can then bring back the same set of subjects and run the experiment again, this time *without* inflation. "If they've lived through an inflationary experience," Camerer explained, "then we've planted a belief in their minds the prices will rise, like seeding clouds to make rain." The result is that "prices do rise, because of this self-fulfilling prophecy based on their common experience."

Shared experience is also key to turning bubbles off. Run the experiment, then bring back the same group for a repeat. This time, investors remember the previous experiment's crash and are more cautious. They don't bid up the prices so high, and they start heading for the exits soon. The crash is milder and earlier. Try the experiment a third time, and there's no crash at all. The prices hardly deviate from the value investor line.

The misfortune of the real market is that memories are short and too much time elapses between bubbles. The investing public as a whole never has the opportunity to make decisions, see their consequences, and change their behavior accordingly. There is no Groundhog Day, and thus investors are condemned to repeat Black Monday.

# Fifty-two

# For the Love of God

In June 2007, the British artist Damien Hirst unveiled the world's most expensive work of art. Titled *For the Love of God*, it was a platinum skull encrusted with 8,601 ethically sourced diamonds. The asking price was £50 million—about $100 million, or more than the gross domestic product of Kiribati. "The skull is extraordinary," said pop artist Peter Blake, adding the jaw-dropping observation that "the price seems right."

Hirst had built a career on creative pricing. When collector Charles Saatchi commissioned the original Hirst shark in formaldehyde, *The Physical Impossibility of Death in the Mind of Someone Living* (1991), the artist set the price at an intentionally outrageous £50,000. That sum was intended as a publicity gimmick, to boost the career of an unknown artist. It worked. *The Sun's* headline was 50,000 FOR FISH WITHOUT CHIPS. In 2004 Saatchi sold the shark to hedge fund manager Steve Cohen for $8 million. The price doubtless would have been higher had the shark been in better shape. Something in the formaldehyde mix was wrong, and the shark had partly decayed. (Hirst replaced it with a brand-new shark for Cohen.) By 2007, other Hirst works of taxidermied live-stock and pharmaceutical cabinets were regularly selling for high seven figures. The price of the 2007 skull was exactly a thousand times that of the 1991 shark. Hirst said the skull's diamonds alone set him back $24 million. "We wanted to put them everywhere," he explained. "They go underneath, inside the nose. Anywhere you can put diamonds, we've put diamonds."

"Is it beautiful?" asked *The New York Times's* Alan Riding. "Compared with what?" Critics have had a love-hate relationship with Hirst, and the skull brought out the haters. "As a trope for human folly and cupidity, a glittering death's head is as tired as it gets," complained *Time* magazine's Richard Lacayo. London critic Nick Cohen snarked, "The price tag is the art."

Hirst's supporters argued that that was the point. The work was a commentary on the insanity of the art market. It was not accidental that Hirst chose to use diamonds, a mineral whose price has been kept artificially high by a cartel. Meanwhile, Hirst detractors predicted that the skull was not long for this world. The diamonds would hold their value better than Hirst's reputation. Whoever ended up owning the thing would one day rip it apart to sell the diamonds.

The skull's short history already tells a tale of that elusive phantom, price. A few days after the work went on view at London's White Cube gallery, Hirst announced that it was "almost sold . . . someone is very interested." The British press named onetime pop idol George Michael as a possible buyer. Then things got quiet. It appeared that the gallery was having a hard time closing the deal. At the end of August, it was announced that the skull had sold to an investment group for the full price of £50 million. A gallery spokeswoman refused to identify the buyers or give further details, except to say that the buyers planned to resell the artwork at a later date.

Resell it at a *higher price*? In any case, it was odd that those financial whizzes had paid full price. Galleries customarily offer a discount to big collectors. Someone buying the world's most expensive artwork would appear to qualify.

The identity of the buyers leaked out. They were none other than Damien Hirst, Jay Jopling (owner of White Cube gallery), and Frank Dunphy—Hirst's accountant. It wasn't hard to understand what happened. The skull's price was an anchor, a canny way of boosting the value of other Hirst pieces. Whether the $100 million skull ever sold was not so important as preserving the credibility of the price. As a publicity gimmick, the skull succeeded too well. Its failure to sell became news. So Hirst and company cooked up a financial arrangement that allowed them to announce that the skull had sold at full price.

It was probably a smart move. On September 15, 2008, Sotheby's began an unprecedented sale of 223 new works by Damien Hirst (and his studio). It was the day Lehman Brothers filed for bankruptcy, but 98 percent of the works sold. The top lot was a pickled "Golden Calf" with 18-karat gold leaf horns and hooves. It went for £10.3 million, setting an auction record for Hirst. The two-day sale total was £111.5 million, or about $200 million.

As for the skull, accountant Dunphy conceded that it's still for sale: "By the way, the price of it now would be double."

## Fifty-three

# Antidote for Anchoring

Thomas Mussweiler, Fritz Strack, and Tim Pfeiffer of the University of Würzburg did an experiment in which they took a ten-year-old car (an Opel Kadett E) to sixty German mechanics and car dealers. A researcher claimed that his girlfriend had dented the car and said he was debating whether it was worthwhile to have it fixed. He mentioned that he thought the car was worth 2,800 marks. "According to your opinion, is this value too high or too low?" He then asked the expert to estimate the current value of the car and the repair cost.

The experts' average estimate of the car's value was 2,520 DM. The researchers went through the same spiel with a different set of mechanics, this time saying they thought the car was worth 5,000 DM. These experts' average estimate was 3,563 DM. That's over 40 percent more.

So far, this was yet another demonstration of anchoring among real-world professionals. The mechanics had the actual car right in front of them. They were still swayed by a casually mentioned price.

The purpose of the Würzburg experiment was to test an antidote for anchoring. It's a technique called "consider the opposite." Hearing a high value for the car prompted the mechanics to think of reasons that might justify the high price. Those reasons remained in active memory and easily accessible, skewing estimates toward the anchor.

This suggests that anchoring could be diminished simply by asking the mechanics to think of reasons the anchor figure might be *wrong* ("consider the opposite"). To test this, the researchers canvassed two further groups of mechanics. After each researcher said he thought his car was worth 5,000 DM (or 2,800 DM), he continued, "A friend of mine mentioned yesterday that he thought this value is too high (low). What would you say argues against this price?"

This prompted the mechanic to list reasons. Then, as before, the researcher asked the mechanic for his estimate of the car's value.

The high-anchor mechanics now gave an average estimate of 3,130 DM (compared to 3,563 without the antidote question). The low-anchor people estimated an average of 2,783 DM (versus 2,520 before). In each case, "consider the opposite" reduced the power of the anchor and made the estimates less extreme. Furthermore, the mechanics who named more reasons were less affected by the anchor.

"Consider the opposite" is not a new idea. In 1650 Oliver Cromwell made a famous plea to the elders of the Church of Scotland: "I beseech ye in the bowels of Christ, think that ye may be mistaken!" Cromwell was trying to convince them that they were wrong to threaten the Commonwealth by supporting Charles II as king. His words fell on deaf ears, yet they echoed down the ages. Three centuries later, Judge Learned Hand said that Cromwell's plea should be "written over the portals of every church, every school, and every courthouse, and, I may say, of every legislative body in the United States."

Judge Hand's point was, look before you leap to conclusions. By considering how your judgment may be wrong, you might come up with an overlooked reason and change your mind. Cromwell and Hand were speaking of the conscious side of decision making. Mussweiler's group believes that "consider the opposite" affects the intuitive and automatic side of decision making too. It can diminish the power of anchors on prices. That can be useful in negotiations, in which it's not always possible to name a number first.

There was an alternate explanation for these results. Half the time, the researchers went to the mechanics with an extremely optimistic view of the car's value. The mechanics may not have wanted to burst a customer's bubble ("the customer is always right"). The researcher had indicated that he would repair the dent only if the car was worth enough to justify it. Any mechanic wanting work would have had reason to give a high estimate. This would have created the same effect as anchoring, making it impossible to tell how much was unconscious heuristic and how much was conscious salesmanship.

Likewise, the researcher's mention of a skeptical friend could have been taken as a conversational hint that he would not be insulted by a dissenting view. By encouraging candor, this could have accounted for the pattern of results seen.

To address this, Mussweiler's team did a second experiment. University of Würzburg students were asked to estimate the chances that German politicians would win the next election. They were asked, for instance, whether Chancellor Kohl's chances were greater or less than 80 percent . . . and then asked what they thought his chances were. This showed the usual anchoring effect. When another group of students was asked to first name three reasons why Kohl would lose, the anchoring effect was greatly diminished, much as it had been with the car mechanics.

"Consider the opposite" is easy to apply. When a dealer, vendor, agent, or employer quotes you a figure, take a deep breath, and don't make any commitments until you've had a chance to think of reasons why that price might be unreasonable. Make a game out of it: try to think of as many reasons as possible.

Many hard-headed businesspeople dismiss such exercises in positive (negative) thinking. But anchoring is real, and we can use all the help we can get.

# Fifty-four

# Buddy System

Car dealers are not crazy about the new breed of buyer who shows up with a sheaf of printouts. Today, anyone with an Internet connection can unlock the mysteries of car dealer profits. A few dollars buys an up-to-the-moment accounting of the dealer cost for any model and its options, including destination charges and holdbacks and other unadvertised incentives. The organizations that sell the information typically advise buyers that 5 percent of the dealer's true cost is a "fair" profit. Consequently, the buyer with printouts comes in knowing exactly what he intends to pay. He is the opposite of a "sucker" and demands a different strategy.

With such customers, bargaining is less about naming prices and more about challenging facts. Dealers have become masters at denial. They insist that *Consumer Reports* is wrong, the Internet is wrong, the buyer's math is wrong. The information in the printouts is outdated (things change daily!); that particular model is on back order locally; whatever the printout says, other buyers are willing to pay the dealer's price and more. The buyer who's done his homework may not quite believe any of this, but it's impossible to discount it completely. There comes a point at which the buyer is so sick of having his every fact and reasonable surmise contradicted that he gives in. He pays more than 5 percent over printout cost. Maybe he believes the dealer's denials, and maybe he just doesn't care anymore.

Car buyers are often advised to use the "buddy system." They should bring along a spouse or friend for support and a second opinion. The buddy system is a social form of "consider the opposite." Your friend provides an opposite opinion to the dealer's where needed. I suspect that the best-informed buyers are the least likely to take advantage of the buddy system, though. When one is armed with the facts, emotional support can seem like a luxury and not a necessity.

One of the classic experiments of social psychology bears on the buddy system. In 1951, Solomon Asch, then at Swarthmore College, published a study of group pressure on decisions. The subjects of his experiment, all undergraduate men, sat at a table with eight others whom they believed to be fellow subjects. These others were confederates playing along with Asch. The experimenter presented a "vision test" consisting of a series of eighteen simple diagrams. The figure below is a facsimile, reproduced at the actual size Asch used. Take a good look at the line on the far left. Now, which of the three lines on the right is the same length as the line on the left?

1          2          3

The group of confederates unanimously agreed the correct answer was . . . line number 1. The experiment was to test whether the lone subject would go along with the outrageously wrong crowd.

The confederates were told to give the correct answers to the first two diagrams, then to alternate wrong and right answers to the following diagrams. The true subject was seated so that he would be one of the last to answer. In the crucial cases, the subject spoke after hearing a number of the ringers give the same *wrong* answer.

Overall, subjects gave a wrong answer 32 percent of the time. Seventy-four percent gave the wrong answer at least once, and a sizable minority caved in to peer pressure three-quarters of the time. That's amazing when you consider how simple the exercise was. In a control group, without confederates, virtually everyone gave the right answer all the time.

Asch tried to uncover what the subjects deferring to group opinion believed. He heard three categories of explanation. Some said the group's bogus answers *did* look wrong, but they reasoned that the group was likely to be right.

Another set of subjects told Asch they *knew* they were right and the group was wrong; they just didn't want to make waves.

Finally, there was a minority of the truly brainwashed. Even after Asch explained the experiment, they insisted they saw the lines the way the group reported them to be.

Participants who gave correct answers often confessed to uncertainty. "You're *probably* right, but you may be wrong!" one told the group during the experiment. Later, after learning the truth and feeling "exultant and relieved," this person told Asch, "I do not deny that at times I had the feeling: 'The heck with it, I'll go along with the rest.' "

Asch also did experiments involving sympathetic "buddies." In one, there were two uncued subjects among Asch's minions. This had a dramatic effect on the line-comparison task. The percentage of wrong answers dropped from 32 percent to 10.4 percent.

The uncued subject who answered first did not have the benefit of hearing the other give the correct answer. He sometimes caved in and went with the majority's answer. That in turn made it harder for the second subject to dissent. Asch therefore tried another setup in which the "buddy" who answered first was a confederate instructed to give the correct answer. This halved the error rate again. The percentage of errors on the part of the one real subject was cut in half, to 5.5 percent.

Asch tried to find out how big a group it takes to sway a lone subject. The answer was three.

When the subject was alone, practically everyone gave the right answer. The situation wasn't much different when the subject went mano a mano against a single confederate giving a wrong answer (*The other guy's crazy!*). When it was two against one, the error rate rose. Nearly the maximum effect occurred with three confederates. It didn't change much with greater numbers. In this case, three is a crowd.

In a car dealership, the "truth" is negotiable. A buddy would be a good idea, and two buddies, achieving that seemingly magic threshold of three, couldn't hurt.

## Fifty-five

# The Outrage Theory

Joan, an inquisitive six-year-old, pried open the "child-proof" cap of an allergy medicine. She swallowed enough pills to require several days in the hospital. Joan's parents sued the drug company. At the trial, company documents submitted in evidence showed that the drug maker was aware that its child-proof caps, though "generally effective," had a failure rate "much higher than any others in the industry." Poor Joan remained "deeply traumatized by pills of any kind. When her parents try to get her to take even beneficial medications such as vitamins, aspirin, or cold remedies, she cries uncontrollably and says she is afraid."

Care to guess how much Austin, Texas, jurors thought Joan's case was worth? Try $22 million.

"Joan" is not a real child, but she figured in an intriguing experiment conducted by Daniel Kahneman, David Schkade, and Cass Sunstein. They wanted to see whether they could induce jurors to award crazy, *Liebeck v. McDonald's* amounts for injuries that weren't all that serious. They also wanted to test a simple, practical remedy, a way of bringing sanity and justice to our tort system.

In their 1998 article, "Shared Outrage and Erratic Awards: The Psychology of Punitive Damages," Kahneman, Schkade, and Sunstein describe their "outrage theory" of jury awards. In effect, they say, juries are psychophysics experiments in which the jurors are rating the outrage they feel at the defendant's actions. The problem is that they are forced to translate outrage into dollars, a magnitude scale with no standard of comparison. "The unpredictability of raw dollar awards," write the authors, "is produced primarily by large (and possibly meaningless) individual differences in the use of the dollar scale."

Citing the work of S. S. Stevens (an authority previously unknown to legal scholars), they show that jury awards have many of the features of magnitude scales. The error or "noise" in psychophysical estimates rises in proportion to the size of the estimate itself. This is true whether you're looking at the repeated estimates of one subject or comparing the estimates of different people. With juries, this would mean that the largest jury awards are likely to be the most off the mark. Furthermore, juries are small samples. Twelve people is too few to sample public opinion with any degree of accuracy. This leads to anomalously high awards (and also to ridiculously low awards, though they rarely get any press).

The experiment involved 899 residents of metropolitan Austin, Texas, which was then Schkade's home base at the University of Texas. The participants were recruited from the voter rolls, the same population that would be called for jury duty. They met in a downtown hotel and read descriptions of hypothetical lawsuits in which a wronged individual was suing a corporation. In each scenario, the corporate defendant had been found guilty and was liable for $200,000 in compensatory damages. The participants' role was to set punitive damages.

One set of participants did this by naming a dollar amount. Another group was asked only to rate the defendant's actions on a scale of "outrage." This was a category scale ranging from 0 ("Completely Acceptable") to 6 ("Absolutely Outrageous").

Still another group was asked to rate the degree of punishment justified, from 0 ("No Punishment") to 6 ("Extremely Severe Punishment").

In each case, the mock jurors filled out their questionnaires alone, without conferring with anyone else. Nevertheless, there was a strong correlation between responses on the two category scales of outrage and punishment. But the dollar awards, the magnitude scale, were all over the map. This is what you'd expect from psychophysics.

The tale of poor little "Joan" got the highest average damage award in dollars. This was absurd for several reasons. It didn't represent a consensus. Though $22 million was the mean award, the median amount was only $1 million. Half the participants thought the damages should be a million or less. There were even a few jurors (2.8 percent) who thought the award should be *zero*.

Do these disparate dollar amounts indicate a split jury? Not so much as you'd think. Looking at the category scale ratings, you find a decent consensus. Jurors rated the drug company's actions an average of 4.19 out of 6 on the outrage scale and 4.65 out of 6 on the punishment scale. Responses were scattered in a rough bell curve around the means.

The consensus fell apart only when jurors had to name a dollar amount. Everyone did this differently. You could have two people in complete agreement that the case merits "severe punishment." To one, severe punishment means $100,000; to another, it's $100 million. The average for Joan was high because of a few high rollers who awarded astronomical sums. Their valuations had an outsized impact when the numbers were averaged.

Now, of course, real juries don't average each juror's separate figure. They debate the amount among themselves and try to talk reason into outliers (as was reported to have happened with the *Liebeck v. McDonald's* jury). Nevertheless, there have been studies showing that deliberating groups, and juries in particular, have no better judgment than the individuals making them up. "Wisdom of crowds" effects work best when everyone makes an independent judgment. Juries may even magnify the biases of their members. This could happen when the first juror to speak names an outrageously high number. "The unpredictability and characteristic skewness of jury dollar awards is readily replicated under laboratory conditions," the research team wrote. "Under these circumstances, we expect judgments to be highly labile, and therefore susceptible to any anchors that may be provided in the course of the trial or in jury deliberations."

The $22 million average award for Joan was way out of line with the dollar amounts for other scenarios. The best proof of that is an alternate version of the Joan scenario that was tested. Some of the jurors read a description in which Joan's overdose permanently weakened her respiratory system, "which will make her more susceptible to breathing-related diseases such as asthma and emphysema for the rest of her life." These jurors gave an average award of $17.9 million—*less* than in the scenario where she's just afraid of pills. This doesn't mean that anyone actually thought permanent respiratory damage was less serious. No juror saw both versions of the story; it was a different randomly chosen group of Metro Austin voters each time (just as would be the case with a real jury). Apparently, the group given the less serious scenario happened to have a few more high rollers.

Again, category scale ratings were more consistent. The permanent-respiratory-damage version of Joan's tale got higher outrage and punishment scores than the afraid-of-pills version, just as logic would demand. These judgments scarcely varied with income, age, or ethnic group. (Women were somewhat harsher than men in their punishment scale ratings.) The researchers concluded that punishment scale ratings "rest on a bedrock of moral intuitions that are broadly shared in society."

And dollar amounts don't. The root of the crazy-jury-award problem is that there is no consensus on how to convert outrage into dollars.


Kahneman, Schkade, and Sunstein used these empirical findings to tackle some philosophical issues. Justice requires consistency, they wrote. Identical crimes deserve identical punishments. In practice, however, every situation is different. That's why we need juries to ensure that punishments accord with community sentiments.

The article sketches several possible reforms. Most involve having jurors use a category scale rather than a dollar scale to set damages. They would rate the degree of punishment, not the dollar amount. Then a "conversion function" would translate the punishment rating into dollars. This conversion function could be set by a judge or a legislature, for instance. A more democratic idea is to let the people decide. Judicial districts, or the nation as a whole, could do experiments much like that done in Austin, to determine just how the public thinks punitive intentions ought to translate into dollar amounts. The empirically derived conversion function would then be used in setting damage awards. The experiment could be repeated every so many years to make sure that the function remained in sync with the public's thinking. As Kahneman, Schkade, and Sunstein wrote, "Many new possibilities are opened by raising the question 'How can we obtain the best estimate of community sentiment?' " It's something that the present system doesn't even ask.

# Fifty-six

# Honesty Box

Eric Johnson is a boyishly enthusiastic Columbia Business School professor, old enough to have taken a Ph.D. under Herbert Simon and to have collaborated with Amos Tversky. One of Johnson's grad students, Naomi Mandel, was reading about priming and wondered whether it would work with a Web page. "I said it was a very cute idea," Johnson recalled, adding, "It will never work." Mandel did some pilot studies anyway. "We just kept doing it, it kept working," Johnson said. "I never expected the data to be that clean, the effect to be that powerful."

Mandel and Johnson's experiment, published in the *Journal of Consumer Research*, has already made a stir in the marketing and Web design communities. The Internet has long been promoted as a level playing field for shoppers. No longer must the consumer accept the prices of the few nearby bricks-and-mortar stores. The Web buyer can comparison-shop the wide world, free of the manipulation of high-pressure sales tactics . . . Well, scratch that last part. Mandel and Johnson found that manipulation could be as simple as a line of HTML code.

Seventy-six undergraduates participated in what they were told was a test of online shopping. Each visited two (bogus) websites, one offering sofas and the other cars. Using the information on the site, they were to choose between two models in each product category. Each posed the familiar trade-off of price versus quality, and the shoppers had to determine which was more important.

The experiment's one variable was the background image of each site's home page. Some visitors to the sofa site saw a wallpaper design of pennies on a green background. Others saw a background of fluffy clouds (suggesting comfort). The car site had either green dollar signs or red and orange flames.

Incredibly, the cheap car's market share rose from 50 percent (with the flames wallpaper) to 66 percent (with the dollar signs). The cheap sofa's share surged from 39 percent (clouds) to 56 percent (pennies).

"It is important to note that our priming manipulation was not subliminal," Mandel and Johnson wrote. "All of our subjects could plainly see the background on the first page, and many recalled the wallpaper when asked." But when asked whether the wallpaper could have affected their decision, 86 percent said no. "This lack of awareness," Mandel and Johnson wrote, "suggests that . . . electronic environments may present significant challenges to consumers."

A second, expanded experiment involved 385 Internet users who had agreed to participate in a survey. The participants were adults from across the United States whose average age and income approximated those of the Internet population. A questionnaire gauged how much experience each user had in buying cars or sofas. This time the website kept track of how much time was spent on each page. The priming effect showed up clearly in the novice buyers' browsing history. When primed with money images, they spent more time comparing prices.

The expert buyers' browsing behavior was not so influenced by the wallpaper images. Their choices, however, were. Mandel and Johnson suspect that seasoned consumers find it easier to judge which sofa is softer or which car is cheaper. The priming affects the facts that experts retrieve from memory. Novices have to construct a similar level of competence from HTML pages. The end result was about the same. The background images could nudge shoppers from a "price matters" to a "quality matters" mind-set.

Already marketers are starting to use the science. Johnson is now helping a major German automaker—he's not allowed to say which one—redesign its website. These applications raise ethical questions transcending the age-old ones of advertising. Our ethics, no less than our economics, has been rendered partly obsolete by decision research. For the most part, we still subscribe to the idea that people have a fixed set of values. Anything that covertly changes those values (a "hidden persuader") is judged to be a violation of personal freedom. The reality is that what consumers want is often constructed between mouse clicks. All sorts of details of context exert measurable statistical effects. No consumer wants to feel "manipulated." But to some degree, that is like a fish not wanting to feel wet.

Consider this: Mandel and Johnson's experiment included a control group of subjects who saw neutral versions of the websites with no background images at all. Their choices were not much different from those of subjects who saw the money backgrounds. This raises the possibility that American consumers focus on price by default. It takes a "manipulation" to get them to pay attention to anything else.

Our bustling, profit-obsessed society rarely grants leisure to ponder "Just how important is money?" That doesn't make the question go away; it just relegates it to the realm of the unconscious and automatic. In a 2004 experiment at Stanford, Christian Wheeler and colleagues had volunteers perform a "visual acuity test" before playing the ultimatum game. The vision test consisted of sorting photographs by size. It was simply a pretext to show the subjects some photographs without arousing suspicions. One group saw pictures relating to business (a boardroom table, a dress suit, a briefcase), and another saw images with no connection to business or money (a kite, a whale, an electrical outlet). This made a difference in how they subsequently played the ultimatum game. Proposers seeing the business pictures offered 14 percent less to responders than the control group's proposers did. The players seeing kites or whales were more inclined to offer fifty-fifty splits rather than to shave a few pennies off. "These are pretty big effects with pretty minor manipulations," Wheeler said. "People are always trying to figure out how to act in any given situation, and they look to external cues to guide their behavior particularly when it's unclear what's expected of them. When there aren't a lot of explicit cues to help define a situation, we are more likely to act based on cues we pick up implicitly."

For many years, a common room at Newcastle University has used an "honesty box" to pay for tea and coffee. Anyone is free to help himself to hot beverages and to deposit the posted price in the honesty box. This saves hiring a checker to take people's money, something that would cost more than the sums collected anyway. The honesty box is a vernacular dictator game. Everyone is supposed to chip in their fair share. They have the option of contributing less, or nothing at all. Based on dictator game research, you'd expect that honesty box compliance has a lot to do with whether people are watching. A 2006 experiment found something more startling.

Psychologists Melissa Bateson, Daniel Nettle, and Gilbert Roberts replaced the poster listing beverage prices with their own posters, identical except for an image banner at the top. Some posters featured a pair of eyes looking directly at the viewer. Others showed an image of flowers. Bateson's group alternated the posters weekly and counted each week's money to detect any differences in payment behavior. (They used milk consumption as a check on how much coffee and tea was actually dispensed.) On the average, they found, people contributed 2.76 times as much money when the eyes posters were up, compared to the flowers posters. "I was surprised how big the effect was as we were expecting it to be subtle," Bateson said. Workplace honesty switched on and off like a lamp.

Dictator game players are apparently conscious of not wanting to appear selfish. No such explanation is possible with a mere poster. "Our brains are programmed to respond to eyes and faces whether we are consciously aware of it or not," Bateson proposed. Another experiment found a similar effect with mirrors. While it's not news that mirrors can change behavior (think of all the ceiling mirrors in honeymoon suites), the effect may be more encompassing than imagined. C. Neil Macrae, Galen V. Bodenhausen, and Alan B. Milne found that people in a room with a mirror were less likely to cheat or display gender or race prejudice, more likely to be helpful and work harder. "When people are made to be self-aware," Bodenhausen said, "they are likelier to stop and think about what they are doing." That in turn can lead to "more desirable ways of behaving."

# Fifty-seven

# Money, Chocolate, Happiness

Charles Darrow patented the game of Monopoly in the Depression year of 1935. He did not actually invent the game but appropriated someone else's idea. Monopoly is an allegory of free-market capitalism, and whether it's for it or against it is never made clear. Though it glorifies profit, the word "monopoly" has always been pejorative. One of the game's precursors, "The Landlord's Game," had an overtly socialist theme.

Monopoly has succeeded because it is so effective at creating an immersive, internally self-consistent world. Players forget whatever is in their wallets and use "Monopoly money," a term that has come to be a metaphor for the unreality of price decisions. The prices in Monopoly make no sense ($100 houses), but the ratios of prices tell the player all he needs to know. The Monopoly universe makes sense on its own terms— as does the planet you and I live on and try to make sense of.

Monopoly figures in a 2006 experiment by Kathleen Vohs, Nicole Mead, and Miranda Goode. It was one of a number of manipulations they used to prime their subjects to think of money. One group played Monopoly; another sat next to a computer monitor with a screen saver of floating dollar bills; another was exposed to a poster of foreign currency; another was asked to imagine being poor or being rich. Vohs's team found that all these kinds of money priming had similar effects. They made people less social and less cooperative. Those subjects who were primed with money:

- *Wanted more "personal space."* The experimenter told each participant she would have a getting-acquainted conversation with another subject. She was instructed to grab a chair from the corner of the room and position it next to her own. Then the experimenter left to fetch the other person. The object of this was to see how closely the subject would position the chair to her own. Those who had been exposed to money primes put more distance between the chairs.

- *Wanted to work alone.* Volunteers were assigned a minor chore and given the option of working alone or with someone else. The vast majority of those exposed to the money screen saver opted to work solo. A majority of the people with a fish screen saver or blank screen wanted to work as a team. There was really no reason *not* to work as a group. The amount of work was the same, whether one person did it or two.

- *Wanted to play alone.* Subjects filled out a questionnaire in which they had to pick their favorite out of pairs of activities. Each choice posed a solitary pastime (reading a novel) against a social one involving family or friends (going to a café with a friend). The participants exposed to money were more likely to choose the solitary activities.

- *Were less helpful to a stranger.* Participants walking from one room to another witnessed a manufactured accident in which a confederate dropped twenty-seven pencils. The people exposed to money primes were less likely to help pick up the pencils, and they picked up fewer pencils on average.

- *Didn't ask for help themselves.* Subjects were given a task that turned out to be impossible. The point was to see how long it would take them to ask someone for help. The people exposed to money primes struggled 48 percent longer before asking.

- *Gave less to charity.* The experimenter gave subjects a private opportunity to donate to the University Student Fund. The participants had no reason to think this was part of the experiment. The money-primed group donated only 58 percent as much as the control group did.

"Others have interpreted our findings as demonstrating that money makes people selfish," Vohs and colleagues wrote. "The idea that money leads to greed or selfishness seems to be part of modern Western cultural lore." They go on to argue that their findings resist quite such a simplistic interpretation.

They asked their participants to describe their emotional states. There was no meaningful difference between those who had and hadn't been exposed to money primes. Thinking about money *didn't* make people "distrusting of others, anxious, or prideful," which might have accounted for some of the findings.

A selfish individual might have immediately demanded help with a difficult task, or might have shared work with a partner to get out of doing it himself. Instead, the money priming made people want to act as individualists. They were like stereotypical male drivers, unwilling to ask anyone else for directions.

Vohs's group adopted *self-sufficiency* as a better term for the behavior triggered by money primes. Like Monopoly, self-sufficiency is a "game" loosely deriving from features of the market economy. The rules of the game say you play as an individual and that money is the way you keep score. Interactions with other players follow rules of fairness and reciprocity. (You don't steal someone's Monopoly money, even though everyone knows it's fake.) To play the game is not to believe that money is everything and personal relationships don't matter, but it is to adopt this as a temporary shared fiction.

Self-sufficiency is just one of the many games humans can play. It plays a big role in American culture and in cultures around the globe with strong market economies. "Priming effects may provide one of the mechanisms by which culture works," Daniel Kahneman has suggested. "Some cultures provide the equivalent of constant reminders of money. Other cultures remind you that there are eyes looking at you. Some make you think in terms of 'we,' others in terms of 'I.' "

Chocolate may be the second most popular motivator in behavioral decision experiments. The way people react to chocolate is much like the way they react to money. They try to be rational chocolate maximizers, constructing magnitude scales of truffles. Sometimes chocoholic avarice makes people do strange things. It is instructive to watch these "economics" experiments in chocolate. There is an uncanny sense of recognition, like watching chimpanzees "ape" too-familiar human foibles.

Christopher Hsee and Jiao Zhang did an experiment in which Chinese university students had to choose between these two options:

(a) to recall and write down a failure in their lives, while eating a large (15-gram) Dove chocolate.
(b) to recall and write down a success in their lives, while eating a small (5-gram) Dove chocolate.

The students had to eat as they wrote and couldn't save the chocolate to take home. As you've probably guessed, most (65 percent) chose the bigger chocolate. The mental commandment appears to be *Never choose less chocolate when you can have more.*

Hsee and Zhang did not give all their participants a choice. Another group was simply told that they had to write about a personal failure while eating a 15-gram chocolate. Afterward, they rated the experience (of writing while eating chocolate) on a 9-point scale of *extremely unhappy* to *extremely happy*. Still another group was instructed to perform option (b) and to rate it on the same 9-point scale. The people assigned (b) were overwhelmingly happier than those assigned (a). The (b) people had a pleasant task *and* got to eat chocolate while doing it. They didn't know their chocolate was smaller than it might have been.

That knowledge—that there was more chocolate to be had—was a spoiler. People couldn't bring themselves to accept less chocolate. Hsee and Zhang see their experiment as "a microcosm of life." Money is the bittersweet chocolate of contemporary existence. We spend our lives searching for the lowest price, the highest salary, the most money— numbers by which to validate our happiness. In the familiar and facile analysis, money doesn't buy happiness, and you can't put a price on human relationships. Hsee and Zhang are adding a radically new gloss on these homilies. It is not so much money as magnitude scales that are the root of all evil. Because money is a number, and numbers are easily compared, it gets too much decision weight compared to everything else. Prices make us a little more thrifty, greedy, and materialistic than we would be in a world without prices.

The most unanswerable question in behavioral decision theory is *What do people really want?* You can't assume that prices *or* choices reflect true values. The problem seems to lie in the question itself. It assumes a fictitious mental exactitude in which there are sharply defined and context-free "true values." There is more evidence than ever that this is not so. Preference reversals (in the broadest sense) are the human condition.

Over the years, behavioral decision theorists have made an art form of devising clever preference reversals. I will close with one of Hsee's. You have your choice of two equally fine chocolates. One is small and shaped like a heart. The other is big and shaped like a cockroach. Which do you prefer?

Hsee has posed this dilemma to students and friends, finding that most choose the cockroach chocolate. The kicker is that when Hsee asks people which chocolate they would *enjoy* more, most admit it's the smaller one, shaped like a heart.

# Notes

# Sources

# Index

# Notes

## 1. The $2.9 Million Cup of Coffee

3 "Stella Awards": See www.stellaawards.com.

3 "defective": Gerlin 1994.

4 180 to 190 degrees: Marinello 1995.

4 Settled for less than $600,000: Robbennolt and Studebaker 1999, 354.

4 Negotiations with McDonald's, settlement amounts: Gerlin 1994.

4 "The jar used to have": *Marketplace* radio show, American Public Media, Jan. 8, 2009. Available at marketplace.publicradio.org/display/web/2009/01/08/pm_ deceptive_packaging/?refid=0.

4 New Skippy jar has 16.3 ounces: *Consumer Reports*, Jan. 2009, 63.

5 physics degree from the University of Chicago: www2.simon-kucher.com/partners /frank-luby.html.

5 Kellogg's phased in thinner boxes: Hirsch 2008.

5 Zest shrinkage: *Consumer Reports*, Oct. 2008, 63.

5 Puffs shrinkage: *Consumer Reports*, Aug. 2008, 67.

6 sixty Ph.D.s: Frank Luby, e-mail, Jan. 29, 2009.

6 SKP history, party at castle: www2.simon-kucher.com/SimonKucher_2008.pdf.

6 SKP clients: www2.simon-kucher.com/clients/.

## 2. Price Cluelessness

9 Coherent arbitrariness: See Ariely, Loewenstein, and Prelec 2003.

10 FREE $ HERE: Southern 1960, 25.

11 "At the time, it was not considered": Kahneman, interview August 30, 2008.

11 Wheel-of-fortune study: Tversky and Kahneman 1974, 1128.

12 23 percent: About 45 of the 192 U.N. member nations are African, counting Mada- gascar and Cape Verde. See www.un.org/members/list.shtml.

12 "The default reaction": Kahneman, interview August 30, 2008.

13 San Francisco, Beatles questions: See Orr and Guthrie 2006, 597, quoting an unpublished study by George Quattrone et al., cited in Plous 1993.

13 "a number in people's heads": Wilson, Houston, et al. 1996, 397.

14  "We suggest that because anchoring effects": Ibid., 398.
14  "Cheap seats don't sell": www.talkinbroadway.com/rialto/past/1999/8_5_99.html.
14  $480 tickets for *The Producers*: Finn 2003.
15  "I now scale all the Orchestra": www.talkinbroadway.com/rialto/past/1999/8_5_99 .html.
15  "advertisers and used-car salesmen": Stanford University News Service 1996.
16  "old hat to marketing experts": Cox 2005, 375.
16  "Many people like myself": Johnson, interview Sept. 9, 2008.


### 3. The Myth of the Boomerang

17  This discussion of the legal ramifications of anchoring is indebted to Orr and Guthrie 2006.
17  Damage awards: Malouff and Schutte 1989, 495.
17  "boomerang effect": Malouff and Schutte 2001, 492.
18  Results of Chapman and Bornstein study: In the paper, the awards are expressed as natural logarithms of the award amounts. I have converted them to dollar amounts.
18  "almost constantly in pain": Chapman and Bornstein 1996, 540.
19  "How likely is it": Ibid., 524.
19  increased modestly with the size of the award: This was significant only at the $p < 0.09$ level (meaning, there's a 9 percent chance this result could have been the result of chance alone).
19  "entrepreneurs": Marinello 1995.
19  "The More You Ask For": Chapman and Bornstein 1996.
19  Jurors should not directly set damage awards: Kahneman, Schkade, and Sunstein 1998; see also Kahneman, Ritov, and Schkade 1999.
20  Birds dying in oil pools: Desvousges, Johnson, Dunford, et al. 1992; see also Kahneman, Ritov, and Schkade 1999.


### 4. Body and Soul

25  Description of optometrist experiment: Glanz and Lipton 2003, 138–41.
25  "Would you please come over here": Ibid., 138–40.
26  "So I began to think": Benson 2003.
27  Fake optometrist office credited with saving lives: Ibid.
28  S. S. Stevens biography: Miller 1975.
29  "I was directed to Dr. Stevens's office": Ibid., 429.
29  "Psychophysics is an exact doctrine": Fechner 1966, 8.
30  "Carving Meat and Setting the Table": Heidelberger 2004, 43.
30  "But then I ruined my eyesight": Fechner's autobiographical note is translated in ibid., 322.
30  "People called Fechner a fool": quoted in ibid., 323.
30  *Little Book on Life After Death*: See ibid., 44.
31  "How much stronger or weaker": quoted in Stevens 1975, 59.
31  Plateau biography: Ibid., 7; en.wikipedia.org/wiki/Joseph_Plateau.
33  power curve rule can be stated in seven words: Stevens 1975, 16.
33  "As an experimental fact": Ekman and Sjöberg 1965, quoted in Stevens 1975, 266.

## 5. Black Is White

34  "tell us how matters stand out there": Stevens 1975, 18.

34  "For example, is it the differences": Ibid., 18.

35  "The print in this book looks black": Ibid., 79.

35  Category and magnitude scales: There is a concise, nontechnical discussion of response scales in Kahneman, Schkade, and Sunstein 1998, 53–55. See also Stevens 1975.

35  suggested that he try dispensing with the modulus: Stevens 1975, 26–27.

36  "I liked the idea": Stevens 1975, 28.

37  "Black is white": Ibid., 79. See also the description of this demonstration in Stevens 1961, 85–86.

## 6. Helson's Cigarette

38  "amateurish experiments": Guildford 1979, 628.

38  "he did have several experiences": Bevan 1979, 155.

39  Experiments with weights: Helson 1947.

39  Fechner and Holbein Madonna: Stevens 1975, 228.

39  "Instead of asking students": quoted in ibid.

39  "The fact is that common principles exist": Hunt 1941, 395.

40  Contrast and assimilation: Ibid., 401.

40  "recency, frequency, intensity": Avant and Helson 1973, 440.

## 7. The Price Scale

42  "Smitty was a close man with a dollar": Miller 1975, 431.

43  "Suppose I were to tell you": Stevens 1975, 6.

43  $35 to $50: Ibid.

44  Indow study: Ibid., 235–37.

44  Social status: Ibid., 244–45.

44  Seriousness of theft: Ibid., 258–59.

## 8. Input to Output

49  Mob types: See Tuohy 2001. Goffstein took over the Riviera after his boss, Gus Greenbaum, was murdered by the Chicago mob (apparently).

49  Murphy biography: See Wikipedia entry, "Charles B. G. Murphy," en.wikipedia .org/wiki/Charles_B._G._Murphy. Murphy's Wood Kalb Foundation also supported psychiatry at Yale.

49  He came up with Ward Edwards: Paul Slovic interview, July 1, 2008.

49  Murphy asked to use the Four Queens for experiments: Phillips and von Winterfeldt 2006.

51  "revealed preference": See Samuelson 1947.

51  "impossible for the behavior": Simon 1945, 79.

51  "How any grown-up": quoted in Mirowski 2002, 454.

52  "Do you think the ratio": Phillips and von Winterfeldt 2006.

53  "was nutty": Barbara Tversky interview, July 8, 2008.

53  "occasional colorful and forthright behavior": Phillips and von Winterfeldt 2006.

53  "Ruth's excellent, if often exotic cooking": Ibid.

53  Paper titled "Behavioral Decision Theory": Edwards 1961.

53  ("a marvelous person"): Lichtenstein interview, July 28, 2008.

53  "was actually interested in the economic theories": Ibid.

53  "comparing incomparables": cited in Goldstein and Einhorn 1987, 250.

53  "Always choose the bet": Edwards 1961, describing "A Study of Decision Making Under Risk" by C. H. Coombs and D. G. Pruitt, published 1960 as Report No. 2900-33-T of the Willow Run Laboratories, University of Michigan, Ann Arbor.

54  1954 *Psychological Bulletin* article: Edwards 1954.

54  "The method of those theorists": Ibid., 381.

55  "a pale wraith of a creature": Heilbroner 1999, 37.

55  "Von Neumann and Morgenstern": Edwards 1961, 474.

## 9. Lunch with Maurice

59  *Econometrica* article: Allais 1953. For another influential challenge to Savage's axioms, see Ellsberg 1961.

59  Zeckhauser conceived Russian roulette as example of certainty effect: Kahneman and Tversky 1979, 283.

60  "His paradox was great": Anonymous interview and e-mail.

60  ("As a matter of fact"): Allais 1995, 252, 254.

61  Mark Machina's website: econ.ucsd.edu/~mmachina/.

61  "We choose between descriptions of options": Tversky 1996, 7.

## 10. Money Pump

62  "When we had written it up": Lichtenstein interview, July 28, 2008.

62  Article with Slovic's name first: Slovic, Lichtenstein, and Edwards 1965.

62  "I sort of followed hubby around": Lichtenstein interview, July 28, 2008.

62  "It was a terrific inducement": Ibid.

63  "I remember we were in Paul's office": Ibid.

65  127 subjects always reversed: Lichtenstein and Slovic (eds.) 2006, 54.

65  "These reversals clearly constitute": Ibid., 63.

66  *endowment effect*: The term was coined in Thaler 1980.

66  A 10/12 chance of winning $9: Lichtenstein and Slovic (eds.) 2006, 71.

66  "If the odds were . . . heavier": Ibid., 48.

67  "The strain of amalgamating different types of information": Ibid., 76.

68  Audio recording on the Web: The audio is on the Decision Research website at www.decisionresearch.org/mp3/PreferenceReversalInterview.mp3.

68  "I see. Well, how about the bid for Bet A?": Lichtenstein and Slovic (eds.) 2006, 65.

69  "Well, now let me suggest": Ibid., 67.

70  "just to make myself look rational": Ibid., 68.

## 11. The Best Odds in Vegas

71  "Roulette Bet," "designed by scientists," "A 25-cent bet": Purcell 1969.

71  "one of the few decision-making experiments": Ibid.

71 "angel" . . . "perfect for Vegas": Lichtenstein interview, July 28, 2008. Other experiments done at the Four Queens include Goodman, Saltzman, Edwards, Krantz (1979) and unpublished work by Slovic and Lichtenstein (Paul Slovic, e-mail Jan. 28, 2009).

72 Pearson . . . had read Edwards's work: Phillips and von Winterfeldt 2006.

72 occupied a balcony: Purcell 1969.

72 Profits to go to a home for unwed mothers: Ibid. Paul Slovic (e-mail, Jan. 28, 2009) is unsure whose idea this was. He doubts there were any profits after expenses.

73 Game unpopular, Ponticello wanted to improve: Slovic interview, July 1, 2008.

74 "The results of this experiment": Lichtenstein and Slovic 2006, 75.

74 "There is a natural concern": Ibid.

76 "I call them as I see them": Tversky and Thaler 1990, 210.

76 "It would be an overstatement": Lichtenstein and Slovic 2006, xvi.

76 "Each of the blind men was partly right": See Wikipedia entry, "Blind Men and an Elephant," en.wikipedia.org/wiki/Blind_Men_and_an_Elephant.


## 12. Cult of Rationality

77 "If you can't talk about a preference": Lichtenstein interview, July 29, 2008.

77 "The first time I talked about it": Lichtenstein interview, July 28, 2008.

78 "I was very young": Camerer interview, Nov. 28, 2008.

78 "would get taken advantage of in the markets": Ibid.

78 Economics and "irrationality": This capsule history is indebted to the more detailed account in Laibson and Zeckhauser 1998.

78 "to discredit the psychologists' work": Grether and Plott 1979, reprinted in Lichtenstein and Slovic 2006, 77.

79 "We knew Charlie Plott": Lichtenstein interview, July 29, 2008

79 "Plott is pretty good at spotting": Camerer interview, Nov. 28, 2008.

79 "In a very real sense": Grether and Plott 1979, reprinted in Lichtenstein and Slovic 2006, 85.

79 "Unsophisticated Subjects," other hypotheses: Grether and Plott 1979.

80 "amplifier": Colin Camerer's word, in Camerer interview, Nov. 28, 2008.

80 Admiring letters from cranks: Ibid.


## 13. Kahneman and Tversky

81 Moshe Dayan witnessed drill: Barbara Tversky, interview July 8, 2008.

81 Panicked soldier saved by Tversky: Everyone tells a slightly different version of this heroic act. This account is based mainly on Daniel Kahneman's account in Stanford University News Service 1996.

81 "Amos was something special": Sarah Lichtenstein interview, July 30, 2008.

81 "You were happy": Stanford University News Service, "Amos Tversky, leading decision researcher, dies at 59" (June 5, 1996).

81 Tversky biography: Stanford University News Service 1996; Barbara Tversky interview, July 8, 2008.

81 "The story is": Barbara Tversky interview, July 8, 2008.

81 "surprised everyone": Ibid.

82 "He didn't like to learn": Ibid.

82 "Growing up in a country": Stanford University News Service 1996.
82 Psychology department massacre; Amos one of first to get degree: Barbara Tversky interview, July 8, 2008.
82 Quiet, unsure about English: Paul Slovic interview, July 1, 2008.
82 English language of "enemy": Barbara Tversky interview, July 8, 2008.
82 "a little mechanical": Ibid.
82 "Amos's writing was perfect": Ibid.
82 "I remember walking home with him": Ibid.
83 "life-changing event": Kahneman Nobel autobiography, nobelprize.org/nobel_prizes/economics/laureates/2002/kahneman=autobio.html.
83 "I will never know": Ibid.
84 leadership test with telephone pole: Ibid.
84 "The story was always the same": Ibid.
85 "most significant intellectual experience": Ibid.
85 "It was a remarkably honest": Ibid.

## 14. Heuristics and Biases

86 "People's intuitions": Tversky and Kahneman 1971, 106.
87 Tossed coin to determine name order: Kahneman Nobel autobiography, nobel prize.org/nobel_prizes/economics/laureates/2002/kahneman=autobio.html.
87 "There was a lot of irony": Kahneman interview, August 30, 2008.
87 "In his presence": Kahneman Nobel autobiography.
87 "was the opposite of Danny": Barbara Tversky interview, July 8, 2008.
87 "a pile of money": Kahneman interview, August 30, 2008.
87 "by far the most productive": Kahneman Nobel autobiography.
87 "They were so *verbal*": Lichtenstein interview, July 29, 2008.
88 "Linda is 31 years old": Tversky and Kahneman 1983, 297.
88 "Linda is a bank teller": Ibid.
89 "a series of increasingly desperate manipulations": Ibid., 299.
89 "Argument 1. Linda is more likely": Ibid.
89 "I thought you only asked": Ibid., 300.
90 Words with r: Tversky and Kahneman 1974, 1127.
90 "the easiest to demonstrate": Strack and Mussweiler 2003, quoted in Orr and Guthrie 2006, 600.
90 "Amos and I didn't quite agree": Kahneman interview, August 30, 2008.
91 Tversky explanation of anchoring: Quattrone, Lawrence, Finkel, and Andrus 1984.
91 Einstein question: Strack and Mussweiler 1997, 442.
91 clutching at straws, "conversational hint": Jacowitz and Kahneman 1995, 1162.
92 "I didn't know about priming": Kahneman interview, August 30, 2008.

## 15. The Devil's Greatest Trick

93 "When it comes to our behavior": Carey 2007.
94 "Anchoring effects are . . . caused by the fact": Transcript of 2008 Edge Master Class, www.edge.org/documents/archive/edge253.html.
94 "What I tell you three times": Carroll 2006.
95 "There are many, many arbitrary numbers": Wilson, Houston, et al. 1996, 389.

### 16. Prospect Theory

97 "I would go batty": Barbara Tversky interview, July 8, 2008.

97 "interesting choices": Kahneman Nobel autobiography, nobelprize.org/nobel_ prizes/economics/laureates/2002/kahneman=autobio.html.

97 Tversky's idea to put a negative sign on amounts: Kahneman Nobel autobiography.

98 "We reasoned that": Ibid.

98 "Our perceptual apparatus": Kahneman and Tversky 1979, 277.

99 "extends to the domain of moral intuitions": Kahneman Nobel autobiography.

101 Loss aversion in real estate: Ibid.

101 Loss aversion their greatest contribution: Ibid.

102 "The major points of prospect theory": Lambert 2006.

102 the most cited article ever to appear in *Econometrica*: Laibson and Zeckhauser 1998, 8, which finds 1,703 citations.

102 Merckle suicide: Moulson 2009.

102 "Humans did not evolve to be happy": Camerer, Loewenstein, and Prelec 2005, 27.

103 "Many of the losses people fear most": Camerer n.d. ("Three cheers—psychological, theoretical, empirical—for loss-aversion"), 9–10.


### 17. Rules of Fairness

104 "spend a lot of money honestly": Kahneman, Nobel autobiography, nobelprize .org/nobel_prizes/economics/laureates/2002/kahneman=autobio.html.

104 Russell Sage biography: Sarnoff 1965. The amount of Sage's fortune was never made public, according to Sarnoff. Estimates range from $63 million to over $100 million.

104 "the improvement of social and living conditions": Russell Sage Foundation website, www.russellsage.org/about/history.

105 "That was the year": Kahneman interview, August 30, 2008.

105 "rules of fairness": Kahneman, Knetsch, and Thaler 1986a, 729.

105 "A hardware store has been selling": Ibid.

106 Football team question: Kahneman, Knetsch, and Thaler 1986b, S287.

106 "A severe shortage of Red Delicious apples": Kahneman, Knetsch, and Thaler 1986a, 734.

106 "We had a very good time": Kahneman interview, August 30, 2008.

107 "A company is making a small profit": Kahneman, Knetsch, and Thaler 1986a, 731.

107 Discontinuing 10 percent bonus: Ibid., 732.

107 "Conventional economic analyses": Ibid., 735; "the gap between the behavior": Ibid., 731.


### 18. Ultimatum Game

109 Plautus dates; earliest complete works of Latin: See E. F. Watling's introduction to Plautus 1964, 7–8.

109 "TRACHALIO: Right, then; listen": Plautus 1964, 131.

110 "The only share you're going to get": Ibid., 133–34.

112 "We were very pleased with the ultimatum game": Kahneman interview, August 30, 2008.

112 "My brother and I": Güth e-mail, August 13, 2008.

113   "That would have been overkilling": Strategic Interaction Group 2002.

113   "the easiest nontrivial": Güth, Schmittberger, and Schwarze 1982, 370.

113   "Are those students in Cologne stupid?": Strategic Interaction Group 2002.

113   "being quite crestfallen": Kahneman Nobel autobiography, nobelprize.org/nobel_
prizes/economics/laureates/2002/kahneman=autobio.html.

114   "All our questions on fairness": Kahneman interview, August 30, 2008.

114   ("If the other player offers you $0.50"): Thaler 1988, 197.

114   average $4.50 offered: Kahneman, Knetsch, and Thaler 1986b, S291. The authors
report three subsamples. For simplicity, I've averaged the three results (weighted by
the number of subjects in each).

114   "It's the resentment": Kahneman interview, August 30, 2008.

114   "The thing that's truly bewildering": Ibid.

114   "Is the Ultimatum Game the Ultimate Experiment?": Halevy and Peters 2007.

114   "money alone does not rule the world": Güth e-mail, August 13, 2008.

115   "Something special had to happen": Kahneman interview, August 30, 2008.

115   Boulware's negotiation strategy: See Boulware 1969.

### 19. The Vanishing Altruist

116   "If you stop construction of that skyscraper": Finch 2007; Lyons 1993.

116   Influence peddling conviction: Lyons 1993.

117   "resistance to unfairness": Kahneman, Knetsch, and Thaler 1986b, S288.

118   The definitive dictator game experiment: Hoffman, McCabe, Shachat, and Smith
1994.

119   less to do with altruism than with manners: Camerer and Thaler 1995.

### 20. Pittsburgh Is Not a Culture

121   "My Israeli game theory professor": "Mind your decisions" (blog) at mindyourdeci
sions.com/blog/2008/01/15/game-theory-tuesdays-the-ultimatum-game-and-hollywood/.

121   Four-city study: Roth, Prasnikar, Okuno-Fujiware, and Zamir 1991.

121   40 percent among Israelis: Robinson 2007, 7.

121   "visibly upset" . . . "I did not earn any money": Zamir 2000, 5.

121   "Pittsburgh is not a culture": Camerer interview, Nov. 28, 2008.

122   "We both expected the Machiguenga": Siegfried 2004.

122   "That's actually a tricky thing": Camerer interview, Nov. 28, 2008.

122   44 percent average offer for Orma: Siegfried 2004.

123   a cultural X-ray: Ibid.

123   "Offering too much money": Ibid.

123   "Adam Smith had this famous quote": Camerer interview, Nov. 28, 2008. I've corrected Camerer's extemporaneous (and near-exact) quotation from Smith's *An
Inquiry into the Nature and Causes of the Wealth of Nations*.

123   Chimp experiment: Jensen, Call, and Tomasello 2007.

124   "It thus would seem": Ibid., 109.

## 21. Attacking Heuristics

125  "I don't know how much [Amos] anticipated": Barbara Tversky interview, July 8, 2008.

125  "I am not really interested in the psychology of stupidity": Kahneman, Nobel auto-biography,  nobelprize.org/nobel_prizes/economics/laureates/2002/kahneman=auto bio.html. For more reactions from philosophers (and others) see Cohen (1981) and comments.

125  "Human incompetence": Lopes 1991, 67.

125  "evident exasperation": Ibid., 76.

126  "woefully muddled": Ibid., 65, quoting an unidentified *Newsweek* article.

126  Gigerenzer's critiques: Gigerenzer 1996.

126  "Gigerenzer was lying": The speaker requested anonymity.

126  "costly": Edwards 1954, 382.

127  "incoherence is more than skin deep": Tversky and Kahneman 1983, 313.

127  a "lapse in judgment" to be "cured": Camerer interview, Nov. 28, 2008.

127  Could not drive cars: Edwards 1975, 292.

127  "We frequently hear about human memory limitations": Ibid., 292.

127  "Not only did he not embrace it": Kahneman interview, August 30, 2008.

## 22. Deal or No Deal

129  Told few people; died three weeks after stopping going to office: Barbara Tversky interview, July 8, 2008.

130  nobody in their right mind would reject $10 or $20: Hoffman, McCabe, and Smith 1996, 292.

130  "Don't be a maryter": Ibid., 293 (footnote).

130  "almost appears to be designed": Post, van den Assem, Baltussen, and Thaler 2008, 39.

131  Average prize value of $131,477.54: This is computed from the 26 prizes of $0.01, $1, $5, $10, $25, $50, $75, $100, $200, $300, $400, $500, $750, $1,000, $5,000, $10,000, $25,000, $50,000, $75,000, $100,000, $200,000, $300,000, $400,000, $500,000, $750,000, and $1 million.

132  76 percent for expected utility v. 85 percent for prospect theory: Post, van den Assem, Baltussen, and Thaler 2008, 27.

133  "as closely as possible in a classroom": Ibid., 29.

133  "a person who has not made peace with his losses": Tversky and Kahneman 1979, 287.

## 23. Prices on the Planet Algon

134  "Here an ordinary cup of drinking chocolate": "Prices on the Planet Algon" sketch from Episode 35 of *Monty Python's Flying Circus* (first aired 1972). See montypython.50webs.com/scripts/Series_3/76.htm.

134  "relatively inexpensive!": Ibid.

135  "I was thinking about what I wanted": Ariely interview, Jan. 9, 2009.

135  MIT auction experiment: Ariely, Loewenstein, and Prelec 2003.

136  Injury, pain of removing bandages: Ariely (n.d.), "Painful Lessons."

136 reading the work of S. S. Stevens and others: Ariely interview, Jan. 9, 2009.

136 the price of everything and the value of nothing: Wilde used this phrase at least twice, in *The Picture of Dorian Gray* (1891) and *Lady Windermere's Fan* (1892). In the latter, the quote is "What is a cynic? A man who knows the price of everything and the value of nothing."

138 "Suppose that a subject": Ariely, Loewenstein, and Prelec 2003, 77–78.

138 "Coherent Arbitrariness" paper: Ibid.

138 "In a few moments we are going to play": Ibid., 80–81.

139 "pain threshold": Ibid., 93.

**24. The Free 72-Ounce Steak**

143 FREE 72 OZ STEAK: See numerous photos on Flickr.com.

143 the signature dish of the Big Texan Steak Ranch: See Wikipedia entry for "The Big Texan Steak Ranch," en.wikipedia.org/wiki/The_Big_Texan_Steak_Ranch.

143 "You don't have to eat the fat": See "Free 72 Oz. Steak" at www.bigtexan.com.

143 *Simpsons* episode about 256-oz. steak: "Maximum Homerdrive" episode, originally aired 1999.

143 Original price $9.95, success rates: See "Free 72 Oz. Steak" at www.bigtexan.com.

144 Questions about meat consumption: Jacowitz and Kahneman 1995, 1163.

145 35 percent discount on a Nikon camera: Hermann Simon interview, Feb. 24, 2009.

145 "willingness to pay": Simon 2008, 214.

146 "Imagine that you are about to purchase a jacket": Tversky and Kahneman 1981, 459.

146 "Why are we more willing": Thaler 1999, 186.

147 "What we're saying": Transcript of 2008 Edge Master Class, www.edge.org/3rd_culture/thaler_sendhil08/thaler_sendhil_index.html.

147 Professional Pricing Society, founded in 1984: See the PPS website, pricingsociety.com/Page4782.aspx.

147 Skeptical about the application of behavioral theory: See Simon 2008, 212, where he calls Thaler's "mental accounting" model a "flop" for business applications.

147 Pack of Wrigley's gum first item scanned: See Wikipedia entry for "Universal Product Code," en.wikipedia.org/wiki/Universal_Product_Code.

147 Simon-Kucher & Partners history: Hermann Simon interview, Feb. 24, 2009.

148 "Indeed, retail pricing software": Michaud n.d., 5.

148 "Pricing is a dangerous lever": Tacke and Luby n.d., 9.

148 increases profit margins by about 2 percentage points: Simon 2008, 215.

148 1 to 4 percent: Michaud n.d., 5.

**25. Price Check**

149 "There's an opportunity to make some margin back": Rendon 2009.

149 Counterclockwise shoppers spend more: Keller 2007.

150 "If you want to get my attention": CBC News 2000.

150 Beer riddle: Thaler 1983.

150 "investing in seemingly superfluous luxury": Ibid., 231.

151 Duke University beer experiment: Huber and Puto 1983, 42.

152 Taste tests show beer drinkers can't distinguish brands: Try Googling "beer blind taste test." See for instance www.strandbrewers.org/reviews/blind98.htm.

153 "safe," a "compromise" choice: Huber and Puto 1983, 38.

153 "less extreme, less expensive": Ibid., 39.


**26. Shilling for Prada**

155 "You sold one thing": Binkley 2007.

155 "with 322 black diamonds": *Robb Report*, Dec. 30, 2008, and www.hublot.com.

156 Eva Longoria photographed with Coach python bag: See www.purseblog.com/coach/eva-longoria-style-coach-python-miranda.html.

156 "a mixture of anger and happiness": Binkley 2007.

156 Breadmaker story: Shafir, Simonson, and Tversky 1993.

156 two commandments of manipulative retail: Simonson and Tversky 1992.

157 "Contrast effects are ubiquitous": Ibid., 281–82.

157 "Luxury goods prices": Von der Gathen and Gersch n.d.

158 Coach allots only one or two ultra-expensive bags: Binkley 2007.

158 over $1,700 per square foot: At its 2001 opening, Prada's SoHo store was said to have cost $40 million for 23,000 square feet. See www.galinsky.com/buildings/prada/index.htm.

158 Prada website: www.prada.com. These figures are from the U.K. online store.


**27. Menu Psych**

159 "Daniel Boulud has a restaurant": O'Dell interview, March 5, 2009.

159 Boulud hamburger, competitors: Wharton 2008; see also the db bistro moderne website at www.danielnyc.com/dbbistro.html.

160 "Places like Chili's and Applebee's": Coomes 2005.

160 *Stars, puzzles*: Hedden 1997.

160 "If you do this with three menu items": Walkup 2006.

160 "By discounting the third item": Ibid.

160 $13 for two scallops: Thaler 1999, 192 (footnote).

161 "The menu turns into a price list": O'Dell interview, March 5, 2009.

162 Scrap the leader dots: Hedden 1997.

164 "We don't want to take it off the menu": Ibid.


**28. The Price of a Super Bowl Ticket**

165 Super Bowl ticket lottery, rules: www.teamonetickets.com/tickets-101/super-bowl-tickets-lottery.html.

165 "fair, reasonable price": Krueger 2001.

165 "virtually screams for non-linear pricing structures": Butscher, Luby, Weber, and Polonetsky n.d., 6.

165 Krueger survey: Krueger 2001.

166 Members of the Miley Cyrus Fan Club: AP news story, "Hannah Montana Tickets Fuel Lawsuit," Nov. 13, 2007.

167 "Mommy get me tickets": "Craig P" comment to ibid.

167   One women won an essay contest: "Mom Goes Too Far for Hannah Montana Tix," ABC News, Dec. 31, 2007.
167   Springsteen and Ticketmaster: Phillips 2009.
167   "transaction utility": Thaler 1983, 230.
168   MRI experiment: Sanfey, Rilling, Aaronson, et al. 2003.
168   "The fact that unfair offers activate": Camerer, Loewenstein, and Prelec 2005, 48.

### 29. Don't Wrap All the Christmas Presents in One Box

169   "How much would you pay for a knife like this?": The original Ginsu commercial is on YouTube at www.youtube.com/watch?v=abLB7aTmnE4.
169   "At the end of the offer": Gottlieb 2008.
169   $50 million sales, Berkshire Hathaway acquisition: Ibid.
169   "Don't wrap all the Christmas presents": Thaler 1985, 202.
169   *Marketing Science* paper: Thaler 1985.
170   "Buy one Snuggie": www.getsnuggie.com/flare/next.
170   "Normally 1 Bottle of Mighty Mendit": www.mightymendit.com/flare/next?tag=OS%7CAF%7C.
170   "What You Get": www.buythebullet.com/whatyouget.php and www.buythebullet.com/howitworks.php.

### 30. Who's Afraid of the Phone Bill?

172   Justine Ezarik's August bill: www.youtube.com/watch?v=UdULhkh6yeA.
173   "With more than 3 million customers every year": Simon 2008, 213, says that ticket prices were $5.50 before and increased to an average of $6.13 paid per ticket.
173   "Companies need to answer several questions": Tacke and Luby (n.d.), 10–11.
174   $3.02 a minute: Lazarus 2009.
174   Netflix prices: See Netflix website, www.netflix.com/Help?action=2&jsEnabled=false&faqtrkid=5&p_faqid=107&p_search_text—embership.
174   Academic studies of causes of flat-rate bias: See Lambrecht and Skiera 2006.
175   the average ticket price paid went up 11 percent: Simon 2008, 213.
175   "Such improvements are not possible": Ibid., 214.

### 31. Breakage and Slippage

176   About a third of all computer gear comes with rebates: Grow 2005.
176   Sperry and Hutchinson Green Stamps history: See www.straightdope.com/columns/read/1940/whatever-happened-to-green-stamps.
177   "The game is obviously": Grow 2005.
177   "If you are using another fulfillment company": Ibid.
177   "further research" . . . "special team": Ibid.
177   a face value of $6 billion: Ibid.
178   "silver lining": Thaler 1985, 202.
178   "Mr. A's car was damaged": Ibid., 204.

**32. Paying for Air**

179  $2,400 for air/vacuum machine: See www.jmesales.com/item/19638/Super-Vac-Air .aspx.

179  "long life and low maintenance": Ibid.

179  Battery life test: "Which AA batteries last?" in *Consumer Reports*, Dec. 2008, 7.

181  A 2008 Consumer Electronics Association survey: Hutsko 2008.

181  an MMS was worth 3.5 times as much as a text message: Stadie, Engelmann, and Elvetico n.d., 6.

181  Real cost of text messages: See www.techcrunch.com/2008/07/01/atts-text-messages-cost-1310-per-megabyte/.

181  the price . . . for text messages doubled: Stross 2008.


**33. Cheap and Cheaper**

182  "If I have 2,000 customers": Meckes, Krohn, and Butscher n.d., 5.

182  Analysis of bargain airlines and price comparisons: Tacke and Schleusener n.d.

183  "Three or four years ago": Sharkey 2009.


**34. Mysteries of the 99-Cent Store**

184  "I'll tell you what brilliance in advertising is": quoted in Arango 2009.

184  "The 79 cents sold better at 99": Arango 2009.

184  99 Cents Only Store history: Chang 2008, Wikipedia entry at en.wikipedia.org/wiki/99_Cents_Only_Stores.

185  "The 99-cent promise": Wilson 2008.

185  "The number 99 is a magic number": Chang 2008.

185  Charm price history: Hower 1943, 52–53; Allen and Dare 2004, 699.

186  "They could be pricing at $3.99": O'Dell interview, March 5, 2009.

186  Taco Bell, 50 Cent promotion: Zambito 2008.

188  "For many years, retail prices": Ginzberg 1936, 296.

188  an unnamed large retailer: Ginzberg mentions that the total edition of the spring catalog was 6 million. A quick search on the Web found claims that the Sears Roebuck catalog had 11 million customers at its peak, but this fell off during the Depression. It had more customers than the rival Montgomery Ward catalog.

188  "as interesting as they were perplexing": Ginzberg 1936, 296.

188  "The vice-president in charge of merchandising": Ibid.

188  boost sales by an average of 24 percent: Liang and Kanetkar 2006, 378.

189  40 percent, twice that of Wal-Mart: Coffey 2002.

189  *Star Wars* underwear deal: Ibid.

190  Nordstrom's doesn't use charm prices: See en.wikipedia.org/wiki/Psychological_pricing.

190  Eddie Bauer and J. Crew charm prices: Anderson and Simester 2003, 106 (note).

190  Costco uses 97-cent endings: *Consumer Reports*, May 2007. See www.consumerreports.org/cro/money/shopping/where-to-buy/warehouse-clubs-5-07/overview/0507_ware_ov.htm.

### 35. Meaningless Zeros
193  Hershey Kisses, Lindt truffles experiment: Ariely 2008, 51–54.

### 36. Reality Constraint
196  "Negotiation at the time was relatively moribund": Neale interview, June 3, 2008.
196  "The argument that we were making": Ibid.
196  "Maggie and I used to have lunch": Northcraft interview, May 30, 2008.
196  "We both had the experience": Ibid.
197  "There's really two ways of looking at this": Ibid.
198  "Science is often portrayed": Northcraft, personal e-mail, May 28, 2008.
199  "I think there are a lot of areas": Northcraft interview, May 30, 2008.
199  "For these judgments": Northcraft and Neale 1987, 96.
199  "It remains an open question": Ibid., 95.
200  "zone of credibility": Ibid., 84.
200  "obviously deviant": Ibid., 88.
200  "At issue here is just how malleable": Ibid., 95.
200  "Back in those days": Neale interview, June 3, 2008.
200  over two hundred citations: Google Scholar listed 233 citations as of June 6, 2008.
200  "they absolutely rejected the findings": Neale interview, June 3, 2008.
201  "I guess I would say there's no shame": Northcraft e-mail, May 30, 2008.
201  "One of the things we've worked on since": Neale interview, June 3, 2008.
201  "The adage 'You can always come down'": Bailey 2008.

### 37. Selling Warhol's Beach House
202  Paid $225,000 for 22 acres in 1971: Cotsalas 2006.
202  Warhol property turned nature preserve: Drumm 2007.
202  "hobbit huts": Ibid.
202  "satin sheets and ice makers": Ibid.
203  "If he would sell it for $25 million": Ibid.
203  The sale price was $27.5 million: Cotsalas 2008.
203  "He seems to be a great guy": Drumm 2007.
204  "This past summer": Lichtenstein 2005, 358.
204  "ARPs work": Ibid.
205  even when the reference price is . . . 2.86 times . . . market value: Urbany, Bearden, and Weilbaker 1988.
205  "your idea of what an item should cost": Lichtenstein 2005, 357.
206  Worms in hamburgers rumor: Ibid., 359.

### 38. Groundhog Day
207  "Anchoring is not a curiosity": Transcript of 2008 Edge Master Class, www.edge.org/documents/archive/edge253.html.
208  "We spend a lot of time talking to real folks": Neale interview, June 3, 2008.
208  Van Leeuwenhoek's findings: See www.ucmp.berkeley.edu/history/leeuwenhoek.html.

208  *Groundhog Day* argument: Heukelom 2007c, 21–22. See also www.mises.org/story/2289.
209  Bargaining experiment: Ritov 1996.
212  "reanchor," "Responding to an initial offer": Bazerman and Neale 1992, 28.

### 39. Anchoring for Dummies
213  "A bat and a ball together": Frederick 2005 and Oechssler, Roider, and Schmitz 2008.

### 40. Attention Deficit
215  "When I build something for somebody": Blair 2005, 262.
215  Experiment with two groups of responders, preference reversal: Bazerman, White, Loewenstein 1995, 42.
216  "Automatic processes": Camerer, Loewenstein, and Prelec 2005, 18 and 38.
216  The amygdala "sees" objects in peripheral vision: Ibid. 43.
216  "a big move covers a small move": Macknik, King, Randi, et al. 2008.
217  Experiment with $400-$400 and $500-$700 payments: Bazerman, White, and Loewenstein 1995, 41.
218  "*Job* A: The offer is from Company 4": Ibid.
218  "Together, our studies suggest": Ibid., 42.

### 41. Drinking and Deal Making
219  12 percent of the retail alcohol market: Mosher 1983. Mosher says that businesses will spend "over $10 billion" on alcoholic beverages in 1982. Adjusted for inflation, this would be about $20 billion in 2008.
219  "ordinary and necessary": quoted in Mosher 1983.
219  "A little bourbon": Haughney 2008.
219  British team's experiment: George, Rogers, and Duka 2005.
221  "How 'bout it, pal": Southern 1960, 13.
221  *alcohol myopia*: The term is coined in Steele and Josephs 1990. See also George, Rogers, and Duka 2005, 168.

### 42. An Octillion Doesn't Buy What It Used To
223  Zimbabwe inflation: Associated Press, Jan. 18, 2009; Dixon 2008; Shaw 2008; Erwin 2009. Z $100 trillion bill: See blogs.usatoday.com/ondeadline/2009/01/zimbabwe-releas.html.
224  Pioneer of behavioral economics: Thaler 1997.
224  "The foisting of Psychology on Economics": Fisher 1925, vi–vii.
224  "shaking out of the lunatic fringe": "Irving Fisher," Wikipedia, en.wikipedia.org/wiki/Irving_Fisher.
224  "Stock prices have reached": Ibid.
225  ("Press stopper I and raise III"): Fisher 1892, 46.
225  "Fearing to be thought a profiteer": Fisher 1928, 7; see also commentary in Thaler 1997.

226 Wine cost survey: Thaler 1999, 191.
227 "Which of the following best captures your feeling": Shafir, Diamond, and Tversky 1997, 362, quoting a then unpublished article by Shafir and Thaler.
227 Wine cost survey responses: Thaler 1999, 191.
227 "Common discourse and newspaper reports": Shafir, Diamond, and Tversky 1997, 344.
228 When prompted by the phrase "in economic terms": Ibid., 352.
229 "California's run-up in housing prices": Connell, Smith, and Watanabe 2008.

**43. Selling the Money Illusion**
230 "My dog is worried": The joke is found widely on Internet quote sites, including www.quotationspage.com/quote/1076.html.
230 Contract A: You agree to sell: Shafir, Diamond, and Tversky 1997, 358.
230 "could have significant consequences": Shafir, Diamond, and Tversky 1997, 358.
231 You agree to sell (version 2): Ibid., 357.
231 You agree to sell (version 3): Ibid.
231 people "naturally" look at things: Ibid., 358.
232 Jensen's tactic: Jensen 2003, 36–37.

**44. Neutron Jane**
234 "the most expensive tryst in history": DePaulo 2002, quoting an unnamed publication in Dublin.
234 Differing estimates; offer: Murray, Silverman, and Hymowitz 2002; Jones 2002. Jack was said to be offering assets valued at "$130 million over the course of Mrs. Welch's life."
235 Kozlowski likened to Welch: *BusinessWeek* Jan. 14, 2002.
235 $4 million salary, $8 million pension: http://en.wikipedia.org/wiki/Jack_Welch.
235 Perks: Murray, Silverman, and Hymowitz 2002.
236 Jack, furious . . . compared to Kozlowksi: Ibid.
236 "They critiqued the existing models": Solnick interview, March 17, 2008.
236 Solnick's background and study: Ibid.
237 "I want at least one of us to get something": Solnick 2001, 193.
237 "women may end up with a smaller share": Ibid., 189.
237 "If women take our first offer": Solnick interview, March 17, 2008.
238 "If you really want to be fair": Ibid.

**45. The Beauty Premium**
239 "There are no productivity issues": Solnick and Schweitzer 1999, 203.

**46. Search for Suckers**
241 "Salesmen . . . categorize people": Quoted in Ayres and Siegelman 1995, 317 (note 29).
241 "lay-down": Ayres 1991, 854 (note 109).

241  instructed on how to dress: Ibid., 825.
242  "honey," "cutie," "You are a pretty girl": Ibid., 846 (note).
242  "studying how sellers negotiate car sales": Ayres and Siegelman 1995, 307 (note 11).
243  "who then proceeded to give them the worst deals": Ayres 1991, 841.
243  "search for suckers": Ibid., 854.
244  "Earlier this year, I asked a car dealer": Ibid., 872.
244  paid an average of $319 less: Ibid. 848.

**47. Pricing Gender**
245  South African lender experiment: Bertrand, Karlan, Mullainathan, et al. 2005.

**48. It's All About Testosterone**
248  Burnham experiment: Burnham 2007.
249  Soccer fans' testosterone levels: Reported in Mazur and Booth 1998, 358.
249  London traders' testosterone levels: Coates and Herbert 2008.
249  Aggressive responses to provocation: Mazur and Booth 1998, 355.
249  Swedish study: Cited in Mazur and Booth 1998, 355.
249  "We essentially create alpha males": Kuchinskas 2007.
250  Button-pushing game: Kouri, Lukas, Pope, and Oliva 1995.
250  Married men have lower testosterone: See Khamsi 2007, which suggests the wedding ring tactic.
251  Ring finger and ultimatum game: Van den Bergh and Dewitte 2006.
251  Ring finger study: Coates, Gurnell, and Rustichini 2009.

**49. Liquid Trust**
252  Oxytocin boosted proposer offers 21 percent: Zak, Stanton, and Ahmadi 2007.
252  Zak fell for "pigeon drop": blogs.psychologytoday.com/blog/the-moralmolecule/200811/how-run-a-con.
253  Liquid Trust: See www.verolabs.com. Another such product is OxyCalm (www.oxycalm.com).
253  the spray made his tips increase fivefold: www.verolabs.com/salestool.php?UID=2009012012550469.239.113.151.
253  "How Salespeople Use Liquid Trust": Ibid.

**50. The Million Dollar Club**
255  $5 million offer to *Seinfeld*: CNN, Dec. 26, 1997.
255  TV star salary demands: *Entertainment Weekly* (no byline) 2006; Silverman 2003.
256  "Wage earners, we suspect": Ariely, Loewenstein, and Prelec 2003, 99.
256  U.S. v. U.K., Japanese CEO pay: www.stateofworkingamerica.org/swa08-exec_pay.pdf.
257  "In the hall of fame of unintended consequences": Nocera 2006.
257  "I absolutely thought [pay] would go down": Ibid.
257  Steve Jobs compensation: DeCarlo 2007.

257 "Lone Ranger theory": Reinhardt 2009.
257 "What's a CEO worth": townhall.com/columnists/WalterEWilliams/2008/01/02/greed,_need_and_money?page=full&comments=true.
258 Immelt as good a manager as Welch: Reinhardt 2009.
258 "Should there be a ratio": *Hardball with Chris Matthews*, transcript for July 12, 2006.

### 51. The Mischievous Mr. Market
261 Graham's stock valuation formula: Graham and Dodd 1934. See also Lowe 1996.
261 Arrow connected Tversky and Kahneman's work to stock market: Arrow 1982.
261 "Does the Stock Market Rationally Reflect": Summers 1986.
264 "They'd say, sure I knew": Camerer 1997, 18.
265 "If they've lived through an inflationary experience": Ibid., 19.

### 52. For the Love of God
266 "The skull is extraordinary": Sandler 2007.
266 That sum was intended as publicity gimmick: Thompson 2008, 2.
266 50,000 FOR FISH WITHOUT CHIPS: Ibid., 2.
266 "We wanted to put them everywhere": BBC News, June 1, 2007, news.bbc.co.uk/2/hi/entertainment/6712015.stm.
266 "Is it beautiful?": Riding 2007.
267 "As a trope for human folly": Lacayo 2008.
267 "almost sold . . . someone is very interested": Sandler 2007.
268 The two-day sale total: Reyburn and Kazakina 2008.
268 "the price of it now would be double": Lacayo 2008.

### 53. Antidote for Anchoring
269 Car value study: Mussweiler, Strack, and Pfeiffer 2000.
269 "consider the opposite": Ibid., 1144.
270 "A friend of mine mentioned yesterday": Ibid., 1145.
270 "I beseech ye," "written over the portals": quoted in Lord, Lepper, and Preston 1984, 1231.

### 54. Buddy System
274 Seventy-four percent gave the wrong answer: Only 13 of 50 subjects made no errors, with the other 37 making at least one error. See Asch 1963, 181.
274 "You're *probably* right, but you may be wrong": Ibid., 182.

### 55. The Outrage Theory
276 "generally effective," "deeply traumatized by pills": Kahneman, Schkade, and Sunstein 1998, 83.
276 "outrage theory": Kahneman, Schkade, and Sunstein 1998; see also Kahneman, Ritov, and Schkade 1999.

276 "The unpredictability of raw dollar awards": Kahneman, Schkade, and Sunstein 1998, 67.
278 "The unpredictability and characteristic skewness," "Under these circumstances": Ibid., 69, 75.
278 "which will make her more susceptible": Ibid., 82–83.
279 "rest on a bedrock of moral intuitions": Ibid., 61.
279 "conversion function": Ibid., 76.
279 "Many new possibilities": Ibid.


**56. Honesty Box**
280 "I said it was a very cute idea": Johnson interview, Sept. 9, 2008.
281 "It is important to note": Mandel and Johnson 2002.
282 "These are pretty big effects": "Even the Furniture Can Affect Business Attitudes," Stanford Graduate School of Business press release, Oct. 2004.
283 "I was surprised how big the effect was": "'Big Brother' Eyes Encourage Honesty, Study Shows," Newcastle University Press Office, June 28, 2006.
283 "When people are made to be self-aware": Angier 2008.


**57. Money, Chocolate, Happiness**
284 History of Monopoly: See Wikipedia entry, "Monopoly (game)," en.wikipedia.org/ wiki/Monopoly_(game).
284 Money priming study (Monopoly, screen saver): Vohs, Mead, and Goode 2006 and 2008.
285 donated only 58 percent as much: Vohs, Mead, and Goode 2008, 210. This is computed from the statement that the money-primed group donated 39 percent of their $2 payment, versus 67 percent for the control group.
286 "distrusting of others": Ibid., 211.
286 "Priming effects may provide one of the mechanisms": Transcript of 2008 Edge Master Class, www.edge.org/documents/archive/edge253.html.
287 "a microcosm of life": Hsee and Zhang 2004.
288 Cockroach chocolate experiment: Hsee 1999.

# Sources

Allais, Maurice (1953). "Le comportement de l'homme rationnel devant le risque: Critique des postulats et axiomes de l'école Américaine." *Econometrica* 21, 503–46.

—— (1995). "The Real Foundations of the Alleged Errors in Allais' Impossibility Theorem: Unceasingly Repeated Errors or Contradictions of Mark Machina." *Theory and Decision* 38, 251–99.

Allen, Marcus T., and William H. Dare (2004). "The Effects of Charm Listing Prices on House Transaction Prices." *Real Estate Economics* 32, 695–713.

*American Psychologist* (no byline) (1983). "Daniel Kahneman and Amos Tversky." *American Psychologist*, Jan. 1983, 2–9.

Anderson, Eric T., and Duncan I. Simester (2003). "Effects of $9 Price Endings on Retail Sales: Evidence from Field Experiments." *Quantitative Marketing and Economics* 1, 93–110.

Angier, Natalie (2008). "Mirrors Don't Lie. Mislead? Oh, Yes." *The New York Times*, July 22, 2008.

Arango, Tim (2009). "Bet Your Bottom Dollar on 99 Cents." *The New York Times*, Feb. 7, 2009.

Ariely, Dan (n.d.). "Painful Lessons." Available at www.predictablyirrational.com/pdfs/mypain.pdf.

—— (2008). *Predictably Irrational: The Hidden Forces That Shape Our Decisions*. New York: Harper.

——, George Loewenstein, and Drazen Prelec (2003). "Coherent Arbitrariness: Stable Demand Curves Without Stable Preferences." *The Quarterly Journal of Economics* 118, 73–105.

—— (2005). "Tom Sawyer and the Construction of Value." FRB of Boston Working Paper No. 05-10. Available at papers.ssrn.com/sol3/papers.cfm?abstract_id=774970.

Arrow, Kenneth J. (1982). "Risk Perception in Psychology and Economics." *Economic Inquiry* 20, 1–9.

Asch, S. E. (1963). "Effects of Group Pressure upon the Modification and Distortion of Judgments." In *Groups, Leadership and Men: Research in Human Relations* (Harold Guetzkow, ed.). New York: Russell & Russell.

Avant, L. L., and Harry Helson (1973). "Theories of Perception." In B. B. Watson (ed.), *Handbook of General Psychology*. Englewood Cliffs, N.J.: Prentice Hall.

Ayres, Ian (1991). "Fair Driving: Gender and Race Discrimination in Retail Car Negoti-ations." *Harvard Law Review* 104, 817–72.

———, and Peter Siegelman (1995). "Race and Gender Discrimination in Bargaining for a New Car." *The American Economic Review* 85, 304–21.

Bailey, Steve (2008). "Timing the Market." *The New York Times*, Dec. 4, 2008.

Bazerman, Max H., and Margaret A. Neale (1992). *Negotiating Rationally*. New York: Free Press.

Bazerman, Max H., Sally Blount White, and George F. Loewenstein (1995). "Percep-tions of Fairness in Interpersonal and Individual Choice Situations." *Current Direc-tions in Psychological Science* 4, 39–43.

Bell, David, Howard Raiffa, and Amos Tversky (1988). "Descriptive, Normative, and Pre-scriptive Interactions in Decision Making." In Bell, Raiffa, and Tversky (eds.), *Deci-sion Making: Descriptive, Normative, and Prescriptive Interactions*. Cambridge: Cambridge University Press.

Benson, Etienne (2008). "The Unexpected Benefits of Basic Science." *Monitor on Psy-chology*, Jan. 2003, 36.

Berfield, Susan (2009). "How to Win Frugal Consumers and Influence Them to Buy." *BusinessWeek*, Jan. 29, 2009.

Bertrand, Marianne, Dean Karlan, Sendhil Mullainathan, Eldar Shafir, and Jonathan Zinman (2005). "What's Psychology Worth? A Field Experiment in the Consumer Credit Market." Yale University Economic Growth Center Discussion Paper No. 918. Available at papers.ssrn.com/sol3/papers.cfm?abstract_id=770389.

Bevan, William (1979). "Harry Helson: 1898–1977." *The American Journal of Psychology* 92, 153–60.

Binkley, Christina (2007). "The Psychology of the $14,000 Handbag." *The Wall Street Journal*, Aug. 9, 2007, D8.

Blakeslee, Sandra (2005). "What Other People Say May Change What You See." *The New York Times*, June 28, 2005.

Boulware, Lemuel R. (1969). *The Truth About Boulwarism*. Washington, D.C.: Bureau of National Affairs.

Brewer, N., and G. Chapman (2002). "The Fragile Basic Anchoring Effect." *Journal of Behavioral Decision Making* 15, 65–77.

Brozan, Nadine (1993). "Chronicle." *The New York Times*, May 3, 1993.

Burnham, Terence C. (2007). "High-Testosterone Men Reject Low Ultimatum Game Offers." *Proceedings of the Royal Society B* 274, 2327–30.

Butscher, Stephan A., Frank Luby, André Weber, and Cory Polonetsky (n.d.). "The Admission of Price." Simon-Kucher & Partners white paper. Available at www2 .simon-kucher.com/index.php/us/publications/white-papers.html.

Camerer, Colin (1997). "Taxi Drivers and Beauty Contests." *Engineering & Science* 1, 10–19.

——— (2003). *Behavioral Game Theory*. Princeton, N.J.: Princeton University Press.

——— (n.d.). "Three Cheers—Psychological, Theoretical, Empirical—for Loss-Aversion." *Journal of Marketing Research*, in press.

———, George Loewenstein, and Drazen Prelec (2005). "Neuroeconomics: How Neuro-science Can Inform Economics." *Journal of Economic Literature* 43, 9–64.

———, and Richard Thaler (1995). "Ultimatums, Dictators and Manners." *The Journal of Economic Perspectives* 9, 209–19.

Carey, Benedict (2007). "Who's Minding the Mind?" *The New York Times*, July 31, 2007.

—— (2008). "You Remind Me of Me." *The New York Times*, Feb. 12, 2008.

Carroll, Lewis (ed. by Martin Gardner) (2006). *The Annotated "Hunting of the Snark."* New York: W. W. Norton.

CBC News (2000). "Paco Underhill: Shopping Scientist." Nov. 7, 2000. Available at www.cbc.ca/consumers/market/files/home/shopping/.

Cervone, D., and P. K. Peake (1986). "Anchoring, Efficacy, and Action: The Influence of Judgmental Heuristics on Self-Efficacy Judgment and Behavior." *Journal of Personality and Social Psychology* 50, 492–501.

Chang, Andrea (2008). "99-Cent Chain May Not Be Able to Buck Inflation Pressures." *Los Angeles Times*, Aug. 29, 2008, A1.

Chapman, Gretchen B., and Brian H. Bornstein (1996). "The More You Ask For, the More You Get: Anchoring in Personal Injury Verdicts." *Applied Cognitive Psychology* 10, 519–40.

Chapman, Gretchen B., and Eric J. Johnson (1994). "The Limits of Anchoring." *Journal of Behavioral Decision Making* 7, 223–42.

Chertkoff, Jerome M., and Melinda Conley (1967). "Opening Offer and Frequency of Concession as Bargaining Strategies." *Journal of Personality and Social Psychology* 7, 181–85.

Chitturi, Ravindra, Rajagopal Raghunathan, and Vijay Mahajan (2007). "Form Versus Function: How the Intensities of Specific Emotions Evoked in Functional Versus Hedonic Trade-Offs Mediate Product Preferences." *Journal of Marketing Research* 44, 702–14.

Coates, John M., Mark Gurnell, and Aldo Rustichini (2009). "Second-to-Fourth-Digit Ratio Predicts Success Among High-Frequency Financial Traders." *Proceedings of the National Academy of Sciences* 106, 623–28.

Coates, John M., and J. Herbert (2008). "Endogenous Steroids and Financial Risk Taking on a London Trading Floor." *Proceedings of the National Academy of Sciences* 105, 6167–72.

Coffey, Brendan (2002). "Every Penny Counts." *Forbes*, Sep. 30, 2002.

Cohen, L. Jonathan (1981). "Can Human Irrationality Be Experimentally Demonstrated?" *Behavioral and Brain Sciences* 4, 317–31.

Connell, Rich, Doug Smith, and Teresa Watanabe (2008). "Census Portrays More of a Melting Pot in Southern California." *Los Angeles Times*, Dec. 9, 2008.

Coomes, Steve (2005). "Engineering a Better Menu." *Pizza Marketplace*, Dec. 22, 2005. Available at www.pizzamarketplace.com/article.php?id=4568.

Cotsalas, Valerie (2006). "The Unsold Warhol." *The New York Times*, Sept. 8, 2006.

—— (2008). "Preservation Deal for Dick Cavett's Land." *The New York Times*, Aug. 16, 2008.

Cowen, Tyler (2006). "A Contrarian Look at Whether U.S. Chief Executives Are Overpaid." *The New York Times*, May 18, 2006.

Cox, Donald (2005). "Good News! Behavioral Economics Is Not Going Away Anytime Soon." *Journal of Product and Brand Management* 14, 375–78.

DeCarlo, Scott (2007). "Ranking the Biggest CEO Paychecks." *Forbes*, May 4, 2007.

Dempsey, John (2004). "Billion Dollar Baby." *Variety*, Dec. 22, 2004.

DePaulo, Lisa (2002). "If You Knew Suzy . . ." *New York*, April 29, 2002. Available at nymag.com/nymetro/news/media/features/5976/.

Desvousges, W. H., F. R. Johnson, R. W. Dunford, K. J. Boyle, et al. (1992). "Measuring Nonuse Damages During Contingent Valuation: An Experimental Evaluation of Accuracy." Research Triangle Institute Monograph 92-1. Research Triangle Park, N.C.: Research Triangle Institute.

Dixon, Robyn (2008). "Zimbabwe Can't Paper Over Its Money Woes." Los Angeles Times, Dec. 20, 2008.

Dreifus, Claudia (2007). "Through Analysis, Gut Reaction Gains Credibility." The New York Times, Aug. 28, 2007.

Drumm, Russell (2007). "'Warhol Estate' in Montauk Is Sold." The East Hampton Star, Jan. 18, 2007.

Edwards, Ward (1954). "The Theory of Decision Making." Psychological Bulletin 41, 380–417.

—— (1961). "Behavioral Decision Theory." Annual Review of Psychology 12, 473–98.

—— (1975). "Cognitive Processes and the Assessment of Subjective Probability Distributions: Comment." Journal of the American Statistical Association 70, 291–93.

Egan, Timothy (2008). "Stranger in a Stadium." The New York Times, Aug. 27, 2008.

Einhorn, Hillel J., and Robin M. Hogarth (1978). "Confidence in Judgment: Persistence of the Illusion of Validity." Psychological Review 85, 395–416.

Ellsberg, Daniel (1961). "Risk, Ambiguity, and the Savage Axioms." The Quarterly Journal of Economics 75, 643–49.

Englich, Birte, and Thomas Mussweiler (2001). "Sentencing Under Uncertainty: Anchoring Effects in the Courtroom." Journal of Applied Social Psychology 31, 1538–41.

Entertainment Weekly (no byline) (2007). "Show Them the Money! (Or the Door)." Entertainment Weekly, March 30, 2007.

Erikson, Charles W., and Harold W. Hake (1957). "Anchor Effects in Absolute Judgments." Journal of Experimental Psychology 53, 132–38.

Erwin, Miles (2009). "Zimbabwe Inflation Hit 500 Billion%." Metro.co.uk, Apr. 30, 2009.

Fechner, G. T., trans. by Helmut Adler (1966). Elements of Psychophysics. New York: Holt, Rinehart and Winston. (Reprint of the 1860 original.)

Finch, Charlie (2007). "A Bizarre Collector." Artnet Magazine, www.artnet.com/magazineus/features/finch/finch7-30-07.asp.

Finn, Robin (2003). "Public Lives: He Put the Rage in Outrageous Prices." The New York Times, Apr. 11, 2003.

Fisher, Irving (1892). "Mathematical Investigations in the Theory of Value and Prices." Yale Ph.D. thesis.

—— (1925). Mathematical Investigations in the Theory of Value and Prices. New Haven: Yale University Press. (Reprint of Fisher's 1892 doctoral thesis.)

—— (1928). The Money Illusion. New York: Adelphi.

Frederick, Shane (2005). "Cognitive Reflection and Decision Making." Journal of Economic Perspectives 19, 25–42.

Gellene, Denise (2007). "Fairness Is Only Human, Scientists Find." Los Angeles Times, Oct. 5, 2007.

George, S., R. D. Rogers, and T. Duka (2005). "The Acute Effect of Alcohol on Decision Making in Social Drinkers." Psychopharmacology 182, 160–69.

Gerlin, Andrea (1994). "McDonald's Callousness Was Real Issue, Jurors Say, in Case of Burned Woman." The Wall Street Journal, Sep. 1, 1994.

Gigerenzer, Gerd (1996). "On Narrow Norms and Vague Heuristics: A Reply to Kahneman and Tversky (1996)." *Psychological Review* 103, 592–96.

Ginzberg, Eli (1936). "Customary Prices." *The American Economic Review* 26, 296.

Glanz, James, and Eric Lipton (2003). *City in the Sky: The Rise and Fall of the World Trade Center.* New York: Times Books / Henry Holt.

Goldberg, Pinelopi Koujianou (1996). "Dealer Price Discrimination in New Car Purchases: Evidence from the Consumer Expenditure Survey." *Journal of Political Economy* 104, 622–54.

Goldstein, William M., and Hillel J. Einhorn (1987). "Expression Theory and the Preference Reversal Phenomena." *Psychological Review* 94, 236–54.

Goodman, Barbara, Mark Saltzman, Ward Edwards, and David H. Krantz (1979). "Prediction of Bids for Two-Outcome Gambles in a Casino Setting." *Organizational Behavior and Human Performance* 24, 382–99.

Graham, Benjamin, and David L. Dodd (1934). *Security Analysis.* New York: McGraw-Hill.

Greenberg, Peter (2007). "What They Won't Tell You About Menus." *Forbes Traveler*, Aug. 16, 2007. Available at www.forbestraveler.com/luxury/menus-printstory.html.

Grether, David M., and Charles R. Plott (1979). "Economic Theory of Choice and the Preference Reversal Phenomenon." *The American Economic Review* 69, 623–28.

Grow, Brian (2005). "The Great Rebate Runaround." *BusinessWeek*, Nov. 23, 2005.

Guildford, J. P. (1979). "Obituary: Harry Helson." *American Psychologist* 34, 628–30.

Güth, Werner (1976). "Towards a More General Study of v. Stackelberg-Situations." *Zeitschrift Für Die Gesamte Staatswissenschaft* 132, 592–608.

———, Rolf Schmittberger, and Bernd Schwarze (1982). "An Experimental Analysis of Ultimatum Bargaining." *Journal of Economic Behavior and Organization* 3, 367–88.

Halevy, Yoram, and Michael Peters (2007). "Is the Ultimatum Game the Ultimate Experiment?" Available at www.cepr.org/meets/wkcn/6/6646/papers/Halevy.pdf.

Hamermesh, D. S., and J. E. Biddle (1994). "Beauty and the Labor Market." *The American Economic Review* 84, 1174–94.

Hammack, Judd, and Gardner Brown (1974). *Waterfowl and Wetlands: Toward Bioeconomic Analysis.* Baltimore, Md.: Johns Hopkins Press, 1974.

Haughney, Christine (2008). "For Apartment Shoppers, Some Liquid Courage." *The New York Times*, Nov. 13, 2008.

Hedden, Jenny (1997). "Maximize Menu Merchandising Power." *Restaurants USA.* May 1997.

Heidelberger, Michael, trans. by Cynthia Klohr (2004). *Nature from Within: Gustav Theodor Fechner and His Psychophysical Worldview.* Pittsburgh: University of Pittsburgh Press.

Heilbroner, Robert L. (1999). *The Worldly Philosophers* (7th ed.). New York: Simon & Schuster.

Helson, Harry (1947). "Adaptation-Level as a Frame of Reference for Prediction of Psychophysical Data." *The American Journal of Psychology* 60, 1–29.

———, and A. Kozaki (1968). "Anchor Effects Using Numerical Estimates of Simple Dot Patterns." *Perception and Psychophysics* 4, 163–64.

Henrich, J., R. Boyd, S. Bowles, Colin Camerer, E. Fehr, H. Gintis, et al. (2001). "In Search of Homo Economicus: Behavioral Experiments in 15 Small-Scale Societies." *The American Economic Review* 91, 73–78.

Heukelom, Floris (2007a). *Kahneman and Tversky and the Origin of Behavioral Economics*. Tinbergen Institute Discussion Paper TI 2007-003/1.

—— (2007b). *What Simon Says*. Tinbergen Institute Discussion Paper TI 2007-005/1.

—— (2007c). *Who Are the Behavioral Economists and What Do They Say?* Tinbergen Institute Discussion Paper TI 2007-020/1.

Hirsch, Jerry (2008). "On Store Shelves, Stealthy Shrinking of Containers Keeps Prices from Rising." *Los Angeles Times*, Nov. 9. 2008.

Hoffman, Elizabeth, Kevin McCabe, Keith Shachat, and Vernon Smith (1994). "Preferences, Property Rights, and Anonymity in Bargaining Games." *Games and Economic Behavior* 7, 346–80.

Hoffman, Elizabeth, Kevin A. McCabe, and Vernon L. Smith (1996). "On Expectations and the Monetary Stakes in Ultimatum Games." *International Journal of Game Theory* 25, 289–301.

Hower, Ralph M. (1943). *History of Macy's of New York 1858–1919*. Cambridge, Mass.: Harvard University Press.

Hsee, Christopher K. (1999). "Value-Seeking and Prediction-Decision Inconsistency: Why Don't People Take What They Predict They'll Like the Most?" *Psychonomic Bulletin and Review* 6, 555–561.

——, and Jiao Zhang (2004). "Distinction Bias: Misprediction and Mischoice Due to Joint Evaluation." *Journal of Personality and Social Psychology* 86, 680–95.

——, Jiao Zhang, Frank Yu, and Yiheng Xi (2003). "Lay Rationalism and Inconsistency Between Predicted Experience and Decision." *Journal of Behavioral Decision Making* 16, 257–72.

Huber, Joel, and Christopher Puto (1983). "Market Boundaries and Product Choice: Illustrating Attraction and Substitution Effects." *Journal of Consumer Research* 10, 31–44.

Hunt, William A. (1941). "Anchoring Effects in Judgment." *The American Journal of Psychology* 54, 395–403.

Hutsko, Joe (2008). "Consumers Want, and Are Skeptical About, Eco-Electronics." *The New York Times*, Dec. 10, 2008.

Jacowitz, Karen E., and Daniel Kahneman (1995). "Measuring of Anchoring in Estimation Tasks." *Personality and Social Psychology Bulletin* 21, 1161–66.

Jensen, Keith, Josep Call, and Michael Tomasello (2007). "Chimpanzees Are Rational Maximizers in an Ultimatum Game." *Science* 318, 107–9.

Jensen, Marlene (2003). *Pricing Psychology Report*. Newtown, Conn.: Jensen-Fann.

Jones, Del (2002). "Welch's Wife Seeks Half of Fortune in Divorce." *USA Today*, March 12, 2002.

Kahneman, Daniel (1992). "Reference Points, Anchors, Norms, and Mixed Feelings." *Organizational Behavior and Human Decision Processes* 51, 296–312.

——, and S. Frederick (2002). "Representativeness Revisited: Attribute Substitution in Intuitive Judgment." In T. Gilovich, D. Griffin, and D. Kahneman (eds.), *Heuristics and Biases: The Psychology of Intuitive Judgment*. New York: Cambridge University Press.

——, Jack L. Knetsch, and Richard Thaler. (1986a). "Fairness as a Constraint on Profit Seeking: Entitlements in the Market." *The American Economic Review* 76, 728–41.

——, Jack L. Knetsch, and Richard Thaler. (1986b). "Fairness and the Assumptions of Economics." *The Journal of Business* 59, S285–S300.

———, Jack L. Knetsch, and Richard Thaler (1991). "Anomalies: The Endowment Effect, Loss Aversion, and the Status Quo Bias." *The Journal of Economic Perspectives* 5, 193–206.

———, Ilana Ritov, and David A. Schkade (1999). "Economic Preferences or Attitude Expressions? An Analysis of Dollar Responses to Public Issues." *Journal of Risk and Uncertainty* 19, 203–35.

———, David A. Schkade, and Cass R. Sunstein (1998). "Shared Outrage and Erratic Awards: The Psychology of Punitive Damages." *Journal of Risk and Uncertainty* 16, 49–86.

———, and Eldar Shafir. "Amos Tversky (1937–1996)." *American Psychologist* 53, 793–94.

———, Paul Slovic, and Amos Tversky (1982). *Judgment Under Uncertainty: Heuristics and Biases.* Cambridge: Cambridge University Press.

———, and Amos Tversky (1973). "On the Psychology of Prediction." *Psychological Review* 80, 237–51.

———, and Amos Tversky (1979). "Prospect Theory: An Analysis of Decision Under Risk." *Econometrica* 47, 263–92.

———, and Amos Tversky (1984). "Choices, Values and Frames." *American Psychologist* 39, 341–50.

———, and Amos Tversky (1996). "On the Reality of Cognitive Illusions." *Psychological Review* 103, 582–91.

Kay, Aaron C., S. Christian Wheeler, John A. Bargh, and Lee Ross (2004). "Material Priming: The Influence of Mundane Physical Objects on Situational Construal and Competitive Behavioral Choice." *Organizational Behavior and Human Decision Processes* 95, 83–96.

Keller, Amy (2007). "The Art of the Aisle." FloridaTrend.com, Oct. 1, 2007. Available at www.floridatrend.com/article.asp?aID=54506009.7270968.618345.8370013.6266116.730&aID2=47556.

Keller, Maryann (2000). "Getting a Premium over List Price." *Automotive Industries*, May 1, 2000.

Khamsi, Roxanne (2007). "Hormones Affect Men's Sense of Fair Play." *New Scientist*, July 4, 2007.

Knetsch, Jack (1989). "The Endowment Effect and Evidence of Nonreversible Indifference Curves." *The American Economic Review* 79, 1277–84.

Knetsch, Jack L., Richard Thaler, and Daniel Kahneman (1986). "Experimental Tests of the Endowment Effect and the Coase Theorem." Simon Fraser University Working Paper, 1988.

Kouri, Elena, Scott Lukas, Harrison Pope, and P. Oliva (1995). "Increased Aggressive Responding in Male Volunteers Following the Administration of Gradually Increasing Doses of Testosterone Cypriate." *Drug and Alcohol Dependence* 40, 73–79.

Krueger, Alan B. (2001). "Seven Lessons About Super Bowl Ticket Prices." *The New York Times*, Feb. 1, 2001.

Kuchinskas, Susan (2007). "Better Living Through Chemistry: Testosterone and Generosity." *American Chronicle*, July 10, 2007.

Lacayo, Richard (2008). "Damien Hirst: Bad Boy Makes Good." *Time*, Sep. 4, 2008.

Laibson, David, and Richard Zeckhauser (1998). "Amos Tversky and the Ascent of Behavioral Economics." *Journal of Risk and Uncertainty* 16, 7–47.

Lambert, Craig (2006). "The Marketplace of Perceptions." *Harvard Magazine*, March–April 2006.

Lambrecht, Anja, and Bernd Skiera (2006). "Paying Too Much and Being Happy About It: Existence, Causes, and Consequences of Tariff-Choice Biases." *Journal of Marketing Research* 43, 212–23.

Lazarus, David (2009). "Talk Isn't Cheap? For Cellphone Users, Not Talking Is Costly Too." *Los Angeles Times*, March 8, 2009.

Liang, Jianping, and Vinay Kanetkar (2006). "Price Endings: Magic and Math." *Journal of Product & Brand Management* 15, 377–85.

Lichtenstein, Donald R. (2005). "Price Perceptions, Merchant Incentives, and Consumer Welfare." *Journal of Product & Brand Management* 14, 357–61.

Lichtenstein, Sarah, and Paul Slovic (1971). "Reversals of Preference Between Bids and Choices in Gambling Decisions." *Journal of Experimental Psychology* 89, 46–55.

—— (1973). "Response-Induced Reversals of Preference in Gambling: An Extended Replication in Las Vegas." *Journal of Experimental Psychology* 101, 16–20.

——, eds. (2006). *The Construction of Preference*. Cambridge: Cambridge University Press.

Lopes, Lola (1991). "The Rhetoric of Irrationality." *Theory and Psychology* 1, 65–82.

Lord, Charles G., Mark R. Lepper, and Elizabeth Preston (1984). "Considering the Opposite: A Corrective Strategy for Social Judgment." *Journal of Personality and Social Psychology* 47, 1231.

Lowe, Janet (1996). *Benjamin Graham on Value Investing: Lessons from the Dean of Wall Street*. New York: Penguin.

Lyons, Richard D. (1993). "Meade Esposito, 86, Former Power in Politics, Is Dead." *The New York Times*, Sep. 4, 1993.

Macknik, Stephen L., Mac King, James Randi, Apollo Robbins, Teller, John Thompson, and Susana Martinez-Conde (2008). "Science and Society: Attention and Awareness in Stage Magic: Turning Tricks into Research." *Nature Reviews Neuroscience*, July 30, 2008.

Malouff, John, and Nicola S. Schutte (1989). "Shaping Juror Attitudes: Effects of Requesting Different Damage Amounts in Personal Injury Trials." *The Journal of Social Psychology* 129, 491, 495.

Mandel, Naomi, and Eric J. Johnson (2002). "When Web Pages Influence Choice: Effects of Visual Primes on Experts and Novices." *Journal of Consumer Research* 29, 235–45.

March, James G., and Herbert A. Simon (1958). *Organizations*. New York: Wiley.

Marinello, Nick (1995). "2.9 Million Served." *Tulane Lawyer*, Fall 1995.

Markovsky, Barry (1988). "Anchoring Justice." *Social Psychology Quarterly* 51, 213–24.

Mazur, Allan, and Alan Booth (1998). "Testosterone and Dominance in Men." *Behavioral and Brain Sciences* 21, 353–97.

Meckes, Rainer, Felix Krohn, and Stephan A. Butscher (n.d.) "Revenue Increase for Book Publishers." Available at www2.simon-kucher.com/index.php/us/publications/white-papers.html.

Michaud, Todd P. (n.d.). "Price Optimization for Retailers." Revionics white paper. Available at www.revionics.com.

Miller, George (1975). "Stanley Smith Stevens." In *Biographical Memoirs*, vol. 47. Washington, D.C.: National Academies Press.

Mirowski, Philip (2002). *Machine Dreams: Economics Becomes a Cyborg Science*. Cambridge, UK: Cambridge University Press.

Mosher, James F. (1983). "Tax-Deductible Alcohol: An Issue of Public Health Policy and Prevention Strategy." *Journal of Health Politics, Policy and Law* 7, 855–88.

Moulson, Geir (2009). "German Mogul Kills Self over Financial Meltdown." Associated Press, Jan. 6, 2009.

Murray, Matt, Rachel Emma Silverman, and Carol Hymowitz. "GE's Jack Welch Meets Match in Divorce Court." *The Wall Street Journal*, Nov. 27, 2002.

Mussweiler, Thomas, and F. Strack (2000). "Numeric Judgments Under Uncertainty: The Role of Knowledge in Anchoring." *Journal of Experimental Social Psychology* 36, 495–518.

———, Fritz Strack, and Tim Pfeiffer (2000). "Overcoming the Inevitable Anchoring Effect: Considering the Opposite Compensates for Selective Accessibility." *Personality and Social Psychology Bulletin* 26, 1142–45.

Nocera, Joseph (2006). "Disclosure Won't Tame C.E.O. Pay." *The New York Times*, Jan. 14, 2006.

Northcraft, Gregory B., and Margaret A. Neale (1987). "Experts, Amateurs, and Real Estate: An Anchoring-and-Adjustment Perspective on Property Pricing Decisions." *Organizational Behavior and Human Decision Processes* 84, 87–93.

Oosterbeek, Hessel, Randolph Sloof, and Gijs van de Kuilen (2004). "Cultural Differences in Ultimatum Game Experiments: Evidence from a Meta-analysis." *Experimental Economics* 7, 171–88.

Orr, Dan, and Chris Guthrie (2006). "Anchoring, Information, Expertise, and Negotiation: New Insights from Meta-Analysis." *Ohio State Journal on Dispute Resolution* 21, 597–628. Available at ssrn.com/abstract=900152.

Phillips, Lawrence D., and Detlof von Winterfeldt (2006). "Reflections on the Contributions of Ward Edwards to Decision Analysis and Behavioral Research." London School of Economics and Political Science, working paper LSEOR 06.86.

Phillips, Tappy (2009). "Springsteen Ticketmaster Troubles." WABC News. Available at abclocal.go.com/wabc/story?section–ews/7_on_your_side&id=6641540&rss=rss-wabc-article-6641540.

Plautus, trans. by E. F. Watling (1964). *The Rope and Other Plays*. London: Penguin.

Plous, Scott (1993). *The Psychology of Judgment and Decision Making*. Philadelphia: Temple University Press.

Post, Thierry, Martijn J. van den Assem, Guido Baltussen, and Richard H. Thaler (2008). "Deal or No Deal? Decision Making Under Risk in a Large-Payoff Game Show." *The American Economic Review* 98, 38–71.

Purcell, Frank (1969). "Roulette Bet May Decide Man's Fate." *Las Vegas Review-Journal*, March 2, 1969.

Quattrone, G. A., C. P. Lawrence, S. E. Finkel, and D. C. Andrus (1984). "Explorations in Anchoring: The Effects of Prior Range, Anchor Extremity, and Suggestive Hints." Unpublished manuscript, Stanford University, Stanford, Calif. Cited in Jacowitz and Kahneman 1995.

Reinhardt, Uwe E. (2009). "Jack Welch and the Lone Ranger Theory." *The New York Times*, Feb. 20, 2009.

Reyburn, Scott, and Katya Kazakina (2008). "How Monet, Freud, Hirst Records Led Art-Market Bubble to Burst." Bloomberg.com, Dec. 29, 2008.

Riding, Alan (2007). "Alas, Poor Art Market: A Multimillion-Dollar Head Case." *The New York Times*, June 13, 2007.

Ritov, Ilana (1996). "Anchoring in Simulated Competitive Market Negotiation." *Organizational Behavior and Human Decision Processes* 67, 16–25.

Robbennolt, Jennifer K., and Christina A. Studebaker (1999). "Anchoring in the Courtroom: The Effects of Caps on Punitive Damages." *Law and Human Behavior* 23, 353–57.

Robinson, Robert C. (2007). "Bounded Epistemology." Social Science Research Network. Available at ssrn.com/abstract=1000697.

Roth, A. E., V. Prasnikar, M. Okuno-Fujiware, and S. Zamir (1991). "Bargaining and Market Behavior in Jerusalem, Ljubljana, Pittsburgh, and Tokyo: An Experimental Study." *The American Economic Review* 81, 1068–95.

Russell Sage Foundation (2007). "Celebrating 100 Years of Social Science Research." Available at www.russellsage.org/about/history/centennialhistory.

Ryerson, James (2002). "The Man Who Wasn't There." *The Boston Globe*, Oct. 20, 2002.

Sahadi, Jeanne (2007). "CEO Pay: 364 Times More Than Workers." CNNMoney.com, Aug. 29, 2007.

Samuelson, Paul A. (1947). *Foundations of Economic Analysis*. Cambridge, Mass.: Harvard University Press.

Samuelson, William, and Richard Zeckhauser (1988). "Status Quo Bias in Decision Making." *Journal of Risk and Uncertainty* 1, 7–59.

Sandler, Linda (2007). "Damien Hirst Says $100 Million Diamond Skull Is 'Almost' Sold." Bloomberg News, June 3, 2007.

Sanfey, Alan G., James K. Rilling, Jessica A. Aaronson, Leigh E. Nystrom, and Jonathan D. Cohen (2003). "The Neural Basis of Economic Decision-Making in the Ultimatum Game." *Science* 300, 1755–58.

Sarnoff, Paul (1965). *Russell Sage: The Money King*. New York: Ivan Obolensky.

Savage, L. J. (1954). *The Foundations of Statistics*. New York: Wiley.

Schkade, David A., and Eric J. Johnson (1989). "Cognitive Processes in Preference Reversals." *Organizational Behavior and Human Decision Processes* 44, 203–31.

Schmid, Randolph E. (2009). "Finger Length May Predict Financial Success." Associated Press, Jan. 12, 2009.

Shafir, Eldar, Peter Diamond, and Amos Tversky (1997). "The Money Illusion." *The Quarterly Journal of Economics* 112, 341–74.

Shafir, Eldar, Itamar Simonson, and Amos Tversky (1993). "Reason-Based Choice." *Cognition* 49, 11–36.

Sharkey, Joe (2009). "Seats Are Cheap Now, but Discounts Won't Last." *The New York Times*, March 19, 2009.

Shaw, Angus (2008). "Zimbabwe Inflation Now over 1 Million Percent." Associated Press, May 21, 2008.

Siegfried, Tom (2004). "Social Thermometers." *The Dallas Morning News*, May 23, 2004.

Silverman, Stephen M. (2003). "Is Gandolfini Killing 'The Sopranos'?" *People*, March 10, 2003.

Simon, Herbert S. (1945). "Theory of Games and Economic Behavior" (review). *American Sociological Review* 50, 558–60.

———. (1947). *Administrative Behavior: A Study of Decision-Making Processes in Administrative Organizations*. New York: Macmillan.

Simon, Hermann (2008). "The Impact of Academic Research on Business Practice: Experiences from Marketing." *Journal of Business Market Management* 2, 203–18.

——, Frank F. Bilstein, and Frank Luby (2006). *Manage for Profit, Not Market Share.* Boston: Harvard Business School Press.

Simonson, Itamar, and Amos Tversky (1992). "Choice in Context: Tradeoff Contrast and Extremeness Aversion." *Journal of Marketing Research* 29, 281–95.

Slovic, Paul, and Sarah Lichtenstein (1968). "The Relative Importance of Probabilities and in Risk-Taking." *Journal of Experimental Psychology Monograph Supplement* 78 (3, pt. 2), 1–18.

——, and Amos Tversky (1974). "Who Accepts Savage's Axiom?" *Behavioral Science* 19, 368–73.

——, Sarah Lichtenstein, and Ward Edwards (1965). "Boredom-Induced Changes in Preferences Among Bets." *The American Journal of Psychology* 78, 208–17.

Solnick, Sara J. (2001). "Gender Differences in the Ultimatum Game." *Economic Inquiry* 39, 189–200.

——, and Maurice E. Schweitzer (1999). "The Influence of Physical Attractiveness and Gender on Ultimatum Game Decisions." *Organizational Behavior and Human Decision Processes* 79, 199–215.

Sorkin, Andrew Ross (2002). "Tyco Details Lavish Lives of Executives." *The New York Times,* Sept. 18, 2002, C1.

Southern, Terry (1960). *The Magic Christian.* New York: Grove Press. (First published in Britain in 1959.)

Stadie, Ekkehard, Ralph Engelmann, and Giuseppe Elvetico (n.d.). "Make Money with Services." Simon-Kucher & Partners white paper. Available at www2.simon-kucher .com/index.php/us/publications/white-papers.html.

Stanford University News Service (1996). "Amos Tversky, Leading Decision Researcher, Dies at 59." June 5, 1996.

Steele, C. M., and R. A. Josephs (1990). "Alcohol Myopia: Its Prized and Dangerous Effects." *American Psychologist* 45, 921–33.

Stevens, S.S. (1961). "To Honor Fechner and Repeal His Law: A Power Function, Not a Log Function, Describes the Operating Characteristic of a Sensory System." *Science* 133, 80–86.

—— (1975). *Psychophysics: Introduction to Its Perceptual, Neural, and Social Prospects.* New York: Wiley.

Strack, Fritz, and Thomas Mussweiler (1997). "Explaining the Enigmatic Anchoring Effect: Mechanisms of Selective Accessibility." *Journal of Personality and Social Psychology* 73, 437–46.

—— (2003). "Heuristic Strategies for Estimation Under Uncertainty: The Enigmatic Case of Anchoring." In Galen V. Bodenhausen and Alan J. Lambert (eds.), *Foundations of Social Cognition: A Festschrift in Honor of Robert S. Wyer, Jr.* Mahwah, N.J.: Lawrence Erlbaum Associates.

Strategic Interaction Group (2002). "An Interview with Werner Güth." Excerpt at http://www.econ.mpg.de/english/research/ESI/gueth_interview.php. The full interview is in *Experimental Economics: Financial Markets, Auctions, and Decision Making,* Fredrik Andersson and Hakan Holm (eds.). Dordrecht, Netherlands: Kluwer Academic Publishers.

Stross, Randall (2008). "What Carriers Aren't Eager to Tell You About Texting." *The New York Times,* Dec. 26, 2008.

Summers, Lawrence (1986). "Does the Stock Market Rationally Reflect Fundamental Values?" *Journal of Finance* 41, 591–602.

Tacke, Georg, and Frank Luby (n.d.). "Selling Content Online." Simon-Kucher & Partners White paper. Available at www2.simon-kucher.com/index.php/us/publications/white-papers.html.

Tacke, Georg, and Michael Schleusener (n.d.). "Bargain Airline Pricing: How Should the Majors Respond?" Simon-Kucher & Partners white paper. Available at www2 .simon-kucher.com/index.php/us/publications/white-papers.html.

Thaler, Richard H. (1980). "Toward a Positive Theory of Consumer Choice." *Journal of Economic Behavior and Organization* 1, 39–60.

—— (1983). "Transaction Utility Theory." *Advances in Consumer Research* 10, 229.

—— (1985). "Mental Accounting and Consumer Choice." *Marketing Science* 4, 199–214.

—— (1988). "Anomalies: The Ultimatum Game." *The Journal of Economic Perspectives* 2, 195–206.

—— (1997). "Irving Fisher: Modern Behavioral Economist." *The American Economic Review* 87, 439–41.

—— (1999). "Mental Accounting Matters." *Journal of Behavioral Decision Making* 12, 183–206.

——, and Cass R. Sunstein (2008). *Nudge: Improving Decisions About Health, Wealth, and Happiness.* New Haven: Yale University Press.

Thompson, Andrea (2009). "Study: You Touch It, You Buy It." LiveScience.com, Jan. 16, 2009.

Thompson, Don (2008). *The $12 Million Stuffed Shark: The Curious Economics of Contemporary Art.* New York: Palgrave Macmillan.

Tuohy, John William (2001). "The Greenbaum Murder." American-Mafia.com, Oct. 2001. Available at www.americanmafia.com/Feature_Articles_264.html.

Tversky, Amos, and Daniel Kahneman (1971). "Belief in the Law of Small Numbers." *Psychological Bulletin* 76, 105–10.

—— (1974). "Judgment Under Uncertainty: Heuristics and Biases." *Science* 185, 453–58.

—— (1981). "The Framing of Decisions and the Psychology of Choice." *Science* 211, 453–58.

—— (1983). "Extensional Versus Intuitive Reasoning: The Conjunction Fallacy in Probability Judgment." *Psychological Review* 90, 293–315.

—— (1991). "Loss Aversion and Riskless Choice: A Reference Dependent Model." *The Quarterly Journal of Economics* 106, 204–17.

Tversky, Amos, and Richard Thaler (1990). "Anomalies: Preference Reversals." *The Journal of Economic Perspectives* 4, 201–11.

Tversky, Amos, Shmuel Sattath, and Paul Slovic (1988). "Contingent Weighting in Judgment and Choice." *Psychological Review* 95, 371–84.

Uchitelle, Louis (2007). "Advocate of Paying Chiefs Well Revises Thinking." *The New York Times*, Sept. 28, 2007.

Underhill, Paco (1999). *Why We Buy: The Science of Shopping.* New York: Simon & Schuster.

—— (2004). *The Call of the Mall.* New York: Simon & Schuster.

Urbany, J. E., W. O. Bearden, and D. C. Weilbaker (1988). "The Effect of Plausible and

Exaggerated Reference Price on Consumer Perceptions and Price Search." *Journal of Consumer Research* 13, 250–56.

Van den Bergh, B., and S. Dewitte (2006). "Digit Ratio (2D:4D) Moderates the Impact of Sexual Cues on Men's Decisions in Ultimatum Games." *Proceedings of the Royal Society B* 273, 2091–95.

Vohs, Kathleen D., Nicole L. Mead, and Miranda R. Goode (2006). "The Psychological Consequences of Money." *Science* 314, 1154–56.

——— (2008). "Merely Activating the Concept of Money Changes Personal and Interpersonal Behavior." *Current Directions in Psychological Science* 17, 208–12.

Von der Gathen, Andreas, and Burkhard Gersch (n.d.). "The Value of Emotions— Pricing for Luxury Goods." Simon-Kucher & Partners white paper. Available at www2.simon-kucher.com/index.php/us/publications/white-papers.html.

Von Neumann, John, and Oskar Morgenstern (1944). *Theory of Games and Economic Behavior*. Princeton, N.J.: Princeton University Press.

Walkup, Carolyn (2006). "Consultant Kalmar: Subtle Price Hikes Boost Sales, Offset Costs." *Nation's Restaurant News*, June 12, 2006.

Weber, Ernst H., trans. by H. E. Ross (1978). *The Sense of Touch*. New York: Academic Press. (Translation of 1834 original.)

Wharton, Rachel (2008). "The $175 Burger Is a Haute Handful for Rarefied Tastes." *New York Daily News*, May 20, 2008.

Wilson, Michael (2008). "Cost of N.Y. Retail Survival: 99 Cents. Or Is It 98 Cents?" *The New York Times*, Aug. 16, 2008.

Wilson, Timothy D., and Nancy C. Brekke (1994). "Mental Contamination and Mental Correction: Unwanted Influences on Judgments and Evaluations." *Psychological Bulletin* 116, 117–42.

Wilson, Timothy D., Christopher Houston, Kathryn Etling, and Nancy Brekke (1996). "A New Look at Anchoring Effects: Basic Anchoring and Its Antecedents." *Journal of Experimental Psychology: General* 4, 387–402.

Wolf, James R., Hal R. Arkes, and Waleed A. Muhanna (2008). "The Power of Touch: An Examination of the Effect of Duration of Physical Contact on the Valuation of Objects." *Judgment and Decision Making* 3, 476–82.

Zak, Paul J. (2008). "The Neurobiology of Trust." *Scientific American*, June 2008, 88–95.

———, Angela A. Stanton, and Sheila Ahmadi (2007). "Oxytocin Increases Generosity in Humans." *PLoS One* 2(11): e1128. doi:10.1371/journal.pone.0001128. Available at www.plosone.org.

Zambito, Thomas (2008). "50 Gets His Taco Bell Rung." *New York Daily News*, Nov. 20, 2008.

Zamir, Shmuel (2000). "Rationality and Emotions in Ultimatum Bargaining." Discussion Paper #222. Available at www.ma.huji.ac.il/~zamir/dp222.pdf.

# Index

Aché people, 123
adaptation level, 38–39, 98
Adelphia, 234
Adelson, Edward H., 36
Adidas Group, 7
adjustment, anchoring and, 12, 88, 91
*Administrative Behavior* (Simon), 51
advertised reference pricing (ARP),
    204–206
Agassi, Andre, 227
Ahmadi, Sheila, 252
Aiello, Greg, 165
Air Force, U.S., 28, 54; Intellectual Func-
    tions Section, 52
airline tickets, 182–83
air-vacuum machines, 179
alcohol, decision-making under influence
    of, 219–22
Alfred P. Sloan Foundation, 104
Allais, Maurice, 56–61
Allais's paradox, 55, 97, 99–101
altruism, 115–19
American Airlines, 182, 183
American Bar Foundation, 241
*American Economic Review, The*, 80
*American Journal of Psychology, The*, 62
amygdala, 216
anchoring, 12–14, 16, 40–41, 45, 94,
    237, 260–61; adaptation levels and, 39;
    and adjustment, 12, 88, 91; alcohol
    consumption and, 219; in art market,

267–68; assimilation, 40; of auction
bids, 135–37; basic effect of, 95–96; of
car repair estimates, 269–70; category
scales and, 36; charm pricing and, 189;
consideration of changes in, 269–70;
contrast, 40; jury award, 17, 19, 20, 278;
in luxury trade, 155–56, 158; memory
and, 138–39; money illusion and, 228;
in negotiations, 207–208, 211, 212; in
nonlinear pricing, 144; preference
reversals and, 74–75, 79–80, 87, 90–
91; in real estate market, 196–201;
reflectiveness versus impulsiveness in
susceptibility to, 213–14; by restaurants, 162; ticket price, 14–15; of top
salaries, 257, 259
Anderson, Eric, 188–91
Anheuser-Busch, 153
Applebee's restaurant chain, 160, 163
Apple Inc., 257; iPhone, 172; iPod, 184
Apple Jacks cereal, 5
appliances, energy-efficient, 181
arbitrariness, coherent, 5, 16
Argentina, 130
Ariely, Dan, 9, 16, 135–36, 138, 193–95,
    256
Arizona, University of, 118, 120, 130, 196
Arrow, Kenneth, 261
art market, 266–68
Asch, Solomon, 273–75
Assem, Martijn van den, 130

assimilation anchoring, 40
Atenga, 6
attention, 216–18; alcohol and, 221–22
attraction effect, 153–54
Au people, 123
Austen Riggs Clinic, 85
automobiles, *see* cars
Ayres, Ian, 241–44

BahnCard, 173
Balthazar restaurant (New York), 162–64
Baltimore Ravens football team, 166
Baltussen, Guido, 130
Barclays Bank, 7
bargaining, 73, 117, 196, 207, 209–11,
    217; buddy system in, 272–75; endow-
    ment effect and, 66; in ancient Rome,
    109, 110; ultimatum, 112–15, 122; *see
    also* negotiations
Bargh, John, 93–94
Barr, Abigail, 122
baseball salaries, 258–59
basic anchoring effect, 95–96
Bateson, Melissa, 283
batteries, 179–80
Baudelaire, Charles, 96
Bayer HealthCare Pharmaceuticals, 6
Bazerman, Max, 102, 212, 215, 217–18
beauty premium, 239–40
Becker-DeGroot-Marschak system, 73
beer, upscale versus downscale, 151–53
*Behavioral and Brain Sciences, The,* 126
behavioral decision theory, 10–11, 28, 53,
    78, 129, 208, 217, 286–88
behavioral economics, 16, 74, 105, 129,
    133, 135; inflation and, 224; practical
    relevance of, 146–47; salaries and, 256
Ben-Gurion University, 209
Berger, Roland, 6
Berkshire Hathaway Inc., 169
Bernoulli, Daniel, 50
Bertelsmann, 6
biases, 87–90, 125, 197
Bielefeld, University of, 146
Big Texan Steak Ranch (Amarillo), 143–
    45, 148

billing plans, 172–75
Black Monday, 265
Blake, Peter, 266
*Blink* (Gladwell), 126
BMW, 7
Bodenhausen, Galen V., 283
boomerang effect, 17–18
Bornstein, Brian, 18–19
Boston Consulting Group, 6
Boulud, Daniel, 159
Boulware, Lemuel, 115
bounded rationality, 52
Boyd, Robert, 121, 122
bracketing, 160
Brawny towels, 149
Brazil, soccer fans in, 249
break-even point, 173
Brennan, Paul, 203
British Airways, 7
British Columbia, University of, 104,
    105
British products, pricing of, 185–86
Broadway shows, ticket prices for, 14–15
bubbles: real estate, 101; stock market,
    261–65
buddy system, 272–75
Budweiser beer, 152, 154
Buffett, Warren, 169, 261
bundling, 160; in infomercials, 169–70
Burke, Edmund, 101
Burnham, Terence, 248–49
*BusinessWeek,* 177

Cabbage Patch dolls, 105–106
Cable News Network (CNN), 228
California, University of: Berkeley, 84,
    194–95; Los Angeles, 121; San Diego,
    60
California Institute of Technology
    (Caltech), 78, 79; Laboratory for
    Experimental Economics and
    Political Science, 263
Call, Josep, 123
Callahan, Thomas, 72
Cambridge University, 251
cameras, 145; batteries for, 179–80

Camerer, Colin, 78, 79, 102–103, 119, 121–23, 127, 208–209, 216, 263–65
Canada, 105
Carroll, Lewis, 94
cars: charm pricing of, 190; price negotiations for, 241–44, 272–73, 275; rebate programs for, 176; repair cost estimates for, 269–70; websites for, 280–82
Cartier watches, 44
cash registers, 186
category scales, 35–36, 277–79
Caterpillar Inc., 7
cell phones: billing plans for, 172–74; text messaging on, 181
CEOs, salaries of, 235, 256–58
cereal boxes, changing size and shape of, 5–6
certainty effect, 60, 61, 99–100, 193
Chapman, Gretchen, 18–19
Charles II, King of England, 270
charm prices, 185–92
CheapTickets, 182
Chicago, University of, 5, 39, 56, 66, 78, 110, 188
Chili's restaurant chain, 160, 163
chimpanzees, 123–24
chocolate, 135, 137, 193, 286–88
Choo, Jimmy, 157
Christian virtues, 99
Claremont Graduate University, 249
Cleese, John, 134
Clemens, Roger, 259
Coach Leatherware, 156, 158
Coates, John, 251
Coca-Cola, 6, 149
Cocoa Krispies cereal, 5
Cognitive Reflection Test (CRT), 213–14
Cognitive Science Society, 104
Cohen, L. Jonathan, 126, 129
Cohen, Nick, 267
Cohen, Steve, 266
coherent arbitrariness, 5, 16
Cologne, University of, 112, 113
Colorado, University of, 204
Columbia University, 188; Business School, 280
compatibility principle, 75

Congress, U.S., 257
Consumer Electronics Association, 181
Consumer Expenditure Survey, 243
Consumer Reports, 179–80, 272; Auto Price Service, 242
contrast anchoring, 40
Coombs, Clyde, 53, 82
Coors beer, 152
Cornell University, 72, 104, 111, 117, 170, 178
Corn Pops cereal, 5
Cornsweet, Tom, 84
Cornsweet illusion, 84–85
Corporate Library, 257
Costco, 151, 180, 190
Cox, Donald, 16
Craigslist, 75
Crandall, Robert, 182
Creed, Greg, 186
Cromwell, Oliver, 270
Cross pens, 156
Crystal, Graef, 257
Cyrus, Miley, 166–67

Darrow, Charles, 284
Dawes, Robyn, 82
Dayan, Moshe, 81
Deal or No Deal (television show), 130–33
decision making, behavioral theory of, see behavioral decision theory
Democratic Party, 116
department stores, 186, 187, 190
Desvousges, W. H., 20
Deutsche Bahn, 173
Deutsche Telekom, 172
Diaconis, Persi, 81
Dial soap, 5
Diamond, Peter, 227, 228, 230–32
diapers, disposable, 153–54
dictator game, 118–19, 283
Discovery Channel, 94
divorces, contentious, 234–36, 238
Doctors Without Borders, 119
Dow Jones, 7; Industrial Average, 262
Drexler, Mickey, 203, 205

Duke University, 151
Dunphy, Frank, 267, 268
Duracell batteries, 180
Dyers (spiritualist couple), 38

eBay, 186
*Econometrica*, 59, 102
economic man, fiction of, 55; gender and, 236
Economic Policy Institute, 256
Eddie Bauer clothing company, 190
*Edmund's New Car Prices*, 242
Edwards, Ruth, 53
Edwards, Ward, 49, 50, 52–55, 62, 71, 72, 82, 86, 126–28
Einhorn, Hillel, 196
Einstein, Albert, 57, 74, 82, 91
Elliman, Douglas, 219
Emerson, Ralph Waldo, 68
Emirates Airlines, 7
endowment effect, 66
Energizer batteries, 180
Enron Corporation, 234
Envirosell, 150
Erasmus University, 133
Erikson, Erik, 85
Eskildsen, Paul, 25–27
Esposito, Meade, 116
*Everybody Loves Raymond* (television show), 255
executive compensation, 235–36, 256
expected utility model, 51
extremeness aversion, 156–57
Ezarik, Justine, 172

Facebook, 195
fairness, 105–108, 110, 124, 218, 286; appearance of, 116; of jury awards, 20; opportunity price increases and, 161; in ultimatum game, 114
*Family Guy, The* (television show), 246
FareCompare.com, 183
Farrelly brothers, 109
fast food: bundling of, 160; charm prices of, 186, 188; *see also* McDonald's

Fechner, Gustav, 29–32, 39, 224
50 Cent, 186, 188
FIFO (first-in-first-out) inventory valuation, 227
Firesign Theatre, 175
Fisher, Irving, 223–26, 232
Fisher, Margaret, 224
flat-rate billing plans, 174
*Forbes* magazine, 189
*For the Love of God* (Hirst), 266
Fortune 500 companies, 208
Foundations of Uncertainty and Risk (FUR), 60
Four Queens Casino (Las Vegas), 49, 71–72
France, anti-Semitism in, 84
*Frasier* (television show), 255
free market, utopian economics of, 56
free offers, 193–95
Freud, Sigmund, 82
Friedman, Milton, 56, 58, 59, 77, 78
*Friends* (television show), 255
Froot Loops cereal, 5
Fruit of the Loom underwear, 189
FSBO (for sale by owner), 186, 205

game theory, 50, 112, 121
Gandolfini, James, 255
gender, 236, 245–47, 283; car sales and, 241–44; jury awards and, 279; salaries and, 237–38, 240; in ultimatum game, 248–52
General Electric (GE), 115, 234–36, 255, 257–58
General Motors, 7
George Mason University, 258
German Institute for the Study of Labor, 213
Germany, 131; car repairs in, 269–71; hyperinflation in, 225–26; Nazi, 83–84; railroads in, 173
Gibbs, Josiah Willard, 224–25
Gigerenzer, Gerd, 126, 129
Ginsu knives, 169
Ginzberg, Eli, 188
Gladwell, Malcolm, 126

Gnau people, 123
Goffstein, Benny, 49, 71
Gold, David, 184, 185, 189
Goldberg, Pinelopi Koujianou, 243, 244
Goldman Sachs, 7
Gompers, Samuel, 207
Goode, Miranda, 284–86
Google, 194
Google Maps, 217
Graham, Benjamin, 260, 263
Grammer, Kelsey, 255
Great Depression, 284
greater fool theory, 264
Greenberg, Hank, 259
Grether, David M., 78–80
*Groundhog Day* (movie), 208–209
*Guinness Book of World Records*, 227
Güth, Werner, 112–14

Halevy, Yoram, 114
Hand, Learned, 270
Hannah Montana tour, 166–67
*Hardball* (television show), 258
*Harvard Business Review*, 234
Harvard University, 28–30, 42–43, 50, 59,
    102, 126, 250; Psycho-Acoustic Labora-
    tory, 28–29, 42
Haughney, Christine, 219
Hebrew University, 82–84, 121
Heilbroner, Robert, 55
Heinrich, Joe, 121–22
Helson, Harry, 38–41
Hermès Group, 155, 156
Hertel, Jim, 149
heuristics, 52, 67, 87–90, 174, 197;
    attacks on, 125–28
Hill, Dan, 156
Hilton Hotels, 7
Hirst, Damien, 266–68
Hoffman, Elizabeth, 118–21, 129–30
Hoffman, Paul, 26–28, 87, 194
Hogarth, Robert, 196
Holbein, Hans, 39
Hollywood Bowl, 15
*Home Encyclopedia* (Fechner), 30
honesty boxes, 282–83

Honey Smacks cereal, 5
Honeywell International, 6
Hooters restaurant chain, 160
*How to Live* (Fisher), 224
HSBC, 7
Hsee, Christopher, 287, 288
Huber, Joel, 151–53, 156
Hublot watches, 155–56
Hunt, William, 40
Hutchinson, Shelly, 176
hyperinflation, 223, 225–26

IBM, 148
Illinois, University of, 18
illusions, 216–17; money, 225–33; per-
    ceptual, 36–37, 84–85
Immelt, Jeff, 258
Indonesia, 123
Indow, Tarow, 44
inflation, 223–32; 99-cent stores and, 185;
    stock market and, 101, 264–65; top
    salaries and, 256–59
infomercials, 169–71, 260–61
Intel Corporation, 6
Internal Revenue Service (IRS), 219
Internet, 35, 181, 232, 253, 280–81;
    airline ticket prices on, 182; rebate
    program for purchases on, 177;
    user-generated content on, 195
inventory valuation methods, 227
Iowa, University of, 125
Israel, 81–84, 88, 121, 136
Italy, soccer fans in, 249

Jacowitz, Karen, 144
James, William, 30
Japan, executive compensation in, 256
J. Crew clothing company, 190, 203, 205
Jensen, Keith, 123–24
Jensen, Marlene, 232
JetBlue Airlines, 182, 183
Jews: Israeli, 81–82; mobsters, 49; Nazi
    persecution of, 83–84
Jobs, Steve, 184, 257
Johns Hopkins University, 52

Johnson, Eric, 280–82
Johnson & Johnson, 6
Jopling, Jay, 267
*Journal of Business*, 110
*Journal of Consumer Research*, 153, 280
*Journal of Experimental Psychology, The*, 65
juries, 197; damages awarded by, 3–4, 17–21, 276–79

Kahn, Irah, 84
Kahneman, Daniel, 16, 83–87, 105, 133, 146, 147, 188, 196, 236; on altruism, 117; on anchoring, 144, 207; economists' hostility to, 77; fairness research of, 106–107, 110, 112–14; heuristics of, 88–89, 125–28, 197; on jury awards, 19, 276–77, 279; at Oregon Research Institute, 28, 87–88; on priming, 92, 94, 286; prospect theory of, 97–99, 101–102, 104, 132; and stock market bubbles, 261; on ultimatum game, 113, 115; United Nations experiment of, 10–12, 90
Kalmar, Tepper, 160, 161
Kelley Blue Book, 75
Kelly, Walt, 76
Kennedy, Edward, 257
Kenya, 122
Klein, Calvin, 246
Knetsch, Jack, 105, 107, 110, 113–14, 117
Kohl, Helmut, 271
Koolhaas, Rem, 158
Kouri, Elena, 250
Kozlowski, Dennis, 234–36
Kozlowski, Karen, 234
Krueger, Alan, 165–66
Kucher, Eckhard, 148–49

Lacayo, Richard, 267
Lagavulin whiskey, 219
laissez-faire capitalism, 108
Lamelera people, 123
"Landlord's Game, The," 284
La Rue, Diane, 167

*Las Vegas Review Journal*, 71
Laube, Jim, 160
laundry detergent, 180
Lauren, Ralph, 155
lawsuits, jury awards in, 3–4, 17–21, 276–79
*Leaves of Grass* (Whitman), 194
Lee, Bob, 144
Leeds, University of, 219
Leeuwenhoek, Anton von, 208
Lehman Brothers, 268
Leipzig, University of, 30
Lichtenstein, Donald, 204–206
Lichtenstein, Sarah, 10, 28, 53, 62–77, 79, 81, 82, 87, 90, 220
*Liebeck v. McDonald's* (1994), 3–4, 17–21, 276, 278
LIFO (last-in-first-out) inventory valuation, 227
Liquid Trust, 253
*Little Book on Life After Death* (Fechner), 30
Loewenstein, George, 9, 102, 135, 138, 194, 215, 216, 218, 256
Lone Ranger theory, 257–58
Longoria, Eva, 156
Lopes, Lola, 125–26
*Los Angeles Times*, 229
loss aversion, 98–103, 174, 220
loyalty cards, 149, 175–77
Luby, Frank, 4, 5, 190
Lufthansa, 7
Luvs disposable diapers, 153–54
luxury, 155–58; superfluous, 151

MacArthur Foundation, 15, 122
Mach, Ernst, 30
Machiguenga people, 121–22
Machina, Mark, 60–61
Macrae, C. Neil, 283
Macy's department store, 186, 187
*Mad Men* (television show), 184
Magic Bullet Blender, 170–71
*Magic Christian, The* (Southern), 9–10, 221
Malouff, John, 17

Mandel, Howie, 130
Mandel, Naomi, 280–82
*Marketing Science*, 169
Marsh's Supermarket (Troy, Ohio), 147
Martin, Katherine, 197
Massachusetts Institute of Technology
    (MIT), 36, 41, 135–39, 188, 195; Sloan
    School, 135, 137
Matthews, Chris, 258
Mauritius, 130
Max Planck Institute for Evolutionary
    Anthropology, 123
Max Planck Institute for Human Develop-
    ment, 126
Maxwell House coffee, 149
Mazar, Nina, 193
McCabe, Kevin, 129–30
McClearn, Karen, 166
McDonald's: hot coffee lawsuit against,
    3–4, 17–21, 276, 278; worm rumors
    about, 206
Mead, Nicole, 284–86
menus, 159–64
Mercedes Benz, 7
Merck & Company, 6
Merckle, Adolf, 102
Merkel, Julius, 31
Mesopotamians, 42
Michael, George, 267
Michaud, Todd P., 148
Michelob beer, 153
Michelson-Morley experiment, 74
Michigan, University of, 49, 52–54, 62,
    82
microscope, invention of, 208
Microsoft Corporation, 6
Mighty Mendit adhesive, 170
*Miljoenenjacht (Chasing Millions)*
    (Dutch game show), 130–32
Miller, George, 42–43
Miller beer, 152, 153
Milne, Alan B., 283
Minolta cameras, 156
Minow, Nell, 257
money illusion, 225–33
*Money Illusion, The* (Fisher), 225
Monopoly (game), 284, 286

Monty Python, 134
Morgan, S. Reed, 3–4, 19–21
Morgenstern, Oskar, 50, 51, 54, 55
Mormons, 28
Morrissey, Paul, 202–203, 205
MRI scans, 168
MSNBC, 258
Mugabe, Robert, 223
Mullainathan, Sendhil, 146–47, 245, 246
Murphy, Charles B. G., 49, 71
Murray, Bill, 208–209
Mussweiler, Thomas, 90, 269–71

Nash equilibrium, 51
National Broadcasting Company (NBC),
    255
National Economic Council, 262
National Football League (NFL), 156–66
*National Geographic*, 93
National Science Foundation, 122, 197
Nature Conservancy, 202
Nazis, 83–84
Neale, Margaret, 196–201, 203, 207, 208,
    212
*Negotiating Rationally* (Bazerman and
    Neale), 212
negotiations, 116, 196, 211–12; anchoring
    in, 207–208, 211; business, 197;
    divorce, 234–36; fairness in, 105, 116;
    gender and, 236–38, 241–44; race and,
    242–44; *see also* bargaining; ultimatum
    game
Nestlé, 6
Netflix, 174–75
Netherlands, 130–33
Nettle, Daniel, 283
neuroeconomics, 249–50, 252
Nevada Gaming Commission, 72
Newcastle University, 282
*Newsweek*, 125–26
New York Giants football team, 166
*New York Times, The*, 185, 203, 227, 235,
    236, 266
Nikon cameras, 145
99-cent stores, 184–85, 189, 190
Nobel Prize, 10, 11, 56, 57, 60, 83, 127

Nocera, Joseph, 236
Nokia, 6
NORAD, 52
Nordstrom's department stores, 190
Norma's restaurant (New York), 159
Northcraft, Gregory, 196–201, 203
Northwestern University, Kellogg Gradu-
ate School of Management, 218

Obama, Barack, 262
O'Dell, Brandon, 159, 161, 186
Oechssler, Jörg, 213–14
Olive Garden restaurant chain, 160
Onassis, Jacqueline, 202
"opportunity" price increases, 161
Oregon, University of, 62
Oregon Research Institute (ORI), 25–28,
49, 62, 68, 79, 87
Organizational Behavior and Human
Decision Processes, 200, 210
Orma people, 122
outrage theory, 19, 276–79
Oxford University, 122, 126, 220
oxytocin, 252–54

packaging, changing size and shape of,
4–6
pain, 138–39; psychophysics of, 136
Palestine, British, 81, 83, 84
Palin, Michael, 134
Palmer, Arnold, 227
Pampers disposable diapers, 153–54
Papua New Guinea, 123
Parago, 177
Paraguay, 123
Parker Meridien Hotel (New York), 159
Parrish, Darrell, 241
Pastis restaurant (New York), 161–62
Pavlov, Ivan, 229
Pearson, Wayne, 72
Pennsylvania, University of, 237
Pepsico, 6
perceptual illusions, 36–37, 84–85
Peru, 121–22
Peters, Michael, 114

Pfeiffer, Tim, 269–71
Philosophical Enquiry into the Origin of
Our Ideas on the Sublime and Beautiful
(Burke), 101
phone bills, 172–73
physical attractiveness, effects on salaries
and prices of, 239–40
Physical Impossibility of Death in the
Mind of Someone Living, The (Hirst),
266
Picasso, Pablo, 116
pigeon drop con, 253
Pinker, Steve, 126
Plateau, Joseph-Antoine Ferdinand, 31–
32, 40
Plautus, 109–10
Plott, Charles R., 78–80, 263
Pogo cartoon, 76
Poincaré, Henri, 57
Ponticello, John, 72, 73
Post, Thierry, 130–33
power curve, 32–33
Prada, 155, 158
preference reversals, 64–70, 72, 78–80,
87; experiments in, 72–75, 78–80, 90–
91; rejection by economists of, 77–78
Prelec, Drazen, 9, 102, 135, 138, 194,
216, 256
price-to-earnings (P/E) ratio, 261, 263
priming, 91–94, 280–81, 284–86; see also
anchoring
Princeton University, 50, 165; Woodrow
Wilson School, 10
Procter & Gamble Company, 6, 153
Producers, The (musical), 14–15
products, changing size and shape of, 5
Professional Pricing Society, 147
prospect theory, 97–103, 132, 147, 170,
172, 220
Prudential Real Estate, 219
Pruitt, D. G., 53
Psychological Bulletin, 54, 55, 86
psychophysics, 8–9, 26–27, 29–36, 39–
40, 53, 146; definition of, 31; experiments in, 26–27, 35, 40; of jury awards,
276–79; luxury trade and, 155; magnitude scales of, 194; of money, 42–45;

origins of, 29–32; of pain, 136; perceptual illusion demonstrations of, 36–37, 84–85; power curve rule in, 32–33; prospect theory and, 98; of rebates, 178
*Psychophysics* (Stevens), 34
Puffs tissues, 5
Puto, Christopher, 151–53, 156

*Quarterly Journal of Economics, The*, 138
Quattrone, George, 12–13
Quilted Northern toilet paper, 5

racial discrimination, 245, 283; in car sales, 241–44
Rand, Ayn, 108
RAND Corporation, 71
Rapp, Gregg, 162–64
rationality: bounded, 52; cult of, 77–78
Ravikovich, Dahlia, 82
Reagan, Ronald, 56, 256
real estate market, 196–206, 211; alcohol and deal-making in, 219; anchoring in, 196–201, 203–205; bargaining in, 115; bubbles in, 101, 264; charm prices in, 186; framing of gains and losses in, 107; incentives in, 176; money illusion in, 229
rebates, 176–78
reference points, 98, 101, 132
reference pricing, 204–206
Remington Rand, Inc., 224
Reserve Bank of Zimbabwe, 223
restaurants, 143–45, 159–64; charm pricing by, 186, 190
Revionics, Inc., 6, 148
RFID tags, 150
Richelieu, Duc de, 219
Riding, Alan, 266–67
Ritov, Ilana, 209–10
Ritty, James, 186
Riviera Casino (Las Vegas), 49
*Robb Report*, 156
Roberts, Gilbert, 283
Robertson, Leslie, 27
Rockefeller, J. Sterling, 49

Rockefeller, Nelson, 116
Rodriguez, Alex, 258–59
Roider, Andreas, 213
Rolex watches, 44
Rolling Stones, 202
Rolodex, 224
Romano, Ray, 255
Romans, ancient, 109–10
*Rope, The* (Plautus), 109–10
Rosenblum, Paula, 177
Russell Sage Foundation, 104
Ruth, Babe, 258–59
Ryan, Nolan, 259

Saatchi, Charles, 266
Saatchi, Diane, 201
Sage, Russell, 104
salaries, 211–12, 218, 287; beauty premium in, 239–40; cuts in, fairness of, 107; gender and, 237–38, 240; psychophysics and, 42–43; of top earners, 235, 255–59
Salary.com, 211
Sam's Club, 151
Samuelson, Paul, 51, 77
S&H Green Stamps, 176–77
Sanfey, Alan, 168
Saturn cars, 243
Savage, Leonard "Jimmie," 56–59, 78, 125, 146
scanners, 147–48
Schiff, Arthur, 169
Schkade, David, 276–77, 279
Schmittberger, Rolf, 113
Schmitz, Patrick, 213
Schutte, Nicola, 17
Schwarze, Bernd, 113
Schweitzer, Maurice, 239–40
*Science*, 12, 88, 90, 125
*Scientific American*, 127, 147
Scion cars, 243
Scotland, Church of, 270
Scott, Robert, 4
Seaney, Rick, 183
Securities and Exchange Commission (SEC), 257

Seinfeld, Jerry, 255
Seinfeld (television show), 3, 255
Sensory Logic, Inc., 156
sensory perceptions, study of, see
    psychophysics
September 11 terrorist attacks, 258
Shafir, Eldar, 227, 228, 230–32, 245–47
Shakespeare, William, 127
Shampanier, Kristina, 193
Shiller, Robert, 262–63
Siegelman, Peter, 241–44
Simester, Duncan, 188–91
Simon, Herbert, 51–52
Simon, Hermann, 6, 145–48, 173, 175
Simon Fraser University, 105
Simon-Kucher & Partners (SKP), 4, 6–7,
    16, 148, 157–58, 165, 172, 173, 181
Simonson, Itamar, 156–58
Simpsons, The (television show), 143
Sinai war (1956), 81
Sizzler restaurant chain, 160
Skinner, B. F., 53
Skippy peanut butter, 4–5
Slovic, Paul, 10, 28, 62–67, 72–77, 79,
    80, 82, 90, 220
Smith, Adam, 77, 123
Smith, Vernon, 10, 129–30
Snuggie blanket, 170
social psychology, 273
Solnick, Sara, 236–40
Sony Ericsson, 6
Sopranos, The (television show), 255
Sorensen, Herb, 150
Sotheby's, 267–68
South Africa, 245–46
Southern, Terry, 9–10
Southwest Airlines, 182, 183
Spacey, Kevin, 95, 96
Sperry, Thomas, 176
Sperry Rand, 224
Springsteen, Bruce, 167
Stack, Fritz, 269–71
Stakes and Odds experiment, 72–76
Standard & Poor's Index, 258, 263
Stanford University, 28, 81, 104, 261, 282;
    Graduate School of Business, 205
Stanton, Angela, 252

Star Wars movies, 189
Stein, Gertrude, 76
Stevens, S. S., 28–29, 32–37, 42–44, 99,
    112, 136, 137, 155, 277
stock market: bubbles in, 261–65; CEO
    compensation and, 257, 258; 1929
    collapse of, 224; risk of bond market
    versus, 101
Stone, Geraldine, 35–36
Strack, Fritz, 90, 269
Summers, Lawrence, 261–62
Sunstein, Cass, 76, 276–77, 279
Super Bowl tickets, 165–66, 168
supermarkets, 149–51; changing size and
    shape of products and packaging in,
    6–7; loyalty cards of, 149, 176; scales
    in, 8; scanners in, 147–48
supply and demand, 156, 224; fairness
    and, 105; top salaries and, 259
Swarthmore College, 50, 62, 273
Swatch watches, 44
Sweden, male aggressiveness in, 249
Swisscom, 172

Taco Bell, 186, 188
Talisker whiskey, 219
TalkingBroadway, 14
Talwalkar, Presh, 121
TCA Fulfillment Services, 177
Tel Aviv University, 136
television stars, salaries of, 255–56
Ten Commandments, 99
testosterone, 248–52
Texas, University of, 277
Texas Instruments, 6
text messages, 181
TGI Friday's restaurant chain, 160
Thaler, Richard, 16, 104–105, 130,
    146, 147, 174, 224, 227, 236; on altru-
    ism, 117, 119; baseball metaphors
    of, 76; beer thought experiment of,
    150–51; on bundling, 160, 169–70;
    on endowment effect, 66; fairness
    research of, 106–107, 110–14; on
    rebates, 178; transaction utility concept
    of, 167–68

*Theory of Games and Economic Behavior* (von Neumann), 50
thought experiments, 150–51
Thurston, Louis Leon, 39
Thyssen-Krupp, 6
Ticketmaster, 167
ticket prices: airline, 182–83; anchoring of, 14–15; fairness of, 165–67; sporting event and concert, 165–68
TicketsNow, 167
*Time* magazine, 267
Timex watches, 44
T-Mobile, 6, 172
Tomasello, Michael, 123
Tom Sawyer experiments, 194–95
Toronto Blue Jays baseball team, 7
Toyota, 7
trade-off contrast, 157–58
transaction utility, 167–68
Treisman, Anne, 104
Trump, Donald, 215
Tucson Realty and Trust, 197
Tversky, Amos, 16, 61, 81–83, 86–87, 133, 136, 146, 147, 188, 196, 280; baseball metaphors of, 76; compatibility principle of, 75; death of, 129; economists' hostility to, 77; heuristics of, 88–89, 125–27, 197; on luxury pricing, 156–58; MacArthur grant awarded to, 15; on money illusion, 224, 227, 228, 230–32; at Oregon Research Institute, 28, 87–88; prospect theory of, 97–99, 101–102, 104, 132; and stock market bubbles, 261; United Nations experiment of, 10–12, 90–91
Tversky, Barbara Gans, 53, 81–82, 87, 97, 125
Tversky, Genia, 81
Tversky, Yosef, 81
Twain, Mark, 194
Twitter, 195
Tyco Electronics Corporation, 234–35

UBS, 7
ultimatum game, 109–15, 120–21, 129–30, 282; altruism and, 116–17; brain-scanning studies of, 168; in contentious divorces, 234–36, 238; cultural factors in, 121–23; hormonal influences in, 248–54; physical attractiveness and, 239–40; two-offer, 215–18
unbundling, 183
Underhill, Paco, 150, 155
Union Square Café (New York), 161
United Airlines, 182
United Kingdom: art prices in, 266–68; executive compensation in, 256
United Nations experiment, 10–13, 90–91
US Airways, 182
*Usual Suspects, The* (movie), 95, 96
Utah, University of, 28
utility, 50–51, 55, 59, 74, 132; transaction, 167–68
Utility Consumers' Action Network, 174
utopian economics, 56

Valenti, Ed, 169
value investors, 264
video rentals, 174–75
Vigneaud, Vincent du, 252
Virginia, University of, 13, 95
Vodaphone Group, 6, 172
Vohl, Kathleen, 284–86
Volkswagen, 7
Volvo, 7
von Neumann, John, 50–52, 54–56
Vuitton, Louis, 186

Wall Street Burger Shoppe (New York), 159
*Wall Street Journal, The*, 238
Wal-Mart, 190
Wanner, Eric, 104–105
Warhol, Andy, 202
Warner Music, 6
watches, *see* wristwatches
wealth effects, 43, 98–99
Weber, Ernest, 31
Web 2.0, 195
Weinstein, Joe, 230

Welch, Jack, 234–36, 238, 257–58
Welch, Jane Beasley, 234–36, 238
Westin Hotel, 159
Wetlaufer, Suzy, 234
Wheeler, Christian, 282
White, Sally Blount, 215, 218
White Cube gallery (London), 267
Whitman, Walt, 194
Whole Foods, 151
Wilde, Oscar, 136
Willard Bishop consulting firm, 149
Williams, Walter E., 258
Williams-Sonoma, 156
Wilson, Timothy, 13–14, 95
Wittgenstein, Ludwig, 84
Wood Kalb Foundation, 71
WorldCom, Inc., 234
World Trade Center, 27; terrorist attack on, 258
Wrigley's gum, 147
wristwatches: anchor pricing of, 155–56;

charm pricing of, 186; social status attached to, 44
Wundt, Wilhelm, 30–31, 53
Würzburg, University of, 269, 271


Yale University, 49, 93, 224, 262; Law School, 241
Yamasaki, Minoru, 27
Young America, 177
YouTube, 172, 195


Zagat guides, 160
Zak, Paul, 249–50, 252–53
Zamir, Shmuel, 121
Zeckhauser, Richard, 59
Zest soap, 5
Zhang, Jiao, 287
Zillow, 205
Zimbabwe, 223, 226